To My

Your Loving Son,

Donald

Sept. 26/89

Calgary

DICTIONARY OF THE AFRICAN LEFT

To My Dear Mother

Dictionary of the African Left:

Parties, Movements and Groups

Donald I Ray

The University of Calgary

Dartmouth

Published by

Dartmouth Publishing Company Limited

Gower Publishing Group
Gower House, Croft Road, Aldershot
Hants. GU11 3HR, England

Gower Publishing Company
Old Post Road, Brookfield, Vermont 05036
USA

British Library Cataloguing in Publication Data
Ray, Donald I. (Donald Iain), 1949-
Dictionary of the African left: parties, movements and groups.
1. Africa. Left wing political movements
I. Title
320.96

ISBN 1-85521-014-2

Printed in Great Britain by
Billing & Sons Ltd, Worcester

Contents

Acknowledgements

I am most grateful to those who helped me in the writing of this book. Margaret O'Reilly, Sue McNaughton and Vivienne Crowe of Gower provided much-appreciated editorial encouragement, patience and guidance. I am grateful to Bogdan Szajkowski for encouraging me to write this book. Lynn Cover, Suzanne Baustad and Daryl Leman provided valuable research assistance for this project. Judi Powell deserves special mention for her excellence in typing this manuscript and for the outstanding way in which she solved numerous problems in the production of the final drafts of this book. The Department of Political Science (Faculty of Social Sciences) and the African Studies Programme (Faculty of General Studies) of the University of Calgary provided the necessary administrative support. The research was funded by the Social Sciences and Humanities Research Council of Canada as well as by Canada Employment's SEED Programme. Most of all I have appreciated the support of my family, and especially my children (Michael, Matthew and Jenny) who constantly had to endure being told that I was busy writing this book.

PART I
THE AFRICAN LEFT: AN INTRODUCTION

1 The Scope, the Uses and the Limitations of This Book

Despite the fact that the left exists in every African state, that it has formed fifty-eight governments in thirty-seven countries, and that it is currently engaged in armed struggle for state power in five countries, there has not been a comprehensive continental survey of the African left. This book breaks this new ground by utilising a dictionary format to list and briefly describe each group for handy reference by the reader.

The melange of names, acronyms and abbreviations associated with political groups confuses many readers; therefore, an information presentation strategy has been established. Following the introductory essay, the various groups are listed in alphabetical order. Each entry analyses the group's history, orientation and composition. Finally there are two indexes, both organised in alphabetical order. The first index lists the acronyms, giving the full title of the group, country and the page on which the group's entry appears. In the second index, groups are listed by country.

This book sets out to provide the most comprehensive survey to date of the various forms of the left in Africa by listing in alphabetical order and briefly describing the various left groups. The dictionary section is introduced by this essay which seeks to provide a context for such a collection of organisations. This diversity of experiences is given coherence by examining the roots of the African left, its growth and the rise to power of leftist governments on the continent.

As the African left has grown, it has had to undertake a very complex series of processes that involved the comprehension, integration, incorporation, rejection, evolution and indigenisation of intellectual and organisational frameworks as well as modes of analysis and action that appear to be drawn mainly from abroad. These particular roots have been drawn from an exceptionally wide variety of European, North American and Asian experiences: from European nationalism, to the black pride movements of the United States, to Cuban proletarian internationalism, to the civil disobedience of Gandhi's India to the successes of the Bolshevik, Chinese and Vietnamese revolutions. Parts of the African left have drawn inspiration variously from European and American democrats and nationalists, from the social democratic Socialist International (Second International), the Leninist Third International or Comintern, the Trotskyist Fourth International and the latter groupings around China and Albania. Today the African left can be categorized by a complex of terms that only hint at the range of nuances of political thought and action in Africa: for example, African Socialism, Afro-communism, Robin Hood nationalism, Marxism without Socialism, Socialism without Marxism, Soviet-style Scientific Socialism, National Democratic revolutions, Pan-Africanism and left-nationalism.

Groups were selected on the basis of their meeting the following criteria. First they had to be in existence as of 1980 or later. This time-frame was largely dictated by the constraint of available research resources, but was also influenced by the fact that such classics as Friedland and Rosberg (1964), Rosberg and Callaghy (1979) and M. and D. Ottaway (1981, 1986) were written or published during the 1960s and 1970s. Thus 1980 is seen as a fruitful starting point for this stage of the research project.

Second, in terms of their scale of operation, they must aim to exercise power at the level of the state and/or the region. The constraints of available research and publication resources as well as the research strategy of focussing on groups exercising or seeking to exercise state power are significant. To include groups of local importance would expand this study beyond its capacity. However, such local groups, or groups who feel that they have been unfairly categorized or treated, are invited to write to this author, enclosing samples of their publications: Dr. Donald I. Ray, Department of Political Science, The University of Calgary, Calgary, AB, T2N 1N4, Canada.

Third, in terms of orientation, they must be socialist or communist or Marxist or left nationalist or left national liberation or left pan-Africanist or anti-imperialist. These orientation descriptors establish, as well as can be done for now, the rather permeable boundaries of the African left for the purpose of this book. Admittedly, the elegance of the book's analysis would be vastly enhanced by the statement of immutable laws for each of the above descriptor categories. But the reality of our understanding does not yet yield such insights. Inevitably someone has to make a judgement on what constitutes each category and what (or who) belongs in each category and justify each decision. Marx and Engels did so in their typology of the 1848 European left in Part III of The Communist Manifesto. Indeed much of what they had to say in 1848 in Europe still applies one hundred and forty years later in 1988 with regard to the categorization of the African left. As will be shortly seen, the examination of the roots and growth of the African left will yield this work's rationale for the choice of categories.

Undoubtedly many will disagree with these categories and the groups which are assigned to them. I invite my constructive critics to write to me: I promise to incorporate, where possible, those comments into future editions of this work. The categories imply neither a demonolatry nor a hagiolatry of the African left but rather the need to understand what the experience of the African left can yield. Furthermore, the boundaries of such categories are notoriously changeable. One person's socialist is somebody else's social imperialist. At times the debate over the categorization of a group appears to be an exercise in political transubstantiation or the alchemist's stone.

These debates reflect both the problems and the state-of-the-art of the analysis of the African left. There are those "Cold War Warriors" who see in each African yet another invincible soldier marching in lockstep in Moscow's 'red hordes' towards Capetown (apartheid South Africa being seen by some strange corollary as the last barrier between 'western civilisation' and 'the evil empire'). These analysts live on a roller coaster of fear and exultation. They examine, with baited breath and pounding pulses, the utterances of each African leader to determine if he has gone over to 'the other side', if the corporate balance sheet is endangered. They see the famines and destruction of war not as the results of the latest apartheid South African raid into a neighbouring state, but as signs of the faltering of socialism. Out of touch with reality, driven by their fantasies, such analysts have little to contribute except to the construction of polemical Maginot lines. Kissinger's National Security Memorandum No. 39 (El-Khawas 1976) ably illustrates the transference of Cold War thinking to Africa. Stockwell's _In Search of Enemies_ demonstrates the results of such thinking.

There are those whose writings portray the African left as an unblemished collection of saints. Too true that they have often suffered as Semyonov's character George Griso has, or as can be confirmed in the files and publications of the International Defence and Aid Fund (for Southern Africa) and Amnesty International. As well as the successes, the mistakes and difficulties of the African left need to be studied if understanding is the goal of analysis. For example, what accounts for the war between the leftist governments of Ethiopia and Eritrea? If Joe Slovo, one of the senior leaders of the South African Communist Party, can discuss past errors of his party, then surely full analysis by others is to be permitted (Davidson, Slovo and Wilkinson, 1976). Surely the point of social science is to use study to prevent past mistakes? The writings of Marx, Engels and Lenin are full of criticisms of what the left was doing in their time (although admittedly it is more blessed to give criticism than to receive it).

Besides the problems of demonology and hagiology, there have been further problems in the epistemology of the African left. One set that this book attempts to address is that of fragmentation and isolation. The African left continues to be analysed on the basis of individual country or movement case studies or else comparisons of several movements or countries. Up to now there has not been a work that attempts to delineate the full extent of the field of the African left. Yet if the full listing of these organisations is not known, any generalizations which have been made on the basis of a particular author's set of choices, especially concerning what the significant examples are, are subject to obvious limitations. As Stretton (1969), Bill and Hardgrave (1973) and Chilcote (1981) argue, single and multiple case study works are valuable both as exercises in the political imagination and in accumulating a body of data, based on case studies, that contribute to theory building. Such theory building can only be done on the basis of the material available for comparison. Macro-level theory in the social sciences demands that the case studies be compiled, that following this a comparative analysis be done. Only then is it possible to test grand theory against the data base and see the degree to which such theory can be operationalised.

Any number of epistemological problems would seem to be possible while these processes are going. Rather than being frozen in awe of them and awaiting for the laws of social science to be presented on stone tablets, in the midst of a burning bush or on ones' computer monitor, if one recognizes the potential fallibility of the tools and conceptual approaches of contemporary social science then the analysts can continue at the levels of the case study and middle-range theory (Bill and Hardgrave, 1973: 21-40; Chilcote, 1981: 15-23), which is really a dialectic between the case study and comparison. [1] An early stage of this process is the construction of categories, based on cases, which are compared and sorted into typologies. To use a cooking analogy, only after you know what cooking ingredients you have, do you know the range of meals that you might cook. Accordingly, this book seeks to establish a typology of the African left as part of the broader comparative process of theory building.

Notes

[1] One quantitative survey of area-studies journals found that few articles engaged in comparative exercises, let alone theory building. Case studies were much more the norm. Ray 1987.

2 Periodization and Typologies in the Literature

A preliminary survey

How has the African left been seen in the literature? There are a host of works which study individual countries or movements of the African left. Only a separate bibliographic volume could begin to address adequately these publications. The main focus of this essay is on a selection of those works attempting surveys and the creation of typologies. As has been argued before, these activities develop broader theoretical schemes.

Hodgkin's work contains outstanding examples of the early work on the African left, most notably the nationalists of the 1950s and 1960s (Hodgkin 1956, 1961). Davidson (1966, 1976) and Saul (1973, 1979). contributed significantly to our understanding of the nationalist movements and parties as well as nationalist liberation movements that have spanned the continent during the 1960s, the 1970s, and the 1980s. The African Liberation Reader contains a useful selection of document extracts from the national liberation movements of Africa. Special mention must be made of the two volume work by Davies, O'Meara and Dlamini (1984) which examines the major political organisations of South Africa and analyses their stand toward apartheid and liberation and of Saul's work (1973, 1979, 1986) on Eastern and Southern Africa. The volumes produced by Friedland and Rosberg (1964) and Rosberg and Callagy (1979) were important skeptical analyses of a range of African countries that proclaimed themselves to be socialist. Solodovnikov et al. (1970) went beyond the consideration of "revolutionary-democratic parties and organizations" to survey the whole political spectrum as it existed by 1970. Markakis and Waller (1986) examined only what they called "military Marxist regimes" in several countries.

M. and D. Ottaway's Afro-communism focuses on a state-level analytical framework. This volume was originally published in 1981 and subsequently republished in 1986 with a new preface and last chapter. The bulk of the analyses, and the case study chapters are based on pre-1981 data. Within this time period the Ottaways suggest that the theory and practice of socialism in Africa has evolved through a three stage model. Starting at independence the Ottaways see the 1960s and up to the mid-1970s as the period of prominence for 'African Socialism'. African Socialism is seen as an amalgam of non-Marxist ideas encompassing social democracy to populist eclecticism. Zambia under Kaunda, Tanzania, Guinea under Toure, and Algeria under Boumediene are briefly considered as examples of African Socialist states. Little consideration is given to the ruling parties as parties of African Socialism. When they are mentioned it is as instruments of the state leader.

'Transitional Socialism' was seen as 'a hybrid mixture of Marxism-Leninism and African Socialism' (Ottaway, 1986:17-18). Ghana under Nkrumah and Guinea under Toure are seen as prime examples of this stage of the African left. This is a confusing stage because contrary to its name it does not appear necessarily to lead the African Socialist governments into Marxist-Leninist governments. Certainly Nkrumah was overthrown and Toure died before this happened. Moreover the Ottaways do not claim that any of the three Afro-communists case study states evolved from the 'African Socialism' stage to 'Transitional Socialism' stage to the 'Afro-communist' stage. Rather the Ottaway's conception of this intermediate stage is better conveyed by the image of the 'hybrid mixture', which is part Marxist, part this and part that rather than the imagery of transition. 'Dog's Breakfast Socialism' might be a less polite way of expressing it.

'Afro-communism' is seen as the third stage. Marxist-Leninist theory and practice is 'Africanised, adapted to

African conditions, to produce the Afro-communist states that emerged after 1974: Ethiopia, Mozambique and Angola. Based on these three country case studies, and having used the 'African Socialism' states as an analytical point of departure, the Ottaways state that the Afro-communist states represent a distinctive ideological formation with its own specific domestic and foreign policy tendencies.

Munslow's edited book, Africa: Problems in the Transition to Socialism (1986), originated in the 1982 conference of that school of mainly European-based scholars clustered around the Review of African Political Economy Like the Ottaways' book, the Munslow book includes both thematic and country case study chapters. Bie Nio Ong examines the question of women in the transition to socialism. Basil Davidson analyses the countries of Guinea-Bissau and Cape Verde, Bertil Egero discusses Mozambique and M.R. Bhagavan appraises the Angolan experience. Barry Munslow, Robin Cohen and Ben Turok contribute three chapters that attempt the building of a scholarly framework for the analysis of the left across Africa with reference to the transition to socialism.

While Munslow (1986) accepts certain aspects of the Ottaways' analysis, he is critical of their typology. He utilises their model to make the point that the political thrust of individual state policies and the ability to carry out the transition to socialism are very much a function of the numerical, organisational and ideological strength of the revolutionary organisations in command of the state. He agrees that it has been a mistake to see African states which aspire to be Marxist-Leninist as being merely poor copies of the Soviet Union. They have struggled to indigenise Marxist theory, and have had considerable success because of their experience as national liberation movements. These African states are not clients or satellites of the Soviet Union or China. Such Marxist-Leninist African states are clearly to be differentiated from the earlier generation of African Socialist states.

Munslow, however, objects to the term Afro-communism because he rejects the Ottaways attempt to draw parallels between Afro-communism and Euro-communism. The common European culture that helped spawn Euro-communism has not African equivalent, he argues. While the Marxist states in Africa do share a common set of ideas such as the necessity of a vanguard party to lead dynamic development, they do not share a common set of experiences with regard to social structure, culture and the method by which they obtained state power. Secondly, unlike the Eurocommunist parties, the African Marxist states have not been motivated by anti-Stalinism and revisionism in their political and theoretical reformulations. Consequently Munslow objects to the 'straightjacket' that the concept 'Afro-communism' imposes on analysing these regimes which are adapting Marxist theory to their specific circumstances. Munslow prefers to use the term, 'Marxist states in Africa'.

Munslow believes that while no state in Africa has succeeded in constructing socialism there have been a number of attempts. These have ranged from the first post-independence wave of African Socialist states to the latest (mainly 1970s) wave of 'Marxist states in Africa'. Thus the questions of the transition are being continually raised even if there has been and remains a lack of the so-called expected preconditions, i.e. a powerful working class and highly-developed productive forces. While denying the validity of the argument that socialism in Africa is structurally doomed to failure, he acknowledges that the transition to socialism in Africa has been taking place within the context of economic dependency, neocolonialism and limited resources, but one in which leadership can play a key role in overcoming or at least dealing with these conditions.

Munslow then attempts to define the transition to socialism in terms of which he defines as "the long-term term goals of socialism": 1) ending of private ownership of the means of production; 2) ending of the bourgeoisie's ability to extract surplus value and hence exploit other classes; 3) establishment of a classless society in which the state is no longer used to suppress other classes for the benefit of the bourgeoisie. Munslow then argues that these goals will be implemented by those policies outlined by Gordon White (1983:2): 1) the state will take over industry and agriculture; 2) market mechanisms will be abolished or considerably reduced as 3) a "comprehensive planning structure" is established and 4) "a politico-ideological system bent on the transition to an ultimate communist society" is created. While there might seem to be some elements of tautology in defining the transition to socialism in terms of how socialism will be achieved, in no small measure this is a reflection of the analytic difficulty of the problem and for how short a time this problem has been actively studied. On another point, Munslow's conceptualization of a socialist state certainly resembles to some degree the Soviet model of a centrally-planned, state-owned economy guided by a party dedicated to a communist society. What Munslow and his fellow authors would make of the rise of 'market socialism', Gorbachev's proposals for the Soviet Union and post-Mao China, let alone Yugoslavian worker self-management, is beyond the scope of this work. Munslow, however, warns that the 'classic' definition of socialism can lead the unwary into "vanguard party directionalism" and a host of traps if the needs to adapt socialist theory to the realities of contemporary Africa and to promote "high levels of popular participation by the labouring classes (workers and peasants) in a self-transformatory exercise" (Munslow 1986:3) are not met.

Munslow endorses Gordon White's view that the transition to socialism has to be analyzed as a process and not as an end product. Consequently Munslow seeks to determine what factors play a major role in determining socialist developments in Africa. Having uttered the usual and necessary espistemological caveats, Munslow identifies six such factors which seem to influence the prospects for socialist transition and the type of socialism adopted.

Munslow's first factor is the route to power of those desiring socialism. He identifies four such routes. The peaceful transition to reformist socialism characterised the first wave of independence in Africa from 1957 to 1968. The regimes of Ghana's Kwame Nkrumah, Mali's Modibo Keita, Guinea's Sekou Toure, and Tanzania's Julius Nyerere are his prime examples. The separation of socialist practice from the nationalist struggle during the drive for independence stunted the application of socialism after independence and resulted in 'African Socialism' rather than 'Marxist states in Africa'.

The radical military coup is the second route to power. Examples of this are cited as Somalia (1969), Benin and Madagascar (1972) and Burkina Faso (1983). Munslow argues that these coups were reactions to neocolonialism and that the coupmakers then faced the problem of having to build a revolutionary party after the seizure of power. Because of this, they tried to create popular revolutionary structures; however, the lack of political cadres has often resulted in the forced substitution of coercion for popular mobilization to achieve revolutionary goals. Rather strangely, Munslow does not mention Ghana under Rawlings (1979 and 1981) where the lack of cadres, inter alia has reduced the success of popular mobilization and forced the government to rely on the security apparatus to stay in power (Ray 1986), although there has been remarkably little exercise of coercion compared to the bloodbaths of Ethiopia, a point on which Munslow is silent.

Instead Munslow characterizes Ethiopia as the example of the third route to power: revolution from above. Despite noting that Markakis (1981) believes Ethiopia to be a prime example of garrison socialism -- a supra-class military clique bent on maintaining a centralised state at the expense of the regions and Eritreans, Munslow accepts the Halliday/Molyneaux thesis of "revolution from above". They argue that "a sector of the pre-existing state apparatus" (i.e. the military coup-makers) rather than a mass movement has initiated revolutionary social and political structural change (Munslow 1986:7 citing Halliday and Molyneaux 1981:26). Munslow does, however, note that while the Ethiopian military regime has had considerable success in eliminating 'feudalism', it has suffered a number of problems as the price for a distorted revolutionary process: little popular participation, oppression of the nationalities, and slowness in party building.

Protracted people's war is the fourth route to power that Munslow examines. Arising out of the theory and practice of the Chinese and Vietnamese revolutions, a number of African revolutionary nationalist movements have applied successfully its precepts. The most notable successes have been in the former Portuguese colonies of Angola, Guinea-Bissau and Mozambique as well as in Zimbabwe. The key concept of this model has been political mobilisation that creates support and then turns it into popular participation in the national liberation movement as this is transformed from a nationalist movement into a socialist party.

In contrast to the Ottaways, Munslow and his fellow authors make class a core concept in their analysis. Consequently Munslow's second factor effecting socialist development is the socio-economic context. The socio-economic context of African revolutions is rather different from those with which Marx was familiar. Based on his European experience, Marx suggested that in Europe socialist revolutions would take place when the proletariat was united as well as being considerable in numbers and when productive forces were very developed. In Africa, however, the proletariat is small in numbers, low in class consciousness and fragmented, while the forces of production are relatively low. Nationalism and anti-imperialism, not class consciousness per se, have motivated the African peasantry to make Africa revolutions.

Because of their particular historical circumstances, when African revolutionaries have come to power they have had to deal with an international context in which their countries are highly integrated in a dependent manner into the global capitalist economy. Consequently they are vulnerable to outside pressures. Munslow concludes that this different formulation of class forces in Africa is attributable to their being part of a social formation of the periphery which thus needs to be carefully considered in the case of each country.

Munslow's third factor influencing socialist development is the development strategy. He notes that while the heavy industrialization model of the Soviet Union and China has carried great prestige in African circles, this strategy has been applied uncritically and with little analysis on how it was originally created and its applicability to a specific African country. Munslow advocates adopting a model adapted from another peripheral socialist economy, i.e. Nicaragua. Peasant production of food and export crops will be encouraged by the state as the means of feeding the proletariat and accumulating capital for the state. Foreign investment and capitalist ownership would be allowed under the direction of the state while the proletariat and socialist leadership grow in numbers, skills and experience. Eventually the transition to socialism will be accelerated and the feasibility of an industrial strategy can be reevaluated.

The fourth factor of Munslow's model is the internal and external opposition to socialism. They are of importance because they have overtly and covertly attacked attempts to establish socialism. Indeed, in countries such as Mozambique and Angola, the socialist regimes have been barely able to survive against racist South African and CIA attacks, let alone build socialist projects. While the socialist governments of southern Africa have borne the brunt of external attacks, the CIA and other intelligence agencies have been identified as being involved in coups and coup attempts in countries ranging from Nkrumah's Ghana (1966) to more recent attempts in Rawlings' Ghana (1982 onwards). Often linked to these external opponents, the bureaucratic and commercial bourgeoisie classes have conducted a class war that has often been very effective in blocking socialist policies, if not always overthrowing socialist governments.

Munslow's fifth factor is the degree of preparedness and maturity of the party. The ideology, organisation and numbers of the revolutionary organisation have had significant effects on the process of socialist transition and the choice and success of state policy during that period. Party building is a key, but very difficult, process.

His sixth factor is the transformation of inherited state apparatus. Socialist governments inherit state structures that are opposed to socialist goals on both or one of two points. The inherited state structures were established by the colonial power. Thus to expect that the former colonial military, police and bureaucracy will help to build socialism was naive. The second point is that the inherited state structures were created by capitalism in the guise of colonialism and therefore contain pro-capitalist class forces which will oppose the closing off of their capitalist options. Yet the revolutionary parties have often been forced to rely on the established state apparatus because of the party's need for the expertise of the bureaucrats and the inability of the working class to take over those structures. Munslow also notes that after independence there has been a tendency for the revolutionary organisations to become absorbed in administration and maintaining state power to the detriment of the mass organisations.

Munslow's six factors "determining" socialist development in Africa are a useful addition to the analysis of the African left. Certainly they aid in the development of criteria on which typologies could be created. Munslow's examples for each of the six factors demonstrates their importance. Whether or not they are really the only six "determining" variables remains open to debate.

Arguing that Marxism in Africa needs to be understood from the perspective of African Marxists, Cohen (1986) offers a periodization of the African left based on the writings of four African/Afro-American political theorists.

George Padmore (originally from Trinidad) and Kwame Nkrumah (founder of Ghana) are seen as the significant political writers for the generation of Pan-Africanist African left that was prominent during the 1940s and the 1950s. As they advocate the unity of Africa, Cohen sees them as bridging the theorising from the previous position of rather unfocussed anti-imperialism to that of arguing for the necessity of first an independent state and then a revolutionary state. Franz Fanon (originally from Martenique but best known for his Algerian experience) and Amilcar Cabral (founder of Guinea-Bissau) are taken to characterise the 1960s and early 1970s. They wrestled with the question of what classes existed in Africa and which were necessary for a revolutionary class alliance during the wars of national liberation that would found a revolutionary state in Africa. Cohen concluded these four writers had demonstrated how Marxism had been Africanised and that the African left could ignore those Cold War Warriors and African mystifiers who claimed that Marxism was an alien ideology.

Turok's typology (1986) is of especial interest because of his lengthy participation in the African left. Turok interprets the African left as consisting primarily of Marxists oriented to the Soviet Union. Other outlooks are mentioned but are usually measured against his main focus. Turok's categories consist of "the bearers of Marxist ideology", "Marxism and national liberation movements," "Marxist states in Africa", and "Marxists against neocolonial regimes".

Turok's overall conclusion is that while there has been a considerable growth in the Marxist left since the 1920s, the various groups and individuals remain focussed within their own countries. Instead of the emergence of a continental Marxist movement capable of providing mutual support, the pan-African organisation that was created was the Organization of African Unity, a vehicle for the state leaders of Africa.

Turok first surveys the bearers of Marxist ideology. These are identified as the Pan-African movement, political figures, academics, journals such as the <u>Review of African Political Economy</u> and the <u>Journal of African Marxists</u> and Marxist parties. He notes that with the exceptions of the Sudan and South Africa, which have long established communist parties, Marxism in Africa is a post-1945 phenomenon. As one measure of its progress, he is able to list twenty-three countries which have Marxist parties. This list appears to exclude those parties which are critical of the Soviet Union.

Turok argues that Marxists have had a very diverse experience with Africa's national liberation movements. Turok is suspicious that national liberation movements are often vehicles for non-Marxist petty bourgeois leaders who will betray socialism at the first chance. He argues that this happened in Algeria, Egypt and the Sudan. However, as the latter two of these three examples did not involve national liberation movements (no where does Turok define the term) this part of his argument is open to question. He is on firmer ground when he argues that the national liberation movements of Angola, Mozambique and Guinea-Bissau provided the training ground for Africans who became Marxists and which movements converted after independence into vanguard parties. Turok does not devote much attention to examining national liberation movements as left organisations per se.

Turok is struck by the rapid yet fragile emergence of Marxist states in Africa. Twelve states accept some version of Marxism as their official ideology, to which Turok is reluctant to add Zimbabwe. Turok is concerned that in the case of the twelve, that the adoption of Marxism as 'more the result of action from above than the expression of a mass proletarian movement led by a communist party...' (Turok 1986:64). Consequently he is not surprised at the difficulties that these governments have in implementing socialist policies. These problems are compounded by these regimes inheriting dependent economies tied to the former colonial power.

Beyond the Marxist states Turok notes that the Soviets see "socialist-oriented countries", a more inclusive category that incorporates a variety of other socialist countries such as social democratic Tanzania and Zambia. Using this broad brush, one in four Africans live under socialism, although Turok notes that social democratic one-party states such as Tanzania proved hostile to Marxists.

Since independence, neocolonial regimes have emerged as the major challenge to African Marxists. African Marxists in these countries have been weakened by repression by the regime, fragmentation amongst the left into different parties. On the other hand, the universities and the junior ranks of the military have provided fresh, if often rather uncontrollable, sources of recruits.

Bie Nio Ong (1986) makes a significant contribution to the analysis of women and the transition to socialism. Having raised a number of important points on the conceptualization of women's oppression, analysing rural women's labour, transforming gender relations, she argues that the experiences of Angola, Mozambique and Zimbabwe point out that the participation of women in the political process depended on three factors. First, the relationship of men and women has to change in tandem with changes in the social relations of production. Second, Ong argues women's organisations must not be subordinated to needs of the men who dominate the party. Third, the production for use by women must be valued by the government just as it includes the value of production for exchange. Until this is done the contribution of African women will always be undervalued, and their participation in the African left will be minimalised.

Concepts

African socialism: the Africanization of social democracy?

'African Socialism' was most clearly articulated by African leaders in the aftermath of the nationalist movement for independence. Before independence, nationalism, the mass parties of nationalism, and the anti-colonial struggle gave coherence and structure to the wishes and actions of many Africans. However, following independence, the leaders of the new African states needed a political ideology that would once again motivate their fellow citizens to achieve a common goal. 'African Socialism' was put forward as such a unifying and motivating force that would propel their countries into 'development' and keep the leaders in power.

At one level, 'African Socialism' is an artificial construct of scholars designed to impose some intellectual uniformity over a variety of often disparate forms in aid of Western social science's reproductive compulsion towards generalizability and theory-building: in short a heuristic device to allow the comparing of uncomparable. At another level when Zambian Kaunda's Humanism is compared to Tanzanian Nyerere's "Ujamaa" (or Familyhood), certain commonalities do appear and a certain resemblance to social democratic socialism does appear.

In this case, 'African Socialism' offers the prospect of an egalitarian society which encourages mass participation in political decisions through the mass party (historically the nationalist party which led the country to independence) and in economic decisions by the encouragement of petty bourgeois enterprises (i.e. small-scale owner-operated farms and business, especially if co-operatives) and state-controlled and -directed large-scale capital intensive economic activity. 'African Socialism' was expected to be readily operationalized, it was stated, because it was rooted in the traditional African values of sharing, hospitality and co-operation of a Golden Age of Pre-Colonial Africa which by custom was classless, non-exploitative, communal and conflict-free. Therefore the job of contemporary African politicians was to create the opportunities for these values to be realized by the African peoples who acted as latent storehouses of 'African Socialism's customs. Yet it has become almost customary to deride 'African Socialism' as simplistic and virtually worthless as an analytical tool. Is this fair?

Julius Nyerere is one of the major architects of credible 'African Socialism'. Nyerere led the nationalist movement for an independent Tanganyika and became its first Prime Minister and President. He created Tanzania when he convinced Zanzibarar to join state power from 1960 to 1985. Thus over a political career of more than thirty years, he had ample time to reflect and act towards the creation of 'African Socialism'.

Nyerere tried to use the concept of 'African Socialism', or "ujamaa" as he called it, as a strategic concept to make the transition from the political and ideological imperatives of a nationalist movement struggling for independence and a ruling post-colonial movement seeking development. As the nationalist leader he needed to demonstrate that he led a people unified in their desire to end colonial rule. Nationalist unity was to be used as a negotiating strategy against the colonial occupier. After independence he needed to preserve the unity of his political power base. Only then could he hope to transform his party (TANU, later CCM) from one goal (independence) to another (development). "Ujamaa" was the ideological key to this transformation.

"Ujamaa" Socialism was defined as 'familyhood', a term culturally appropriate to Tanzanians who valued the extended family. Classes were seen as the result of foreign, European experience and hence intrinsically alien to Africa. Class conflict in Africa was alien, and in any case such tensions were not antagonistic, i.e. immutably hostile. Consequently Nyerere and other 'African Socialist' leaders rejected the vanguard party in favour of the mass party. Persuasion, not force, was to be used by 'African Socialist' governments: voluntarism not coercion was part of the theory if not the practice of 'African Socialism'. Accordingly African socialist leaders were to design and implement policies that rolled back accumulations of wealth based on exploitation. Land became the property of the whole people; agriculture, the economic base of 90% of Tanzanians, was to be organised along co-operative and communal lines; large-scale economic activities were to be organised socially, by the state; and health and education services were to be organised and funded for the benefit of the whole people. In short, ujamaa for Nyerere meant social democracy, as it did for Kenneth Kaunda of Zambia who called 'African Socialism' by the name of

'Humanism'. While the Ottaways claim that Leopold Senghor, long-time President of Senegal, who was also an 'African Socialist' (p.14), Senghor was more renowned for his writings on 'negritude' in which he argued that Africans were oriented to spiritual, humanistic matter rather than the Marxist materialism of Europe. All three leaders shared a rejection of Marxism, to varying extents, and certainly of the Soviet model and leadership.

This was especially apparent in the sphere of foreign policy. In its 'purest' form, 'African Socialism' implied that as neither capitalism nor communism were to be the motive force for domestic policy, the impetus of foreign policy of 'African Socialism' was to seek alignment with neither the Western nor the Soviet blocs, in other words: non-alignment. This implied membership in the Non-Aligned Movement (NAM). In practice it often meant a refusal to follow necessarily the voting wishes of the major powers at the UN, a willingness to establish diplomatic relations with members of the various blocs and to accept aid from all donors. Another component of 'African Socialism's' foreign policy was African unity. In order for all Africans to be able to fully express themselves, and thus for 'African Socialism' to flourish, African Socialist government supported measures which would end foreign rule and enhance African unity. However, neither non-alignment nor African unity were the exclusive preserves of the 'African Socialists', contrary to what some sources argue (Ottaway 1986: 14-15). Rather they were values held and honoured, to varying degrees, by a wide range of African governments and groups on the left and right.

The Ottaways argue that while 'African Socialism' dominated the thinking of African socialists during the 1960s, by the end of the 1970s it had been "totally discredited" and had been replaced by the Soviet interpretation of Marxism-Leninism (Ottaway 1986:13) as adapted to Africa in the form of Afro-communism. Their argument is somewhat overstated on this point. They claim that 'African Socialism' in some form was advocated by the leaders of Ghana, Zambia, Tanzania, Senegal and Guinea. True that what these leaders said and wrote may be interpreted as 'African Socialism', but then so did Kenyatta of Kenya claim to be implementing African Socialism while he and his friends amassed considerable fortunes. True the concept of 'African Socialism' has considerable interpretive plasticity, but the concept is in danger of losing its ability to structure argument. Moreover the Ottaways do not, at this point in their argument, take into account four other points. First, a considerable number of other African socialist leaders in the 1960s and 1970s were Marxist-oriented: the Ottaways never demonstrate that these socialists went through, en masse, an African Socialist phase. Second, a good number of these 'African Socialists' were really social democrats as Nyerere (Pratt 1976) and Kaunda (see his Humanism) have been and who have been influenced by British and Canadian social democrats. Third, others, such as Senghor of Senegal, were really centrist liberals and radicals of the French ilk. Fourth, to the extent that there is common intellectual core to 'African Socialism', it seeks to Africanize the ideologies of their European (former colonial) class counterparts as they take over African states created by capitalism. In order to do this, 'African Socialists' have strong political motives to obscure class and ethnic divisions, as the Ottaways correctly point out (pp.15-17), and so appeal to the liberal and social democratic beliefs that classes should not exist and if they do, then class conflict is not inevitable nor necessary.

Finally, it should be noted that even if the Ottaways' selection were taken as constituting the total population of African socialist leaders (which is not true), Kaunda of Zambia, Nyerere of Tanzania, Senghor of Senegal never accepted the Soviet model. Not one of the Ottaways' 'African Socialist' country leaders became the leader of an 'Afro-communist' state; although Nkrumah might have been willing to do so if he had not been overthrown. Leaders such as Nyerere and Kaunda were 'African Socialists' at independence and have remained so up to the present. The Afro-communist state leaders of the Ottaways were drawn from entirely different leadership and inspirational pools. There is little proven leadership or ideological overlap between 'African Socialism' and 'Afro-communism'.

'Transitional socialism'

'Transitional Socialism' is the least satisfactory of the Ottaways' analytical categories for their typology of the African left. In large measure, perhaps this is a reflection of the difficulties of analysing those diverse phenomena who and which are lumped into this catch-all category. The Ottaways conceptualise 'Transitional Socialism' as being "a hybrid mixture of Marxism-Leninism and African socialism"(pp.17-18) which was generated as a second stage of socialist activity by certain of those African leaders who had become dissatisfied with 'African Socialism'. State leaders such as Ghana's Nkrumah, Guinea's Toure, Algeria's Ahmed Ben Bella and Mali's Modibo Keita were reacting to their problems in implementing 'African Socialism' in their countries. Specifically, the Ottaways argue these leaders became 'Transitionalists' because they found that while the mass party structure had mobilised everybody for the nationalist struggle, it also offered positions of power to capitalists and bureaucrats from which they could oppose socialist policies and the mobilization for socialism. These leaders therefore sought out alternatives including the experience of the Marxist-Leninists, which the Ottaways interpret as a wholly-Soviet experience. These 'Transitional Socialism' country leaders attempted to utilise some items of Marxism-Leninism, but never enough of them for a long enough period of time for the 'ML formula' to work and put these countries into the transition to socialism. Interestingly, all these leaders die or are overthrown before they can establish socialism as something that survives their individual hold on power. In any case these leaders lacked the understanding of Marxism-Leninism and the commitment to it to be able to use it to achieve socialism. Perhaps in fairness to some of these leaders, especially Nkrumah (Card 1975), the Chinese, Soviets and U.S. were right: it is difficult to build socialism without socialists. Lenin made the key point: a socialist party is needed to build socialism.

The Ottaways' use of the term 'Transitional' is indicative of the problems of analysing social phenomena that contain both Marxist and non-Marxist elements. They see this 'hybrid mixture' as containing only Marxism-Leninism and 'African Socialism'. However, it seems difficult to argue that 'African Socialism' was the only non-Marxist component to 'Transitional Socialism' when in fact there were numerous other ideas that were lumped in with 'African Socialism'. For example, the Ottaways do not have separate categories for the nationalists, Pan-Africanists, Islamic radicals and so on. Nkrumah mixed traditional Ghanaian ideas of politics with nationalism, Pan-Africanism, anti-colonialism, anti-imperialism, social democracy, Marxism-Leninism and Christianity but not Islam which was significant in the Algerian case. Moreover, 'Transitional Socialism' is seen primarily, nearly exclusively, from the perspective of the choices of individual leaders of countries. While there is much to be said for examining the statements of state leaders as part of a research strategy, to do so without considering the others who made up the rest of that leader's party, group, movement and/or power based is to miss important parts of the picture.

While clearly there is much utility in the Ottaways' category of 'Transitional Socialism' in pointing out there were those who clearly were not 'African Socialists' or Marxist-Leninists, 'Transitional Socialism' remains another catch-all category that needs to be further analysed and broken up into its component parts.

Afro-communism

Afro-communism is the most useful and original category of the Ottaway's model because it points to the existence of African governments which aspire to the Marxist-Leninist model. Paradoxically at no point do they attempt a concise definition of the concept. Instead they define it by citing examples (eg. p.213) and then distilling the key elements of the concept from these examples drawn from the governments of Angola, Ethiopia and Mozambique.

By an inductive process, Afro-communism is thought to be a belief system of governments (virtually no attention is given to movements, etc. out of power) that is composed of six major points. First, Marxism-Leninism is a scientific socialism that is non-area specific but which is capable of being utilised everywhere. Therefore, there cannot be an 'African Socialism' which has its scientific laws peculiar to a region. Second, unlike 'African Socialism', Afro-communism uses a class analysis that expects class conflict, and moreover such conflict is seen as the motive force for social change. Third, the state is to be a 'dictatorship of the proletariat', to use the classical concept, in which the working class leads the other labouring classes (e.g. peasantry) in establishing and exercising state power. However, although the Ottaways do not develop this point, there seems to be a contradiction between this concept of the 'dictatorship of the proletariat' and the concepts of 'people's democracy' and the 'national democratic revolution'. The first concept is based on a party and state organised from and definitively led by the working class, whereas the latter two are based on a coalition state and amalgam party that contains significant elements that are not drawn from the working class. There seems thus a contradiction between the two concepts based on the class criteria who should be permitted to exercise power. This contradiction is perhaps in part attributable to the very concept of 'Afro-communism' but in part is also due to the complex realities of the states that generated Afro-communism, and as well to the theoretical problems that many Marxist-Leninists have had in trying to understand and implement the transition to socialism that often started from a nationalist/national liberation movement (as in the case of Angola and Mozambique) or a coup d'etat by elements of the military (as remains the case in Ethiopia).

Fourth, the socialist revolution is to be led by a vanguard party, i.e. a party of selected cadres chosen for their revolutionary dedication, political experience and knowledge of Marxism-Leninism and who are proletarian in origin. With such high standard, the vanguard party will be small in numbers but able to provide revolutionary leadership under the most strenuous conditions as argued. Fifth, the Ottaways (p.28) argue that 'Afro-communists' distinguish themselves from 'African Socialists' on the issue of coercion. The former cheerly incorporate coercion into their philosophy of the state, while the latter reluctantly implement, but do not philosophically accept, violence against their opposition, a source of enormous relief to their victims. At this point the Ottaways have fallen into the rather hopeless American Cold War mind-trap, best epitomised by an U.S. ambassador who once stated that authoritarian regimes were not to be criticised because they belonged to the U.S. but that totalitarian regimes were to be attacked because they belonged to them (i.e. the Soviets).

Sixth, the foreign policies of the Afro-communist states are dominated by 'proletarian internationalism' and an anti-imperialist interpretation of non-alignment. In contrast to earlier generations of the African left, the Afro-communists are claimed to be little interested in Pan-Africanism (Ottaway 1986:29), although this is not really proven or explained. Certainly Mengistu's Ethiopia placed a lower priority on Pan-Africanism than did Nkrumah's Ghana, but this would seem to be more of a function of the new possibilities for policies of proletarian internationalism than a rejection of Pan-Africanism per se. Certainly Mozambique and Angola have borne the brunt of the external battles against the apartheid regime by African states for the liberation of the people of South Africa: very definitely Mozambique and Angola have thus operationalised the Pan-African tenet of struggling to end colonial rule of African peoples. Moreover, as active participants in the Organization of African Unity and as founders of the SADCC which is designed to promote regional co-operation in southern Africa as a defence against racist rule in South Africa, these two Afro-communist states have been promoting African unity, another core idea of Pan-Africanism. But where Pan-Africanism was a dominant element of earlier left regimes, e.g. Nkrumah's Ghana, for the Afro-communist states Pan-Africanism is subsumed within their commitment to 'proletarian internationalism' and non-alignment. Both of these latter two elements are seen from the perspective that there are two major groups of states in the post-1917 world. There is the anti-imperialist camp led by the 'socialist' or proletarian countries, most prominently the Soviet Union, and the capitalist camp led by the imperialist, or bourgeois countries, most notably the USA. Marx's classes are transformed from the level of people to the level of countries. Thus all proletarian elements fighting against imperialism and for socialism are supposed to co-operate with each other and to have foreign policies that reflect this imperative. In a similar fashion non-alignment is interpreted as a foreign policy that is not aligned with imperialism, even if one of the co-operantes has not accepted socialism per se but has agreed to fight imperialism.

Left nationalism

The term "Left Nationalism" encompasses a range of orientations, organisations, individuals and political problems. Nationalist movements, national liberation movements, Pan-Africanism (and Pan-Arabism for North Africa) and national democratic/new democratic revolutionary organisations are different expressions of Left Nationalism. There is, alas, no spectroscopic analysis possible to prove that any one political movement definitively belongs to a given category. The core orientations that define Left Nationalism include anti-colonialism, populism but not a class analysis that sees class antagonism as inevitable, a mixed economy with a public sector but not an anti-capitalist economic strategy, and a political organisation strategy based not on a vanguard party but on a loosely-organised mass party or a more structured national liberation movement.

Eclectic socialism

Into what category can a country like Somalia be put? Somalia declared itself to be a Marxist-Leninist state, set about building a vanguard party under Soviet guidance, opened its ports to the Soviet navy and then once it realised that it had been traded in for new Soviet interests in Ethiopia, socialist Somalia backed away from the Soviet bloc and appealed for Western help. Eclectic Socialism describes those governments and organisations which have had some socialist content but which now contain significant, if not now dominant, non-socialist influences.

3 Phases and Growth of the African Left

Pre-European contact roots of the African left

Was there an African left that predates European contact? Such a question is of importance not only because it addresses the questions of the indigenisation and authenticity of leftist ideas and actions in Africa as well as the history of the left in Africa but also because it makes explicit the need to understand the contributions and assumptions that Africans have brought to their leftist ideas, actions and organisations.

This in turn implies two further factors to be considered: (a) what 'cultural baggage' or political preconceptions did Africans bring to their interpretation of left ideas and actions, and (b) what aspects of African society contributed to the fund of leftist ideas and actions. These two questions raise two further problems. First, given the vast number of African societies in the pre-European period, can one talk of one set of African reactions or contributions to the body of leftist ideas and actions? Despite the attempts of African leaders such as Nyerere of Tanzania and Kaunda of Zambia to create a picture of a golden pre-colonial age of African socialism, we really know very little about this period in terms of the questions that we now raise. There are fragments which have emerged as parts of studies focussing on other subjects, but an integrated study of the African indigenous left on a regional, let alone continental, basis remains to be undertaken. Such a study should probably include consideration of the following variables: degree and nature of political participation, public control of leaders, public control of land, public control of production, trade and distribution, ideas of hospitality and responsibility as well as Islamic contributions. At the very least the movements of the primary resistance to the imposition of colonial rule need to be examined in light of these criteria.

This mention of Islam raises again the problem of whether it is appropriate to phrase the original question of an African left as existing before 'European contact'. As North Africa has been in constant contact with the European side of the Mediterranean Sea, it seems hard to conceive of this part of Africa existing in a 'pre-European contact' period. Indeed for some time Islam acted as a unifying force throughout much of the Mediterranean basin and North America. If, however, sub-Saharan Africa is being discussed, then the mid-fifteenth century can be taken as the time from which continuous European contact takes place. The initial form of this contact was mainly restricted to the coastal areas of Africa until the latter half of the nineteenth century. When the conquest and colonization of Africa was virtually complete by 1900, then nearly all Africans were forced face to face with the real nature of their subjugators, which was not European but rather capitalism with colonialism as its political face. Thus the emergence of an African left which, at the least, is critical of capitalism and colonialism becomes possible across the continent as a major part of the reaction to colonialism and capitalism.

The colonial period: the birth of the anti-colonial left

Colonialism, as the political face of expanding capitalism, was the decisive force in shaping the African left in the period from the middle of the nineteenth century until the latter part of the twentieth century. As Africans came to experience and understand colonialism, and hence capitalism and imperialism, numbers of them began to organise resistance to these phenomena. The anti-colonial resistance by what became the African left manifested itself in a variety of organisational and ideological forms.

The first reactions of many Africans to the colonial conquest and forcible incorporation into the capitalist system by imperialism were those of confusion and resentment, then a growing understanding of how the colonial system and the search for models to deal with colonialism. The adaptive models initially ranged from conversion to Christianity to the adoption of Western education, manners and mores. Other responses included collaboration (e.g. joining the colonial police and armies) and the search for organisational forms capable of being recognised by and of dealing with or resisting capitalism.

Such new forms included ethnic welfare associations and other voluntary associations, trade unions, movements for the rights of indigenous peoples in the churches (i.e. from the Africanisation of the 'mother' churches in the colonies to the creation of independent African churches) and in the colonies. In addition to these new types of organisation, traditional African organisations were sometimes adapted to deal with this new problem. One notable example of this was the utilisation of traditional grain threshing groups by the nationalist movement in Tanzania to expand their political base. These new organisations were the training ground for African nationalists, numbers of whom became leftists, and the building blocks for the nationalist movements and national liberation movements.

The heyday of these particular new organisations may be considered to be from 1900 to 1945. The nationalist organisations were most important from 1945 to 1965. National liberation movements emerged in Algeria and Kenya during the 1950s, but it was not until around 1965 that they assumed continental significance. Colonial racism was especially well entrenched in southern Africa. Consequently armed resistance by Africans organised into national liberation movements became necessary in Angola, Zimbabwe, Mozambique, Namibia and South Africa, as well as the Portuguese outposts in Guinea-Bissau and (indirectly) Cape Verde and Sao Tome.

By the end of the 1980s, colonialism and apartheid had been formally pushed back from these countries except for the apartheid bunker of South Africa and occupied Namibia. South Africa continues to attack these countries whenever possible. Another type of national liberation movement emerged in the Western Sahara and in Eritrea where the indigenous African peoples have had to fight off attempts of the neighbouring African states of, respectively, Morocco and Ethiopia to absorb them.

Writers on nationalism agree that the core criteria for the existence of any nationalism is that at least some people share a consciousness of that nationality. [1] The European experience, which gave birth to the concept of nationalism, took place in a situation in which there were peoples who shared a common language, culture, economy and history. Often these peoples had been subjugated and incorporated into imperial structures that did not recognize the legitimacy of their nationalism. In Africa, however, the general lack of consolidation of the precolonial states and polities and the tremendous diversity of separate peoples, often of relatively small numbers, meant that a common nationalist consciousness emerged only in reaction to the colonial experience. Thus the actions of the European empires on the African peoples created the nationalisms of Africa which have been defined by the colonial boundaries. Each colony gave birth to its own nationalist or national liberation movement.

At first glance the difference between nationalist movements and national liberation movements may seem rather obscure. Certainly both start by being motivated by nationalism. Saul in his article on Frelimo (the Mozambique Liberation Front) made the important point that there was an underlying political difference between the two types of movements that went beyond the fact that African nationalist movements of the post-1945 period did not use armed struggle to end colonial rule but that the national liberation movements did. The significant difference was that national liberation movements were by their nature oriented not to the nationalist elites but to the masses. National liberation movements contained within themselves the germ of socialism. Sacrifices inherent in armed struggle seemed to demand post-independent states that used available resources for the benefit of the people not just the elite. Now that national liberation movements have won independence throughout the former Portuguese empire in Africa and in Zimbabwe, they are attempting to set up some sort of socialist states. Indeed the former national liberation movements of Angola and Mozambique have declared themselves to be Leninist vanguard parties and have attempted to move from the national liberation phase of the revolution to the socialist phase.

During the colonial period, a variety of social democratic, socialist and communist parties movements and groups were established. Some organisations and individuals operated publicly, and some had to act in the underground. At the beginning these ideas and models of organisation were transferred to Africa mainly by Europeans but also by Africans who had travelled and studied in Europe and, to a much lesser extent, North America. Gradually these ideas and organisational models were indigenised during the colonial period as techniques of dealing with colonialism and capitalism.

Other left responses to colonialism and capitalism in Africa were contained in Pan-Africanism, Pan-Arabism, Negritude and religion. In response to the humiliations of colonial rule, some Africans came to the conclusion that until all of Africa was united in one country, Africans would remain the prey of imperialist predators. Some Arab-Africans believed that they were part of the Islamic Arab-speaking world, and that unless they united, they would suffer a similar fate. Some Pan-Africanists and Pan-Arabists were inspired by socialist ideals, many were not. Negritude, pride in being a black African, developed amongst African students and intellectuals as a reaction to the racism of French colonialism. Across the spectrum of the religions of Africa, there appeared from time to time religious movements that were anti-colonial. All were opposed to colonialism and in that aspect may be considered to be part of the left in general if not necessarily consciously.

Independence: the left in power

As independence swept across Africa during the four decades of 1950s, 1960s, 1970s, and 1980s, the left found itself in power in a number of countries. The route to power at independence varied from peaceful negotiations and elections to the negotiated surrender by the colonial power following its defeat by the national liberation movement. In the wake of independence, the left has been brought to power by elections, coups and revolutions. The left has been forced to deal with state building, poverty, development strategies, counter-revolution formented at home and by foreign powers to break efforts for full economic independence, attempts at neocolonialism by the former colonial power and by imperialist forces to ensure that the formalities of constitutional independence remain undermined by continued foreign control of the economy, wars of national liberation, and in southern Africa with the attacks against the Front-line States and the vicious repression by the apartheid regime of its own people in South Africa.

During the thirty-six years between 1952 and 1988, the left has formed governments in thirty-seven African countries (including Eritrea and Western Sahara) and as fifty-eight regimes. This latter category counts one left regime as existing from the moment it comes to power until it loses power and is replaced. Thus one country, such as Ghana has had four left regimes: Nkrumah (CPP) 1957-1966; Rawlings (AFRC) 1979; Limann (PNP) 1979-1981; Rawlings (PNDC) 1981-1988 onwards.

Yet this listing would be challenged by some. While there would be nearly unanimous agreement that Nkrumah's governments were a good example of African Socialism/Social Democracy-Left Nationalism with currents of Pan-Africanism and proto-Marxism, the qualifications necessary to describe this regime demonstrate the difficulty of categorising the left, let alone developing an effective typology.

Similar difficulties occur in the analysis of the other regimes. Most observers of Ghana would agree that the first Rawlings regime (the Armed Forces Revolutionary Council) was left-nationalist in orientation, although a vigorous debate would break out on whether it was a coup, an uprising or a revolution. While Turok (1986: 66, 71) classifies Limann's Peoples National Party as a member of the social democratic Inter-African Socialist Organisation (IAS), founded in Tunis on February 26-28, 1981, and while the PNP certainly contained a variety of leftists, other analysts would reject the idea that the PNP government was social democratic in nature.

Nearly all analysts agree that at the beginning of the second Rawlings regime (the Provisional National Defence Council), it was revolutionary and that a variety of left nationalists, social democrats, Marxists and other socialists provided the driving force for the revolution. As time passed, a number of left organisations and individuals had differences with Rawlings and left the government. These observers deny that the PNDC is either revolutionary or left.

These analytic problems are multiplied as a continental perspective is assumed. One scholar's "socialist government" is another person's counter-revolutionary puppet. If we declare ourselves to be undaunted by these epistemological (and indeed emotional) problems, it is possible to arrive at a preliminary typology of African leftist regimes. There are four major categories, each of which contain variations: Left Nationalism, African Socialism/Social Democracy, Afro-Communism and Communist, as well as Eclectic Socialism.

From 1952 to 1988, sixteen countries have had twenty Left Nationalist governments. African Socialism grew in popularity and influence during the late 1950s and during the 1960s. It was an attempt to move closer to socialism while avoiding Marxism and the Leninist vanguard party. In large measure African Socialism has been social democracy. From 1952 to 1988, twenty countries have had twenty-seven Left Nationalist governments. Afro-communism and Marxism were adopted by a number of left organisations that gained power during the 1970s and 1980s. Between 1952 and 1988 nine countries have had nine Afro-communist and Marxist governments. Between 1952 and 1988 two countries have had two Eclectic Socialist governments.

The left struggling for power

By 1988, the left had either achieved state power or was struggling to obtain it, in all the countries of Africa. With only the exception of the Ivory Coast, every African country had left groups organised as political parties, groups or movements. In the Ivory Coast, the left was displaced into sectors of society other than the overt party by the ruling party.

Categorising these groups by their strategy for obtaining power, most groups had an electoral-style strategy but at least sixty-two groups had a strategy of armed struggle. The Eritrean People's Liberation Front had come close to establishing Eritrea as an independent state while POLISARIO still faced a considerable battle to free Western Sahara from Morocco. SWAPO continued its combined strategy of armed and peaceful resistance to the apartheid South African occupation of Namibia.

Within South Africa, the left has experienced perhaps the most rapid growth in all of Africa because of its involvement in the anti-apartheid movement.

Some Conclusions

Three sets of conclusions emerge. First, that the growing significance of the African left demands that we pay greater attention to its nature and evolution. Second, the left is now an indigenous and integral part of African life. Third, the growing complexity of the African left is often manifested in unexpected forms: contrary to certain preconceptions, the Soviet model has not yet proven dominant.

Notes

[1] Authors ranging from Kohn (1965) to Stalin (1913) have discussed this topic.

Sources cited

Bill, James A. and Hardgrave, Robert L., (1973), Comparative Politics: The Quest for Theory, Columbus, Ohio, Merrill.

Braganca, Aquino and Wallerstein, Immanuel (eds.), (1982), The African Liberation Reader, London, Zed Press.

Card, Emily, (1975), "The Political Economy of Ghana" in The Political Economy of Africa. R. Harris (ed.), New York, John Wiley, pp.51-91.

Chilcote, Ronald H., (1981), Theories of Comparative Politics: The Search For a Paradigm, Boulder, Westview Press.

Davidson, Basil, (1966), Africa: History of a Continent, London, George Weidenfeld and Nicolson Ltd.

Davidson, Basil; Slovo, Joe; Wilkinson, Anthony, (1976), Southern Africa: The New Politics of Revolution, Harmondsworth, Pelican Books.

Davies, Rob; O'Meara, Dan and Dlamini, Sipho, (1984), The Struggle for South Africa: A Reference Guide to Movements, Organizations and Institutions, two volumes, London, Zed Books.

El-Khawas, Mohamad A. and Cohen, Barry (eds.), (1976), The Kissinger Study of Southern Africa: National Security Memorandum 39, Westport, Conn., Lawrence Hill and Company.

Friedland, William H. and Roseberg, Carl C., (1964), African Socialism, Stanford, Stanford University Press.

Hodgkin, Thomas, (1956), *Nationalism in Colonial Africa*, Harmondsworth, Penguin.

______, (1961), *African Political Parties: An Introductory Guide*, Harmondsworth, Penguin.

Kaunda, Kenneth, (n.d.), *Zambian Humanism*, Lusaka, University of Zambia.

Kohn, Hans, (1965), *Nationalism: Its Meaning and History*, Revised Edition, New York, D. Van Nostrand.

Markakis, John and Waller, Michael (eds.), (1986), *Military Marxist Regimes in Africa*, London, Frank Cass.

Munslow, Barry (ed.), (1986), *Africa: Problems in the Transition to Socialism*, London, Zed Books.

Ottaway, Marina and Ottaway, David, (1986), *Afrocommunism*, Second Edition, New York, Africana Publishing.

Pratt, Cranford, (1976), *The Critical Phase in Tanzania 1945-1968*: *Nyerere and the Emergence of a Socialist Strategy*, London, Cambridge University Press.

Ray, Donald I., (1986), *Ghana: Politics, Economics and Society*, London, Frances Pinter Publishers.

______, (1987), "African Studies: A Preliminary Quantitative Survey of Selected Area Studies Journals for Africa, Latin America and the Middle East", Edmonton, Canadian Association of African Studies.

Rosberg, C.G. and Callaghy, T.M. (eds.), (1979), *Socialism in Sub-Saharan Africa: A New Assessment*, Berkeley, Institute of International Studies, University of California.

Saul, John, (1973), "FRELIMO and the Mozambique Revolution" in *Essays on the Political Economy of Africa*, Arrighi, Giovanni and Saul, John. New York, Monthly Review Press.

______, (1979), *The State and Revolution in Eastern Africa*, London, Heinemann Educational Books.

Saul, John S. and Gelb, Stephen, (1986), The Crisis in South Africa, Revised Edition, New York: Monthly Review Press.

Semyonova, Julian, (1987), TASS Is Authorized to Announce..., Oakville, Ontario, Mosaic Press, translated by Charles Buxton from the Russian language edition published by Druzhba Narodov, 1979.

Solodovnikov, V.G.; Letnev, A.B. and Manchkha, P.I. (eds.), (1970), Political Parties in Africa, Moscow, translated and published in English (1971) by Joint Publications Research Service, Washington.

Stalin, J.V., (1954, orig. 1913), Marxism and the National Question, Moscow, Foreign Languages Publishing House.

Stockwell, John, (1978), In Search of Enemies, New York, Norton.

Stretton, Hugh, (1969), The Political Sciences: General Principles of Selection in Social Science and History, London, Routledge and Kegan Paul.

Turok, Ben (ed.), (1980), Revolutionary Thought in the 20th Century, London, Zed Press.

Appendix A: Chronology of Left States in Africa

This chronology sets out the rise and fall left governments in Africa between 1952 and 1988.

1952

Egypt:

July 23. King Farouk was overthrown by a group of left nationalists ultimately led (1954) by Col. Gamel Abdel Nasser.

1956

Tunisia:

March 20. Habib Bourguiba's Neo-Destour Party (later the PSD) became the first government of independent Tunisia.

1957

Ghana:

March 6. Under Kwame Nkrumah's Convention People's Party (CPP) became independent. Nkrumah attempted to establish a pan-African, socialist-type, one-party state, but equivocated on Marxism and the strategy to establish socialism, until his overthrow in 1966.

1958

Guinea:

October 2. Guinea became independent under Sekou Toure's Parti Democratique de Guinee (PDG). He established a one-party state based on an eclectic amalgam of Marxism, pan-Africanism, Maoism, Islam and African socialism.

1960

Mali:

June 20. Mali became independent under the leadership of Modibo Keita's Soudanese Union Party. He attempted to move towards the Soviet interpretation of a Marxist state until his overthrow in 1968.

Zaire (Congo):

June 30. At independence Patrice Lumumba (Mouvement National du Congo-MNC) became Premier.

September 14. Col. Mobutu overthrew Lumumba.

Tanganyika:

Tanganyika, later Tanzania, became independent under the leadership of Julius Nyerere's Tanganyika African National Union (TANU). He began to implement a non-Marxist social-democratic form of African Socialism which has continued to date.

Senegal:

August 20. Senegal became independent under the leadership of President Leopold Senghor's UPS (renamed PS in 1976)

Mauritania:

November 28. President Moktar Ould Daddeh's PPM (Parti du peuple mauritanien) led the country to independence.

1961

Zaire (Congo):

Following Lumumba's assassination on January 17, parties allied to him formed a "Nationalist" coalition government in Stanleyville (Kisangani) that controlled eastern Congo until their reconciliation with the right-wingers, including Mobutu in August.

1962

Algeria:

July 3. Algeria became independent under the leadership of Ahmed Ben Bella's Front de Liberation Nationale (FLN). Ben Bella attempted to transform the FLN from a national liberation movement to a vanguard party until his overthrow in 1965.

Uganda:

October 9. Uganda became independent under Milton Obote's UPC.

1964

Zaire (Congo):

Mid-1964. The Comite National de Liberation (CNL), an alliance of Lumumbist left-nationalist parties, established the People's Republic of the Congo with Christopher Gbenye (leader of the MNC-L) as President. They were based in Stanleyville (Kisangani), controlling the eastern Congo.

November. Belgian troops and mercenaries overthrew the People's Republic of the Congo.

Zambia:

October 24. Kenneth Kaunda led his social democratic party, UNIP, to power.

1965

Algeria:

June 19. Ben Bella's socialist government was overthrown by the military who converted the FLN into a mass party based on social democracy.

1966

Ghana:

February 23. Nkrumah and the CPP were overthrown by the military.

1967

Tanzania:

Nyerere made his "Arusha Declaration" which signalled the elaboration of a social democratic programme.

Sierra Leone:

March 21. Dr. Siaka Stevens' APC won the election but was then overthrown by a military coup.

1968

Mauritius:

March 12. Mauritius became independent under the leadership of the MLP.

Sierra Leone

April. The Anti-Corruption Revolutionary Movement restored Stevens' APC to power.

Mali:

November 19. Keita was overthrown by the military.

1969

Congo (Brazzaville):

Congo (Brazzaville) became Africa's first lasting 'People's Republic' with Marxism-Leninism as its political outlook.

Libya:

September 1. Col. M. Qadhafi overthrew the King and started the revolution.

Somalia:

October 21. Col. Mohamed Siad Barre came to power in a coup and created the increasingly pro-Soviet Marxist-Leninist SRC.

Uganda:

December. President Obote declared a one-party state based on the social democratic "Common Man's Charter."

Sudan:

May 25. Col. Nimeri overthrew the elected government and banned all political parties except for the Sudanese Communist Party which played a significant role in his initially left nationalist regime.

1970

Egypt:

September 28. President Nasser died.

1971

Sudan:

July 19-21. Elements of the SCP seized power and established a government before their overthrow. Following the coup attempt President Jaafar Nimeri suppressed the SCP and broke relations with the Soviet Union.

1972

Madagascar:

May. President Philibert Tsirana resigned in favour of left nationalist Major General Gabriel Ramanantsea.

Egypt:

President Anwar Sadat expelled Soviet military advisers, ending military assistance from the Soviet Union.

Benin:

October 26. Lieutenant Mathieu Kerekou launched the revolutionary process by seizing power.

Sudan:

October. Col. Nimeri created the SSU as his social democratic political vehicle.

1973

Guinea-Bissau:

September 24. Under the leadership of PAIGC, Guinea-Bissau's National Assembly declared the country's independence from Portugal.

1974

Guinea-Bissau

September 10. Portugal recognised the independence of Guinea-Bissau.

Somalia:

July. The government signed a Treaty of Friendship and Cooperation with the Soviet Union, the first such treaty with sub-Saharan Africa.

Ethiopia:

September. The military overthrew Emperor Haile Selassie.

The military government established ties with the Soviet Bloc.

Benin:

November. Lt. Col. M. Kerekou declared Marxism-Leninism as the regime's framework for theory and practice.

1975

Madagascar:

June. Navy commander Didier Ratsiraka became the head of the military-run Supreme Ruling Council which came to accept Marxism-Leninism.

Mozambique:

June 25. FRELIMO (Frente de Libertacao de Mozambique) under the leadership of Samora Machel led Mozambique to independence. FRELIMO began the transition from a national liberation movement to Marxist-Leninist vanguard party.

Sao Tome and Principe:

July 12. Dr. Manuel Pinto Da Costa's Movimento de Libertacao de Sao Tome e Principe (MLSTP) led the country to independence under a mixture of social democratic and Marxist policies.

November. The Movimento Popular de Libertacao de Angola (MPLA) declared Angola to be independent. The MPLA, led by Agostinho Neto, took power during 1975 and 1976 after winning a civil war, and receiving troops from Cuba and equipment from the Soviet Union to expel a South African invasion. The MPLA began to change from a national liberation movement into a vanguard Marxist-Leninist party.

Comoros:

Ali Solilih led a coup on August 3 and established a National United Front which attempted to carry out a Maoist-style anti-feudal programme.

Rwanda:

July 5. MRND was created by the military as the new ruling party.

1976

Somalia:

July 1. Barre led the SRC into the SRSP, a Soviet Marxist-Leninist vanguard party.

1977

Seychelles:

June 5. Prime Minister France A. Rene's SPUP overthrew President J.R. Mancham's Seychelles Democratic Party. Rene's SPUP became the SPPF in 1978.

Djibouti:

June 27. President Hassan Gouled's LPAI (reorganised as the RPP in 1979) assumed power at independence.

Eritrea:

The EPLF had established a government over most of the country.

1978

Comoros:

May 12-13. President Ali Solilih was overthrown by some fifty French-led mercenaries. Solihih was shot on May 29 by the new regime of Ahmed Abdallah.

Mauritania:

Daddeh's PPM government was overthrown.

1979

Ghana:

June 4. The left nationalist Armed Forces Revolutionary Council (AFRC) overthrew the corrupt military government and supervised the elections and handover to civilian rule.

September 24. Rawlings and the AFRC handed power over to elected President Hilla Limann and his social democratic People's National Party (PNP).

Chad:

August 20-21. Woddei's Frolinat-FAP formed the core of the new ruling GUNT.

1980

Guinea-Bissau:

November 14. Brig. Gen. Vieira replaced President L. Cabral as head of state and PAIGC. Relations were broken between the Cape Verde and Guinea administrations and parties.

Cape Verde:

November. Cape Verde separated from Guinea-Bissau. This led to the formation of PAICV in Cape Verde.

1981

Somalia:

February 26-28. Barre's SRSP became a founding member of the Inter-African Socialist Organisation, thus formally marking its transition from Soviet Marxism-Leninism to social democracy.

Ghana:

December 31. Flt. Lt. J.J. Rawlings overthrew President H. Liman, bringing a variety of left forces to power under the aegis of the Provisional National Defence Council.

1982

Chad:

June 7. Habre's Frolinat-FAN seized power from Woddei's GUNT.

Mauritius:

June 15. The MMM coalition having defeated the MLP coalition, became the government.

Lesotho:

Relations between the BNP government and the Soviet Union thawed. The BNP had strengthened its criticism of the apartheid government of South Africa.

1983

Mauritius:

March. The MMM split. Jugnauth's MMM faction formed the MSM and became the government.

Burkina Faso:

August 4. Captain Thomas Sankara seized power on behalf of the revolutionary CNR government.

1984

Guinea:

March 26. President Toure died while having heart surgery in the USA.

Guinea:

April 3. Toure's PDG was overthrown by a rightist military coup.

Chad:

June 22. Habre's ruling Frolinat-FAN became the UNIR.

1985

Sudan:

April 6. Nimeri and his SSU were overthrown.

Uganda:

July 27. Brigadier B. Okello overthrew Obote's UPC government.

1986

Lesotho:

January 19. Because of its anti-apartheid stance, the BNP was overthrown by a South-African backed military coup.

Uganda:

January 27. Museveni's NRM/NRA overthrew General Tito Okello's military government and assumed power.

1987

Burkina Faso:

Capt. T. Sankara was murdered by his 'close friend', Capt. Blaise Compaore, who seized control of the government.

PART II
DICTIONARY OF THE LEFT PARTIES, MOVEMENTS AND GROUPS OF AFRICA (A-Z)

Explanation of Entry Categories

Each party, group or movement has been allocated one primary entry. Secondary entries were allocated to a group, movement or party if they had changed names (e.g. the SACP was known earlier as the CPSA) or were known by other names ("a.k.a." means "also known as", and "k.a." means "known as").

For each primary entry, information on the movement, party or group was organised into the following fourteen categories:

1. TITLE: The names and acronyms of the organisation are listed as is the shortened country name for greater ease in identifying organisations with similar names but often from different countries.

2. COUNTRY: The formal name and estimated population of the country are listed.

3. DATE ESTABLISHED: The date that the organisation was established or first known to exist is listed.

4. ORGANISATIONAL TYPE: Organisations are characterised as being "vanguard parties" (parties based on democratic centralism); "mass parties" (parties with mass membership, but not operating on democratic centralist principles); "national liberation movements" (parties with membership open to all nationalists, operating along disciplined lines and using armed struggle against the occupying power); "coalitions" (an organisation comprised of still-existing organisations) and "other".

5. ORGANISATIONAL NATURE: The main executive and legislative organs and auxiliary organs of the organisation are listed.

6. MEMBERSHIP: This category too often reflects the fertile imaginations of people. Estimates of numbers should be treated with caution. Where numbers seemed too improbable, an attempt has been made to note the socio-economic classes and

groupings from which the organisation is claimed to have been recruiting.

7. STATUS: The key distinctions listed here is whether the organisation is considered to be legal or illegal by the government, and whether the organisation is the ruling party or an opposition party.

8. PUBLICATIONS: The newspapers, magazines, radio and television stations that an organisation owned or to which it had access are listed.

9. ORIENTATION: The main types of political worldview listed here are: left nationalism, socialism (including social democracy and African socialism), eclectic socialism and Marxism. These types are discussed in chapter two.

10. STRATEGY: The main distinction was whether an organisation claimed to have adopted armed struggle, negotiations or elections as the route to power.

11. INTERNAL AFFILIATIONS: Organisations which are internal to the country and which are affiliated or allied with the main entry organisation are listed here.

12. EXTERNAL AFFILIATIONS: Organisations operating with regard to other countries but which are affiliated or allied with the main entry organisation are listed here.

13. HISTORY: A brief history of the organisation is outlined.

14. LEADERSHIP: The senior leadership by name, with party office (and government office in parentheses), are listed. In some particularly difficult cases, the name commonly used as a surname has been highlighted.

The number was not used to introduce the first category. Availability of information determined the completeness for each entry. All information used in the entries was in the public domain. This practice is, of course, in accordance with The University of Calgary's code of ethics for research, and is designed to protect individuals. Given the parameters of the project, while I have taken the utmost care to ensure the accuracy of the information in the entries, this information (especially for numbers "9" and "10") is not to be taken as having any legal standing.

AFRICAN NATIONAL CONGRESS OF SOUTH AFRICA (ANC: South Africa)

2. Republic of South Africa (34,577,000)

3. Date Established: 1912

4. Organisational Type: National liberation movement (nationalist movement prior to 1960)

5. Organisational Nature: Imprisoned leaders such as Nelson Mandela and Walter Sisulu constitute a national symbol of inestimable value, importance and loyalty for the vast majority of South Africans. Since the banning of the ANC in 1960, and the subsequent arrest or forced exile of much of its top leadership, the nature of the ANC has changed from a legal if harassed nationalist movement with a nationwide organisational structure to that of an underground national liberation movement. Umkhonto We Sizwe (MK) has been the ANC's army since 1961 and now operates throughout South Africa on the basis of the initial stages of protracted people's war. SACTU (South African Congress of Trade Unions) has been the trade union ally of the ANC. The ANC has had an extensive diplomatic presence throughout the world since the 1960s. Congresses and consultative conferences act as legislative bodies. The National Executive Committee consists of thirty members. The Revolutionary Council directs the armed struggle. The senior executive officers are the President-General, the Secretary-General and the Treasurer-General.

6. Membership: Thousands

7. Status: Illegal; underground; exiled elements

8. Publications: _Sechaba_ (monthly), clandestine publications, MK published _Dawn_; SACTU published _Workers' Unity_. The ANC's radio arm has been "Radio Freedom, Voice of the African Nationalist Congress and Umkhonto We Sizwe, the People's Army"

9. Orientation: Left nationalist, anti-apartheid

10. Strategy: National liberation revolution, political mobilisation, armed struggle to achieve the national democratic phase of the revolution.

11. Internal Affiliates: Besides the previously mentioned relations with SACTU and MK, the ANC has been formally allied with the SACP. Numerous organisations such as the UDF has adopted the ANC's "Freedom Charter" but are not affiliated to the banned ANC.

12. External Affiliations: The ANC has been allied with SWAPO (Namibia), ZAPU (Zimbabwe), MPLA (Angola), FRELIMO (Mozambique), PAIGC (Guinea-Bissau), the Derg/WPE (Ethiopia). The ANC has been supported by most African states and has been recognised by the Organisation of African Unity as one of two liberation movements in South Africa. The Soviet Union and its allies have provided consistent support to the ANC.

13. History: The ANC has the distinction of being Africa's senior political movement; no other political party or movement presently in existence has had such a long continuous history. Created in 1912 as the South African Native National Congress, the ANC (name change in 1923) was designed to lobby the white-controlled South African government for improved conditions and legal status for Africans as well as overcoming tribalism by creating an African national consciousness. By and large, the ANC remained a nationalist movement of the chiefs and the emerging African small business, clerks and intelligentsia until the 1940s. In 1943 the ANC by adopting a new constitution and programme as well as establishing the Congress Youth League (CYL) laid the structural basis for its transformation into a mass nationalist movement. The ANC accepted the CYL programme as its own "Programme of Action" in 1949. The ANC used this strategy of mass mobilisation and Gandhian civil disobedience throughout the 1950s with such great success that the ANC was banned in 1960 by the apartheid regime. Membership had risen to the range of 100,000 and the ANC had organised the Congress of the People on 26 June 1955 which adopted the Freedom Charter. This remains the blueprint for independence. Following the closing-off of non-violent means by its 1960 banning, the ANC and the SACP established in 1961 MK to carry out the armed

struggle. The apartheid security forces were able to disrupt and immobilise much of the ANC's structure, culminating in the 1963 capture of the High Command of MK (including most of the top ANC leaders, such as Nelson Mandela). The ANC spent the rest of the 1960s and until 1976 rebuilding the organisation, mainly in exile, in preparation to expanding the scope and level of resistance within South Africa.

The 1969 Morogoro (Tanzania) consultative conference adopted the policies of membership open to all democratic South Africans, the need for 'economic emancipation', the importance of organising the working class in order to end the 'Colonialism of a Special Type' in which blacks are an 'internal colony' who have to overcome first their colonisation by the whites (national democratic phase of the revolution) and then overall capitalist exploitation. The 16 June 1976 Soweto uprising marked a dramatic upsurge in popular resistance and then brutal state repression. Many participants went on to join the ANC and its armed wing, MK, thereby effectively recognising the primacy of the ANC in process of liberation. Since then MK has greatly increased the number and effectiveness of its attacks on military and economic targets of the apartheid regime.

The 16-23 July 1985 Kabwe (Zambia) conference expanded to thirty the National Executive Committee, elected the leadership (which included people of all so-called races) as well as discussing policy.

14. Leadership: Nelson Mandela (imprisoned); Walter Sisulu (imprisoned); Oliver R. Tambo (President General); Alfred Nzo (Secretary General); T. Nkobi (Treasurer General)

AFRICAN PEOPLES' DEMOCRATIC UNION OF SOUTH AFRICA (APDUSA: South Africa).

See also, UMSA

AFRICAN YOUTH BRIGADE (AYB: Ghana)

2. Republic of Ghana (12,205,000)

3. Date Established: c.1983

4. Organisational Type: Mass party

6. Membership: Several hundred to over one thousand, mainly among secondary students of the Volta, Brong Ahafo and Greater Accra Regions.

7. Status: Legal

9. Orientation: Left nationalist

10. Strategy: Peaceful change

13. History: The AYB split from the AYC

14. Leadership: Kwabla Davour, National Secretary; Dr. M.M. Owusu-Ansah, Patron

AFRICAN YOUTH COMMAND (AYC: Ghana)

2. Republic of Ghana (12,205,000)

3. Date Established: 1974

4. Organisational Type: Mass party

6. Membership: Thousands of youth (7-50 years of age)

7. Status: Legal

8. Publications: The Command (newspaper)

9. Orientation: Left nationalist (Pan-Africanist), elements of Marxism

10. Strategy: Peaceful cooperation with African governments to promote development and Pan-African unity

11. Internal Affiliations: Since the AYC's founding, it has worked with all the governments of Ghana, including the PNDC. The AYC has cooperated especially with the Movement for Peace and Democracy and the Ghana Peace and Solidarity Council.

12. External Affiliations: The AYC has affiliates in Nigeria, Togo, Sierra Leone, Ivory Coast, Liberia, Gambia and Senegal.

13. History: The AYC was formed as a Pan-African youth organisation in response to an Organisation of African Unity meeting in Accra. The AYC has concentrated on establishing a number of educational and employment projects and programmes for youth.

14. Leadership: Dr. F.W.A. Akuffo, President (Ghana); S.S. Baffuor-Awuah, Ghana National Secretary and Continental Deputy Secretary-General.

AFRO-SHIRAZI PARTY (ASP: Tanzania)

See also CCM.

AL HAKIKA (The Truth: Tunisia)

2. Republic of Tunisia (7,224,000)

3. Date Established: Existed in 1981

6. Membership: Few

7. Status: Illegal

9. Orientation: Left nationalist (Arab nationalist)

12. External Affiliations: Pro-Soviet

14. Leadership: Ahmed Hafnaoui

AL-HIZB AL-SHUYU'I AL MISRI (HSM-Egypt) a.k.a. ECP

AL-HIZB AL-SHUYU'I AL-SUDANI (HSS: Sudan) a.k.a. SCP

AL HURRIYA (Liberty: Tunisia)

2. Republic of Tunisia (7,224,000)

3. Date Established: Existed in 1981

6. Membership: Few

7. Status: Illegal, in exile

9. Orientation: Left nationalist (Iraq Baathist) and Libyan eclectic socialism.

12. External Affiliations: Iraq, Libya

14. Leadership: Mohammed Messouad Chebbi

ALL ETHIOPIAN SOCIALIST MOVEMENT (AESM-Ethiopia) a.k.a. MEISON

ALLIANCE DEMOCRATIQUE SENEGALAIS (ADS-Senegalese Democratic Alliance: Senegal)

See also, LD-MPT, MRDM, OST, PDS, UDP

2. Republic of Senegal (6,710,000)

3. Date Established: July 1985

4. Organisational Type: Alliance of parties

7. Status: Illegal

9. Orientation: left nationalist with Trotskyist, Maoist and Albanian versions of Marxism-Leninism

10. Strategy: Coordination of anti-imperialist opposition forces.

11. Internal Affiliations: The ADS is composed of the left nationalist PDS, the Maoist MRDN, the pro-Albanian UDP and the Trotskyist LD-MPT and OST.

13. History: Following the doctor's strike and the PS government's bulldozing of a squatter housing area, in July 1985 the five parties created the ADS to improve opposition coordination. The PS government, having outlawed electoral coalitions, responded by outlawing the ADS and harassing the leaders. This did not have any significant immediate effect on the ADS.

14. Leadership: Dr. Abdoulaye Bathily (LD-MPT), Chairman.

ALL-PEOPLE'S CONGRESS (APC: Sierra Leone)

2. Republic of Sierra Leone (4,105,000)

3. Date Established: 1960

4. Organisational Type: Mass party

5. Organisational Nature: One-party state

6. Membership: Thousands

7. Status: Ruling party in one-party state.

8. Publications: Through the government, the APC has access to the government newspapers (Daily Mail; 13,000 daily), radio and television.

9. Orientation: Elements of left nationalism.

10. Strategy: Electoral, regime maintenance.

13. History: Formed in 1960, the year before independence, the APC led by Dr. Siaka P. Stevens won the 1967 election, defeating Sir A.M. Margai's SLPP (Sierra Leone People's Party). However a military coup led by Lt. Col. A. Juxon-Smith prevented the APC from assuming office until 1968 when the Anti-Corruption Revolutionary Movement (mainly non-commissioned officers) restored Stevens' APC to constitutional power. Under the 1978 Constitution, the APC became the sole, ruling party of Sierra Leone. Major-General Joseph Saidu Momoh was chosen by APC members at the 1-4 August 1985 Congress to be the new Secretary General of the APC. Momoh thereafter became President of Sierra Leone on 28 November 1985.

14. Leadership: Secretary General Maj. Gen. Joseph Saidu Momoh (President of the Republic); Francis Misheck Minah (First Vice-President of the Republic; Chairman, Dr. Siaka Probyn Stevens).

AND-JEF (Senegal) a.k.a. MRDN/AND-JEF

ANTOKO'NY KONGRESI'NY FAHALEO-VANTENAN'I MADAGASIKARA (AKFM-Congress Party for an Independent Madagascar:

Madagascar) a.k.a. KDRSM

2. Democratic Republic of Madagascar (9,490,000)

3. Date Established: 1958

4. Organisational Type: Mass party

7. Status: Constituent 'revolutionary association' in the ruling FNDR coalition

8. Publications: Imongo Vaovao (circulation 10,000)

9. Orientation: Pro-Soviet Marxism-Leninism and left nationalism

10. Strategy: Electoral, building a socialist society

11. Internal Affiliations: The AKFM was associated with the AREMA, VITM/VONJY, MPP/MFM, MONIMA, VSM and UDECMA/KMTP as constituent parts of the ruling FNDR.

12. External Affiliations: Pro-Soviet Union

13. History: Founded in 1958, AKFM was an important nationalist movement in the capital, Antananarivo, amongst the radicalised professionals and other middle classes of Protestant Christian Merina background, both during the colonial period and as an opposition party during the first republic (1960-1972). AKFM was made part of the ruling FNDR at its creation in 1975. Its inability to project itself beyond the capital and the better-off people have been reflected in loss of seats in the National Assembly between the 1977 elections (sixteen seats) and those of 1983 (9/137).

14. Leadership: Pastor Richard Andriamanjato, leader; Gisele Rabesahala (Minister of Revolutionary Culture and Art)

ARAB SOCIALIST BAATH PARTY-COUNTRY OF SUDAN (ASBP-CS)

2. Republic of Sudan (23,089,000)

3. Date Established: Existed in 1984

4. Organisational Type: Mass party

6. Membership: More than a few

7. Status: Legal

9. Orientation: Left nationalism (Iraqi Baathist), possibly more Sudanese nationalist than pan-Arabist

10. Strategy: Electoral

11. Internal Affiliations: the ASBP-CS belonged in 1984 to the anti-Nimeri National Salvation Front (NSF), which included, inter-alia, the Umma Party, the Democratic Unionist Party and the SCP.

12. External Affiliations: Iraq

13. History: Drawing its inspiration from Iraqi Baathism, the ASBP-CS existed in open illegality during Nimeri's regime. After his 1985 downfall, the ASBP-CS contested, amongst other areas, ten Khartoum area seats in the 1986 elections.

14. Leadership: Badr el Din Mudathir, leader; Taisir Mudathir

ARAB SOCIALIST BAATH PARTY - ORGANISATION OF SUDAN (ASBP-OS: Sudan)

See also PNF

2. Republic of Sudan (23,089,000)

3. Date Established: Existed in 1984

4. Organisational Type: Mass party

6. Membership: Few

7. Status: Legal

9. Orientation: Left nationalist (Syrian Baathist; Pan-Arabism)

10. Strategy: Electoral

11. Internal Affiliations: The ASBP-OS contested the 1986 elections as part of the leftist Progressive National Front (PNF).

12. External Affiliations: Syria

ASSOCIATION DES STAGIAIRES ET DES ETUDIANTS COMORIENS (ASEC - Association of Comoran Students and Trainees: Comoros)

2. Federal Islamic Republic of the Comoros (410,000)

3. Date Established: Existed in 1985

7. Status: Paris-based exile group

AVANT-GARDE ARABE EN TUNISIE (AGAT - Tunisian Arab Vanguard: Tunisia)

2. Republic of Tunisia (7,224,000)

3. Date Established: Existed in 1981

6. Membership: Few

7. Status: Illegal

8. Publications: <u>Actualities Tunisiennes</u> (Paris-based)

9. Orientations: Left nationalist (Iraq Baathist)

AVANT-GARDE DE LA REVOLUTION MALGACHE (AREMA-Vanguard of the Malagasy Revolution)

2. Democratic Republic of Madagascar (9,490,000)

3. Date Established: March 1976

4. Organisational Type: Mass party/party of notables

5. Organisational Nature: AREMA is the key constituent 'revolutionary association' of the FNDR. In the past AREMA depended on local administrators and other notables, some of whom were alleged to be corrupt, to

project its voice beyond the capital. Its Executive Bureau has seventeen members.

7. Status: Main party within the ruling (coalition) FNDR

9. Orientation: Socialist

10. Strategy: Building and administering a socialist state, regime maintenance, electoral, mixed economy

11. Internal Affiliations: The AREMA was associated with the AKFM, VITM/VONJY, MPP/MFM, MONIMA, VMS and UDECMA/KMTP as constituent parts of the ruling FNDR.

12. External Relations: Non-aligned with pro-Soviet, pro-Palestinian and anti-apartheid components

13. History: AREMA was organised as the personal political vehicle for President Ratsiraka in March 1976, following the 21 December 1975 establishment of the second republic and the rise to power on 15 June 1975 of then Captain Ratsiraka. AREMA won the National Assembly elections in 1977 and 1983 (117/139 seats) as well as having its leader elected President of the Republic in the 1982 presidential election.

14. Leadership: Admiral Didier Ratsiraka, Secretary General (President of the Republic); Lt. Col. Desire Rakotoarijaona (Prime Minister)

AZANIAN PEOPLE'S REVOLUTIONARY PARTY (APRP - South Africa)

2. Republic of South Africa (34,577,000)

3. Date Established: 1977

4. Organisational Type: Mass party

6. Membership: Very few

7. Status: Illegal, defunct

9. Orientation: left nationalist, black consciousness

10. Strategy: Revolution, protracted people's war

13. History: The APRP was formed in 1977 after the Ntantala faction was purged from the PAC by the Leballo faction. Templeton Ntantala, who had been the commander of the PAC armed unit, favoured the protracted people's war strategy in contradiction to the Leballo group's preference for urban guerrilla war. Upon their being purged, the Ntantala faction accused Leballo and two other PAC Control Committee members of being paid agents of western intelligence agencies. The APRP were readmitted to the PAC in 1981 by the then new PAC Chairman, John Pokela.

AZANIAN YOUTH REVOLUTIONARY COUNCIL (AYRC: South Africa) a.k.a. SAYRC

AZANIA PEOPLE'S ORGANISATION (AZAPO: South Africa)

2. Republic of South Africa (34,577,000)

3. Date Established: May 1978

4. Organisational Type: Mass party

6. Membership: Mainly black intelligentsia, urban petty bourgeoisie in the parts of the Transvaal, Orange Free State and Cape provinces

7. Status: Legal toleration

9. Orientation: Black consciousness, left nationalism

10. Strategy: Peaceful mass mobilisation by race to overcome apartheid

11. Internal Affiliations: Informal links through individual AZAPO leaders to other black consciousness organisations and the UMSA

13. History: AZAPO was created as a second generation black consciousness organisation to replace the first generation ones that were crushed in October 1977. Following AZAPO's founding congress in May 1978, the apartheid regime detained the AZAPO executive. In the ensuing debates AZAPO decided to continue to exclude whites but to begin to adopt elements of a class analysis. Following its second congress (March 1982)

it had some success in recruiting drives. The election of former UMSA members and other anti-ANC people to the AZAPO leadership at its 1983 conference has continued the split in the resistance.

14. Leadership: Lybon Mabasa (President); Saths Cooper (Vice-President); Safako Nyaka (National Organiser); Muntu Myeza (General Secretary); Ismael Mkhabela (Publicity Secretary)

BASOTHO CONGRESS PARTY (BCO-Lesotho)

2. Kingdom of Lesotho (1,497,000)

3. Date Established: 1952

4. Organisational Type: Mass party

6. Membership: 75,000

7. Status: Quasi-legal

9. Orientation: elements of anti-Soviet left nationalism; Pan-Africanism, some Maoist elements; anti-apartheid.

10. Strategy: Internal faction -- electoral, negotiations; External faction -- i.e. the Lesotho Liberation Army (LLA) conducted armed struggle from c.1979-1982.

12. External Affiliations: China, SWANU

13. History: The BCP (first named the Basotholand African Congress, then the Basotholand Congress Party, then the BCP) was founded in 1952 as a result of the post-1945 decline of the emerging commercial/intelligentsia-based Progressive Association (KTL, founded 1907) and the peasant-based Lekhotla la Bafo (founded 1913). The BCP was a Pan-Africanist nationalist movement utilising negotiations and elections throughout the 1950s and 1960s. The OAU recognised the BCP as a national liberation movement. The BCP had had offices in Tanzania, Ghana and Egypt. However, Tanzania expelled the BCP in April 1967 on the grounds that Lesotho had gained independence on 4 October 1966. The BCP was split on 2 February 1967 when some members created the pro-apartheid Lesotho Democratic Party. Following the Sino-Soviet split, some members of the BCP helped

create the CPL, while the BCP found itself becoming oriented towards China and being excluded from pro-Soviet forums. The BCP became sharply critical of the Soviet Union. When it appeared that the BCP under Ntsu Mokhele was about to win the 1970 elections, Jonathan's BNP government voided the election and banned the BCP. Mokhele went into exile and his faction formed the LLA which at its height (1979-1982) comprised 500-1,000 fighters and was responsible for organising numerous attacks on the BNP and its government. After the 1970 banning, George P. Ramoreboli led his "internal" faction of the BCP into an alliance with the BNP and consequently participated in the provisional National Assembly which was overthrown by the 19 January 1986 military coup.

14. Leadership: Ntsu Mokhehle, leader of the LLA faction; Nathaniel Nkuatsana and George P. Ramoreboli, leaders of the "internal" faction, Geoffrey Kolisang, Secretary General of the internal faction.

BASOTHO NATIONAL PARTY (BNP-Lesotho)

2. Kingdom of Lesotho (1,497,00)

3. Date Established: 1958

4. Organisational Type: Mass party

6. Membership: 150,000

7. Status: Ruling party 1966 (independence) until it was deposed on 19 January 1986 by the military coup.

9. Orientation: Variable-elements of anti-apartheid left nationalism with some links to the Soviet Union after 1982.

10. Strategy: Electoral, power maintenance.

11. Internal Affiliations: Lesotho Peace and Solidarity Committee.

12. External Affiliations: Pro-west but some links to the Soviet Union and China, especially from 1982-1986.

13. History: Following its 1958 founding, the BNP, under Dr. Leabua Jonathan, formed the Lesotho government after independence in 1966 until its overthrow on 19 January 1986 by a military coup led by Maj. Gen. Justin Metsing Lekhanya. Although the BNP was anti-Soviet, anti-communist and willing to accommodate apartheid South Africa on these matters, friction with South Africa grew, especially over the BNP's unwillingness to turn ANC refugees over to the apartheid regime. Finally in 1982 the BNP government achieved an understanding with the Soviet Union. In October 1983, the BNP Secretary General became the chairman of the newly named Lesotho Peace and Solidarity Committee. Later the Student Council of Lesotho joined the International Union of Students and the CPL regained significant elements of its legal status that had been taken away in 1970. All of this had to be seen in the context of two themes. When it appeared that the BNP was losing the 1970 election to the BCP, the BNP government voided the election and banned the other political parties. Also the BNP had been in conflict with the king for constitutional supremacy.

14. Leadership: Dr. Leabua Jonathan, Leader; E. Sekhonyana, National Chairman; V.M. Makhele, Secretary General.

BATH, LE (Renaissance: Tunisia)

2. Republic of Tunisia (7,224,000)

3. Date Established: Existed in 1981

6. Membership: Few

7. Status: Illegal, in exile

9. Orientation: Left nationalist (Iraq Baathist)

12. External Affiliations: Iraq

13. History: Le Bath existed in Paris

14. Leadership: Mabrouk Mansouri

BLACK PEOPLE'S CONVENTION (BPC: South Africa)

2. Republic of South Africa (34,577,000)

3. Date Established: July 1972

4. Organisational Type: Mass party

7. Status: Illegal

9. Orientation: Black consciousness, elements of left nationalism

10. Strategy: Peaceful mass mobilisation by race to overcome apartheid

11. Internal Affiliates: South African Students Organisation (SASO, founded 1969 by black university students).

12. History: The BPC was established in 1972 in large measure by SASO in order to incorporate more sectors of the black population than students. Several key leaders were arrested after BPC/SASO refused to cancel a September 1974 celebration of the FRELIMO traditional government in Mozambique. In December 1974 at the Black Renaissance Convention, BPC and SASO delegates split the conference over the issue of black consciousness. In April 1976 the BPC adopted the 'Black Communalism' programme which emphasised that blacks must be the authors of their own liberation, and that whites had a marginal role to play. Following the Soweto uprising that started on 16 June 1976, Steven Biko was murdered by the South African Police on 12 September 1977 and the BCP was banned (along with seventeen other black consciousness groups) in October 1977, thus being forced underground and into exile.

14. Leaders: Mxolisi Mvovo (previously Acting President), President Kenneth Rachidi (previously detained).

BOTSWANA INDEPENDENCE PARTY (BIP-Botswana)

2. Republic of Botswana (1,143,000)

3. Date Established: 1964

4. Organisational Type: Mass party

7. Status: Legal opposition party

9. Orientation: Social democracy, Pan-Africanism

10. Strategy: Electoral

13. History: The BIP was created by a dissatisfied BPP faction in 1964. The BIP lost its sole seat in the 1979 election and failed to regain it in the 1984 election.

14. Leadership: Motsamai K. Mpho, President; J.G. Gugushe, Vice President; Emmanuel R. Mokobi, Secretary General.

BOTSWANA NATIONAL FRONT (BNF-Botswana)

2. Republic of Botswana (1,143,000)

3. Date Established: 1967

4. Organisational Type: Mass party

7. Status: Leading opposition party; legal.

8. Publication: Puo Pha (Straight Talk), monthly.

9. Orientation: left nationalist, Marxist.

10. Strategy: Electoral, emphasizing social justice.

13. History: Formed in 1967, the BNF won the second largest number of votes in the 1969, 1974, 1979 and 1984 elections. In the 1984 election the BNF defeated two cabinet ministers and increased its vote, and number of seats from two to four out of thirty-four elected members.

14. Leadership: Dr. Kenneth Koma, Leader; ex-Chief Bathoen II Gaseitsiwe, Parliamentary Leader; Mareledi Giddie, Secretary General.

BOTSWANA PEOPLE'S PARTY (BPP-Botswana)

2. Republic of Botswana (1,143,000)

3. Date Established: 1960

4. Organisation Type: Mass Party

7. Status: Legal opposition party

8. Publication: Masa (Dawn), monthly

9. Orientation: Social democracy, Pan-Africanism

10. Strategy: Electoral

13. History: Founded in 1960, the BPP (formerly the Bechuanaland PP) was the principal opposition party until 1969 when it was overtaken by the BNF. The BPP retained its sole seat in the 1984 election.

14. Leadership: Dr. Knight Maripe, President; Kenneth Mkhwa, Chairman; John Mosojane, Secretary General.

CHAMA CHA MAPINDUZI (CCM-Revolutionary Party of Tanzania: Tanzania)

See also ASP and TANU

2. United Republic of Tanzania (22,415,000)

3. Date Established: 1954

4. Organisational Type: Mass party

5. Organisational Nature: The Chairman, Vice-Chairman Secretary-General and most of the National Executive Committee (NEC - one hundred and seventy-two members) are elected by the national conference. The NEC elects the Central Committee (eighteen members). There were national youth, women's, trade union, parents' and cooperatives affiliates of CCM.

6. Membership: Thousands

7. Status: Ruling, sole legal party

9. Orientation: Social Democracy

10. Strategy: Electoral; building and administering socialism

13. History: The CCM itself was founded in 1977 by the merger of TANU (founded in 1954 by Julius Nyerere) and the ASP (founded 1957); the party merger following on from the 1964 union of Tanganyika and Zanzibar. Nyerere was the Chairman of the CCM and President of the Republic from 1977 until 1985 when he resigned as President but stayed on as CCM Chairman until 1987 when he retired. Ali Hassan Mwinyi became the President of the Republic in 1985 and Chairman in 1987. Nyerere made his Arusha Declaration in 1967 and developed the notion of ujamaa, a form of social democracy.

14. Leadership: Ali Hassan Mwinyi, CCM Chairman and President of the Republic.

CHOIX REVOLUTIONNAIRE, LE (CR-Revolutionary Choice: Tunisia)

See AT

COMITE DE LIBERTACAO DE SAO TOME E PRINCIPE (CLSTP-Committee for the Liberation of Sao Tome and Principe-CLSTP: Sao Tome and Principe) Later a.k.a. MLSTP

COMITE NATIONAL DE SALUT PUBLIC (CNSP-National Committee for Public Salvation: Comoros)

See also, FNUK, UNIKOM and FNUK-UNIKOM

2. Federal Islamic Republic of the Comoros (410,000)

3. Date Established: Existed in 1981

7. Status: Exile group

11. Internal Affiliations: FNUK and Unikom and coalition partners.

13. History: On October 3, 1981 the CNSP, joined the FNUK-Unikom coalition.

14. Leadership: Said Ali Kemal

COMMISSION FOR ORGANISING THE PARTY OF THE WORKING PEOPLE OF ETHIOPIA (COPWE: Ethiopia)

See also WPE

2. Socialist Ethiopia (35,210,000)

3. Date Established: December 1979

4. Organisational Type: Party-building organisation

5. Organisational Nature: COPWE had a Chairman (Col. Mengistu), an Executive Committee (seven members), a Central Committee (ninety-three members), fourteen Provincial Committees, nine political organisation committees, and a Plenary Session (two thousand representatives). Mass organisations included the Revolutionary Ethiopia's Women's Association, Revolutionary Ethiopia's Youth Association, All-Ethiopian Trade Union, All-Ethiopian Peasants' Association, and the Kebeles.

6. Membership: Plenary sessions were attended by some two thousand representatives.

7. Status: 1979-1984, legal pre-vanguard party organisation subordinated to the ruling PMAC government; 1984, dissolved into the WPE.

8. Publications: Serto Ader (Working People: weekly c.100,000)

9. Orientation: Pro-Soviet Marxism-Leninism

10. Strategy: Revolutionary - build a vanguard party, support the administration of socialism.

11. Internal Affiliations: See the mass organisations of (5) above.

12. External Affiliations: Pro-Soviet parties, especially those of the Soviet Union and Cuba.

13. History: Formed in December 1979 at the instigation of Mengistu's PMAC, COPWE held its First Congress in June

1980, its Second Congress on 3-6 January 1984 and the Third Congress 6-10 September 1984 at which COPWE constituted itself into the vanguard party WPE.

14. Leadership: Chairman-Lt. Col. Mengistu Haile-Mariam; Executive Committee (seven members) - Mengistu Haile-Mariam, Legasse Asfaw, Berhanu Bayeh, Lt. Col. Fikre-Selassie Wogderess, Lt. Gen Tesfaye Gebre-Kidan, Addis Tedlay, Fisseha Desta

COMMUNIST PARTY OF LESOTHO (CPL-Lesotho)

2. Kingdom of Lesotho (1,497,000)

3. Date Established: May 5, 1962

4. Organisational Type: Vanguard Party

5. Organisational Nature: Democratic centralism. The final decision-making body of the CPL was the Congress which also elected the Central Committee. There were also committees at the district and village level.

6. Membership: Several hundred

7. Status: Quasi-legal

8. Publications: Tokoloholo (published c.1966-c.1979)

9. Orientation: Soviet interpretation of Marxism-Leninism, anti-Maoist.

10. Strategy: Electoral, party-building, alliances to build the national democratic revolution which would eventually lead to the next stage of the revolution-socialism. The national democratic revolution must be constructed by bringing together a 'broad front of National Resistance' against South African imperialism.

11. Internal Affiliations: The Lesotho Congress of Trade Unions and the Lesotho Workers' Union contained some but not many CPL members. During the 1960s the CPL supported the royalist Marema Tloe Freedom Party because its anti-apartheid stand was shared by the CPL and contrasted with the then collaborationist attitude of the ruling BNP. After the 1982 thaw in relations

between the BCP government and the Soviet Union and the concurrent growing condemnation of apartheid South Africa, the CPL came to support critically the BNP government. The CPL was instrumental in founding the Lesotho Peace Council (LPC), the affiliate of the World Peace Council. Following the 1982 warming of relations between the BNP and the Soviet Union, in October 1983 control of the LPC passed to the BNP, whose then Secretary General, Vincent M. Makhele became the chairman of the newly named Lesotho Peace and Solidarity Committee (LPSC). Shortly after this, the Student Council of Lesotho joined the International Union of Students.

12. External Relations: The CPL has close links with the Communist Party of the Soviet Union and the Communist Party of South Africa.

13. History: The CPL was formed during 5 May 1962 out of elements of the BCP (founded in 1952) and others influenced by the CPSA and the ANC of South Africa. Until the 1970 electoral blow-up, the CPL operated as a legal party contesting elections. While many of its members were jailed in the aftermath of the near loss of power by Dr. Leabua Jonathan's BNP in 1970, the BNP government released many members of the CPL in 1972. The Sixth Congress was held May 1, 1982. Following the 1982 warming of Soviet-BNP relations, the CPL issued a statement of critical support for the BNP government. It may be that at least one CPL affiliate was handed over to the BNP as part of CPL strategy of creating a broad united national democratic government under BNP leadership with the CPL as a junior partner. In 1984, the BNP government partially legalised the CPL as both parties prepared to enter the BNP-proposed elections. These electoral preparations were overturned by the 19 January 1986 coup by Maj. Gen. Justin Metsing Lekhanya.

14. Leadership: R. Matji, chairman; Jacob M. Kena, secretary general; John Motlohela, secretary; Jacob/Jeremiah Mosotho.

COMMUNIST PARTY OF SOUTH AFRICA (CPSA: South Africa) a.k.a. SACP

CONSEIL NATIONAL DE LA REVOLUTION (CNR-National Revolutionary Council: Burkina Faso)

2. Republic of Burkina Faso (8,130,000)

3. Date Established: 4 August 1983

4. Organisational Type: Revolutionary Council

5. Organisational Nature: Starting at the locality and gradually expanding their geographic scope, a series of committees known as the CDR's (Committees for the Defense of the Revolution-Comites pour la Defence Revolutionnaire) were established to mobilise revolutionary energy and exhort popular control over the country.

7. Status: Government: Ruling council

8. Publications: The CNR controls a number of daily newspapers: Bulletein Quotidien d'Information (1500) Sidwaya (5000) and Dunia; as well as weeklies: Carrefour Africain and Journal Officiel du Burkina. The CNR also controls radio and television broadcasting.

9. Orientation: Anti-imperialist, socialist, left nationalist

10. Strategy: Having seized power by means of a military coup, the CNR under Sankara sought to establish a non-aligned revolutionary state that would empower the ordinary people and eliminate all traces of their exploitation by imperialism and the remains of the chiefly power. This meant the consolidation of the national democratic phase of the revolution and the transition to a new form of socialism.

11. Internal Affiliations: The CNR was supported by the ULC, GC, UCB, ROC and (up until 1984) LIPAD.

12. External Affiliations: Sankara's CNR was closely associated with Rawling's PNDC of Ghana.

13. History: The CNR came to power on 4 August 1983 under Captain Thomas Sankara, having overthrown the military government of Major Jean-Baptiste Ouededraogo's Conseil de Slut du Peuple (CSP-People's Salvation Council). In

1984 a split between the CNR and LIPAD occurred. Sankara was murdered by a fellow member of the CNR, Captain Blaise Compaore, in late 1987.

14. Leadership: Captain Thomas Sankara, Chairman, 1983-1987; Captain Blaise Compaore (leader 1987-)

CONSEIL POUR LA LIBERATION DU CONGO (CLC-Council for the Liberation of the Congo- CLC: Zaire)

2. Republic of Zaire (33,927,000)

3. Date Established: 1980

4. Organisational Type: Coalition of groups

6. Membership: Several thousand indirect members (i.e. by being members of groups belonging to the CLC)

7. Status: Illegal

9. Orientation: Elements of Marxism, socialism, left nationalism, liberalism and conservatism

10. Strategy: Revolution

11. Internal Affiliates: The CLC included the following groups, amongst others: PSC, ECP and the Mouvement pour l'Union et la Reconciliation an Zaire (MNUR).

13. History: Formed in Belgium in 1980 by a broad spectrum of groups, by 1982 the CLC had been at least partially eclipsed by the new FCD coalition.

14. Leadership: Bernardin Mungul-Diaka, President

CONSEIL SUPREME DE LA REVOLUTION (CSR-Supreme Revolutionary Council: Chad)

2. Republic of Chad (5,308,000)

3. Date Established: August 1985

4. Organisational Type: National liberation/civil war movement

7. Status: Civil war opposition, alternative government.

10. Strategy: Negotiation and civil war

11. Internal Affiliations: The most important creators of the CSR were Woddei's Frolinat-FAP and Kamougue's FAT/MRP which had been combined with the GUNT (later reorganised and renamed as the CNL).

12. External Affiliations: Pro-Libya

13. History: The CSR grew out of those GUNT/CNL factions that remained or became pro-Libyan.

14. Leadership: Goukouni Woddei, Chairman; Lt. Col. Wadal Abdelkader Kamougue, Vice-Chairman.

DEMOCRATIC FRONT FOR THE LIBERATION OF SOMALIA (DFLS: Somalia) a.k.a. SDLF

DEMOCRATIC FRONT FOR THE SALVATION OF SOMALIA (DFSS: Somalia) a.k.a. SDSF

2. Somali Democratic Republic (4,450,000)

3. Date Established: 5 October 1981

4. Organisational Type: Coalition

5. Organisational Nature: The March 1983 DFSS congress elected the Chairman, the Vice-Chairman, the Executive Committee (nine members) and the Central Committee (twenty-one members) as well as approving a programme and a constitution.

6. Membership: Through its constituent organisations (the SSF, SWP and SDLF) the DFSS had thousands of members.

7. Status: Illegal, but from 1983 onwards was really the SSF

8. Publications: The DFSS had access to the Ethiopian-based Radio Kulmis.

9. Orientation: Left nationalist, Marxist-Leninist elements

10. Strategy: Armed struggle to overthrow Barre's SRSP government

11. Internal Affiliations: The DFSS consisted of the SSF, SWP and SDLF from 1981 to 1983, and of only the SSF afterwards.

12. External Affiliations: Ethiopian Derg, South Yemen and Libya

13. History: The DFSS was founded at a conference between the SSF, SWP and the SDLF during 19 September to 5 October 1981. While it was initially quite successful in its guerilla campaign against the Barre regime, the attempt of the SSF to take over the organisation destroyed it in 1983 shortly after its first (May 1983) congress. Following the split, the DFSS/SSF had several hundred of its fighters accept Barre's amnesty. It then operated from Ethiopia, Djibouti and Kenya.

14. Leadership: Col Abdullahi Yusaf Ahmed, Chairman (and chairman of SSF); Abderahman Aydeed Ahmed, Vice-Chairman (and leader of the SDLF before his 1983 defection).

DERG (Armed Forces Coordinating Committee a.k.a. DERGUE a.k.a. PMAC (Ethiopia)

DFSS/SSF (Somalia) a.k.a. SSF

ECH-CHOOLA-EL-WATAD (SF-Strong Flame: Tunisia) a.k.a. SF: Strong Flame (a.k.a. FDP Flame Democratic Patriots)

EGYPTIAN COMMUNIST LABOUR PARTY (ECLP: Egypt)

2. Arab Republic of Egypt (48,832,000)

3. Date Established: Existed in 1979

7. Status: Illegal

9. Orientation: Marxism-Leninism

10. Strategy: Revolution

13. History: The ECLP was an offshoot of the ECP.

EGYPTIAN COMMUNIST PARTY (**ECP: al-Hizb al-Shuyu'i al-Misri**: **Egypt**)

2. Arab Republic of Egypt (48,832,000)

3. Date Established: 1921

4. Organisational Type: Vanguard party

5. Organisational Nature: Democratic centralism

6. Membership: 500

7. Status: Illegal

8. Publications: Leaflets; _al-Wa'i_ (Consciousness) circulars

9. Orientation: Pro-Soviet Marxism-Leninism, pro-Palestinian, POLISARIO and Kurdish

10. Strategy: Revolution; creation of a national democratic united front to carry out the national democractic phase of the revolution leading to socialism; party-building amongst students and workers

11. Internal Affiliations: Unofficial but close relationship with the NPUP. In 1981, the ECP participated in the Damascus-based Egyptian National Front which sought to overthrow President Sadat. Led by General Saadeddin Shazli, former Chief of Staff, the Front also included a Lebanese-based group of Egyptian leftists, a pro-Libyan Nasserite group and a Muslim group.

12. External Affiliations: Pro-Soviet parties, especially Arab communist parties, as well as the Syrian Arab Ba'th Party. In 1978, the Soviet Union recognised the ECP as the official communist party in Egypt.

13. History: Expatriates, including Joseph Rosenthal, founded the Egyptian Socialist Party (al-Hizb al-Ishtiraki al-Misri) in Alexandria during 1921. Changing its name to the ECP, in 1923 it was admitted to the Comintern. The ECP's history has been one of being suppressed and repeated fragmentation since 1921.

It reformed as the Mouvement democratique de liberation nationale in 1947, and again in 1958 as the Unified Egyptian Communist Party, decided to dissolve in April 1965 and merge into Nasser's ruling Arab Socialist Union (where it achieved some influence), and reemerged in 1972 (when President Sadat moved to the right and expelled Soviet personnel). On 4 August 1975, the Secretariat of the ECP published a Manifesto, in al-Safir, a Beirut newspaper, which denounced the Sadat government but argued for a strategy of burrowing from within. In September 1980, the ECP held its first congress in Egypt.

14. Leadership: Farid Mujahid (possibly), Secretary General; Michel Kamel, Politburo member; Farid Mujahid and Yusef Darwish, Central Committee members

EGYPTIAN WORKERS COMMUNIST PARTY (EWCP-Egypt)

2. Arab Republic of Egypt (48,832,000)

3. Date Established: Existed in 1979

7. Status: Illegal

9. Orientation: Pro-Soviet Marxism-Leninism

10. Strategy: Revolution, clandestine literature, including leaflet, distribution

11. Internal Affiliations: Unofficial but close relationship with elements of the NPUP

12. External Affiliations: Pro-Soviet

13. History: On 4-5 November 1981, sixty-five members of the EWCP and the ECP were arrested by the Egyptian state security forces.

EL AMAL EL TOUNSI (AT-Tunisian Worker: Tunisia)

2. Republic of Tunisia (7,224,000)

3. Date Established: Existed in 1981

7. Status: Illegal

9. Orientation: Marxism-Leninism: one pro-Albanian faction, one pro-Chinese faction

10. Strategy: Revolution (Pro-Albanians); Critical support of Bourguiba's PDS (Pro-Chinese)

13. History: AT has split into a number of factions. The main groupings are the 'Albanians' and the 'Chinese'. The 'Albanians', who wished to make a common front with other democratic and socialist groups to overthrow the PDS regime, have had Le Choix Revolutionnaire (CR-Revolutionary choice) split from them over this issue.

14. Leadership: 'Chinese' - Abdel Waheb Megdoub, Brahim Razgallah; 'Albanian' - Mohammed Benjennt, Ahmed Negib Chebbi; CR-Hamma Hamami.

EL HARAKA EL WATANIYA LIBYA (HWL-National Libyan Movement: Libya)

2. Socialist People's Libyan Arab Jamahiriya (4,108,000)

3. Date Established: Existed in 1981

6. Membership: Active student units.

7. Status: Illegal opposition group in exile

8. Publications: Sawt el Talia (Voice of the Vanguard) and cassettes of speeches, etc.

9. Orientation: left nationalist, Baathist.

EL HOR a.k.a. FREE MAN (Mauritania)

EL JABHA EL WATANIYA DEMOCRATIYA (JWD-National Democratic Libyan Front: Libya)

2. Socialist People's Libyan Arab Jamahiriya (4,108,000).

3. Date Established: Existed in 1981

6. Membership: Youth concentration

7. Status: Illegal opposition group based in Switzerland

8. Publications: <u>Al Watan</u>

9. Orientation: Socialist

EPUN (Elan Populaire pour l'Unite Nationale: Madagascar) a.k.a. VONJY

ERITREAN LIBERATION FRONT

2. Eritrea (3,000,000) (partial Ethiopian occupation)

3. Date Established: 1958

4. Organisational Type: nationalist movement

5. Organisational Nature: The Eritrean Liberation Army was the ELF's armed wing.

6. Membership: Possibly 1000

7. Status: Losing side in Eritrean civil war with the EPLF, illegal to Ethiopia, exists mainly in exile

9. Orientation: Muslim elitist nationalism

10. Strategy: Armed struggle, negotiations

12. External Affiliations: Saudi Arabia and some other Arab countries have provided recent support.

13. History: The ELF was formed in 1958 as a reaction to the failure of an earlier generation of nationalists; however, the elitist orientation of the ELF led to a split which resulted in the formation of the EPLF which defeated the ELF in 1981 and absorbed the ELF (Central Command) in 1987. ELF fragments remained abroad.

ERITREAN PEOPLE'S LIBERATION FRONT (EPLF: Eritrea)

2. Eritrea (3,000,000) (partial Ethiopian occupation)

3. Date Established: 1970

4. Organisational Type: Vanguard movement/national liberation movement

5. Organisational Nature: The EPLF has been one of the best organised political parties or movements in Africa. The National Congress of the EPLF is comprised of some nine hundred delegates elected by the Eritrean People's Liberation Army (EPLA) and the mass organisations for women, youth, students, peasants, workers and professionals. The National Congress elects the Central Committee (thirty-seven members) which in turn elects the Politburo, comprising the General Secretary, Vice General Secretary and eleven other members who administer the various departments. An inner cabinet, the Standing Committee, is composed of the General Secretary, the Vice General Secretary, the chair of the 'Political Committee' departments and the chair of the 'Military Committee' departments.

6. Membership: 60,000

7. Status: Ruling movement fighting partial Ethiopia occupation

8. Publications: Saghim (in Tigrinia and Tigre languages); Adulis (English monthly, EPLF Foreign Relations Bureau); EPLF radio in five languages; Information Department also publishes extensive list of texts, school textbooks, etc.

9. Orientation: left nationlist; Maoist-Cuban Marxism-Leninism

10. Strategy: National democratic phase of the revolution being carried out by people's protracted war and political mobilisation (including women: 11% of the 1977 Congress delegates were women, who constituted 30% of the EPLF membership and 15% of the EPLA, including fighting units).

11. Internal Affiliations: See (5) above for the mass organisations. The ELF (Central Leadership) joined the EPLF during the EPLF's Second (1987) Congress.

12. External Affiliations: The EPLF has cooperated with the TPLF and Oromo Liberation Front (OLF). The EPLF received military and political support from the Soviet Union, Cuba and other Soviet bloc countries until the

Soviets traded in Eritrea and Somalia for PMAC/Derg Ethiopia in 1977.

13. History: The EPLF was created in 1970 by a group who left the ELF over its mechanical military and repressive policies. In 1972 they formed themselves into the ELF-PLF (Popular Liberation Forces), renaming themselves the EPLF at the 1977 First Congress which established the policy and organisational framework. Following the Soviet betrayal in 1977, the EPLF was forced to concede a number of urban areas to the massively Soviet-rearmed Ethiopian forces; however, they maintained control of the EPLF rural base areas. Following the EPLF-ELF civil war (1970-1974) an attempt at forming a common front was made in 1977. Following the ELF attacks on EPLF positions in early 1981, the EPLF militarily dissolved the ELF, leaving it as a diplomatic husk. In 1987 the EPLF held its Second National Congress. In 1988, the EPLF made a number of important strategic gains.

14. Leadership: Secretary General: Ramadan Mohammad Nur; Vice Secretary General-Isaias Afewerki

ETHIOPIAN OPPRESSED REVOLUTIONARY STRUGGLE EORS-I.Ch.A.T.: Ethiopia)

2. Socialist Ethiopia (35,210,000)

3. Date Established: Existed in 1975

6. Membership: Leadership predominantly Oromo

7. Status: Legal during the mid-1970s

9. Orientation: Marxism-Leninism

10. Strategy: Party-building with PMAC (during 1977-1978 through the mechanism of UEMLO)

11. Internal Affiliations: EORS joined with LL, RF, MEISON and MLRO to form the short-lived UEMLO in February 1977 in an attempt to unify the pro-PMAC left into a vanguard party.

13. History: EORS supported PMAC.

ETHIOPIAN PEOPLE'S DEMOCRATIC MOVEMENT (EPDM-Ethiopia)

2. Socialist Ethiopia (35,210,000)

3. Date Established: Existed in 1986

4. Organisational Type: Revolutionary united front

7. Status: Illegal, civil war participant

9. Orientation: left nationalist, Marxism-Leninism

10. Strategy: Revolution, preparation for the creation of a unified all-Ethiopian vanguard party

11. Internal Affiliations: TPLF provided all of the EPDM's military supplies.

ETHIOPIAN PEOPLE'S REVOLUTIONARY PARTY (EPRP: Ethiopia)

2. Socialist Ethiopia (35,210,000)

3. Date Established: 1972

7. Status: Illegal party, civil war participant from 1976 onwards

8. Publications: <u>Democracia</u> (c.mid-1970s)

9. Orientation: Marxism-Leninism

10. Strategy: Armed overthrow of the DERG (or PMAC) government

11. Internal Affiliations: Some elements tried to coordinate their efforts with the anti-Derg, but conservative Ethiopian Democratic Union (EDU). In 1980 this was to have been formalised under a coalition grouping, the Ethiopian National Democratic Front (ENDF).

13. History: From 1974 to 1976 the EPRP tried to influence the PMAC. From mid-1976 onwards, the EPRP tried to forcibly overthrow the PMAC, though with little success. By 1980, the EPRP forces had been pushed out of Tigre by the TPLF.

ETUDIANTS CONGOLAISE PROGRESSISTE (ECP-Progressive Congolese Students PCS: Zaire)

2. Republic of Zaire (33,927,000)

3. Date Established: Existed in 1980

4. Organisational Type: Mass party type

6. Membership: Numbers of students, especially those overseas

7. Status: Illegal

8. Publications: some

9. Orientation: Left nationalist (Lumumbist), socialist and Marxist elements

10. Strategy: Revolution

11. Internal Affiliations: The ECP had some relations with the PRP and was a member of the CLC coalition.

13. History: The ECP has been active mainly in Belgium (especially Louvain-la-Neuve), has published numerous items but has been plagued by agents of the Mobutu dictatorship.

FLAME DEMOCRATIC PATRIOTS (FDP: Tunisia) a.k.a. SF-Strong Flame (pref. translation)

FNUK-UNIKOM (Comoros)

See also, FNUK, UNIKOM and CNSP

2. Federal Islamic Republic of the Comoros

3. Date Established: 1981

7. Status: Exile group based in Paris

11. Internal Affiliations: the FNUK and Unikom formed the FNUK-Unikom in mid-1981. The CNSP joined on October 3, 1981.

13. History: see above.

14. Leadership: Abubakar Ahmed Nurdin

FORCE DES OPPRIMES DU CONGO-KINSHASA, LE (FOCK-Force of the Oppressed of Congo-Kinshasa: FOCK: Zaire)

2. Republic of Zaire (33,927,000)

3. Date Established: Existed in 1982

6. Membership: Few

7. Status: Illegal

9. Orientation: Left nationalist (Lumumbist)

10. Strategy: Revolution

11. Internal Affiliation: The FOCK had some relations with the PRP.

13. History: The FOCK appears to have been based in Belgium.

FREE MAN (FM-EL Hor: Mauritania)

2. Islamic Republic of Mauritania (1,888,000)

3. Date Established: Existed c.1980

4. Organisational Type: Mass party (clandestine)

5. Organisational Nature: El HOR held an underground congress in 1983.

6. Membership: Mainly descendants of freed slaves (a.k.a. Harratines)

7. Status: Secret, tolerated

9. Orientation: Left nationalist, anti-slavery

10. Strategy: Reform, negotiations to end slavery and its enduring stigma by forming alliances with other exploited classes

11. Internal Affiliations: Possible contact with the MND and with the trade union, UTM-Union des Travailleurs Maurtianiens

13. History: El Hor has a considerable constituency: some twenty-five per cent of Mauritanians are Harratines, descendants of or actual slaves, especially of mixed Black-Berber parentage. In 1983, El Hor decided at its clandestine congress to change its definition from being an ethnic organisation to being a political movement seeking an end to exploitation of all disadvantaged classes in Mauritania.

14. Leadership: clandestine; possibly Hamoyd Boitgel

FRENTE DA LIBERATACAO DE MOCAMBIQUE (FRELIMO-Mozambique Liberation Front: Mozambique)

2. People's Republic of Mozambique (14,525,000)

3. Date Established: 1962

4. Organisational Type: Vanguard party

5. Organisational Nature: Formerly a national liberation movement, since 1977 FRELIMO has been transforming itself into a Marxist-Leninist vanguard party of the Soviet model. Operating on the principle of democratic centralism, the Congress was the supreme decision-making body. Between congresses, the executive powers were exercised by the Secretary General, the Politburo, the Secretariat and the Central Committee. Locals form the constituent unit of the party. Mass organisations included the OMM (Organizacao da Mulher Mocambicana-Organization of Mozambican Women), the Mozambique Youth Organisation (OJM), the local group, the production councils and the trade unions. The party has the constitutional right to direct government policy.

6. Membership: 110,323 (1983)

7. Status: Ruling party supreme over state structures

8. Publications: FRELIMO controlled all government newspapers (Noticias-daily circulation 42,000, Maputo; Diario de Mocambique - daily circulation 18,000, Beira;

Jornal do Povo; *Domingo*, Sunday weekly; *O Tempo*, weekly magazine) as well as the Central Committe - published *Voz da Revolucao*. The same relationship applies to all television and radio, including the Voice of FRELIMO.

9. Orientation: Marxism-Leninism

10. Strategy: Following the use of armed struggle political mobilisation against Portuguese colonialism, FRELIMO since independence has used similar strategies since it had to deal with the attacks of the Smith regime (until 1980) and the apartheid South African government and their puppet force, the MNR. Regime maintenance has emerged as a major concern during these attacks, which have gravely crippled FRELIMO's efforts at development: party-building and the creation of a socialist society.

11. Internal Affiliations: The mass organisations of FRELIMO have consisted of the OMM, OJM, the local group, production councils and the trade unions.

12. External Affiliations: FRELIMO has relations with pro-Soviet parties, the Chinese Communist Party, Tanzania's Chama Cha Mapinduzi, Zimbabwe's ZANU, and the ANC of South Africa. In addition, FRELIMO has a foreign policy that has also sought better relations with the West.

13. History: UDENAMO (Uniao Democratica Nacional de Mozambique), UNAMI (Uniao Africana de Mocambique Independente), and MANU (Mozambique African Nationalist Union) agreed in June 1962 to dissolve themselves and form FRELIMO. The First Congress, convoked during September in Dar es Salaam, focussed on the need to build and organise popular support. Dr. Eduardo Mondlane was elected President. In 1964, FRELIMO launched the armed struggle against the Portuguese, emphasizing that the political aspect was primary over the military. In 1968 FRELIMO, having created liberated zones, held its Second Congress inside Mozambique. FRELIMO emerged as a national liberation movement with considerable talent for winning and organising popular support based in large part measure on the Chinese Maoist experience and with its distinctive interpretation of left-nationalism/socialism. Mondlane was assassinated by the Portuguese in 1969. After a debate over the goals of FRELIMO, Samora Machel

was chosen as President of FRELIMO and as President of the Republic at independence on June 25, 1975. The 1977 Third Congress decided to transform FRELIMO from a national liberation movement with mass membership into a Marxist-Leninist vanguard party with stricter criteria for membership. The Fourth Congress (26-29 April 1983) increased participation in the party by more than doubling Central Committee membership from fifty-five to one hundred and thirty. Following apartheid South Africa's massive attacks on Mozambique, Mozambique signed the 1984 Nkomati Accord in an attempt to stop South Africa's attacks, although the apartheid regime did not keep its word. One significant result of these attacks was that FRELIMO turned to the West, including the World Bank, for much more humanitarian, military and financial aid. In 1986, Secretary-General Machel was murdered by the South African government. Politburo member and Minister of Foreign Affairs Joaquim Alberto Chissano then became the third leader of FRELIMO and the second President of independent Mozambique.

14. Leadership: Secretary General: Joaquim Alberto Chissano; Politburo: Joaquim Alberto Chissano, Marcelino dos Santos, Alberto Chipande, Armando Emilio Guebuza, Jorge Rebello, Mariano de Araujo Matsinhe, Sebastiao Marcos Mabote, Jacinto Soares Veloso, Mario de Graca Machungo, Jose Oscar Monteiro, one other.

FRENTE PARA A LIBERTACAO E INDEPENDENCIA DA GUINEE-BISSAU (FLING-Guinea-Bissau Front for Liberation and Independence: Guinea Bissau)

2. Republic of Guinea-Bissau (873,000)

3. Date Established: Pre-1981

7. Status: Dissolved

9. Orientation: Elements of left nationalism

13. History: Based in Dakar, Senegal, FLING represented Guinean elements that rejected unification of Guinea with Cape Verde. Losing their raison d'etre after the 1980 Guinea coup broke the links with Cape Verde, FLING members dissolved that organisation and joined PAIGC in March 1981.

FRENTE PARA UNIDADE NACIONAL E DESENVOLVIMENTO (FUND-Front for National Unity and Development: Guinea Bissau)

2. Republic of Guinea-Bissau (873,000)

3. Date Established: 1981

7. Status: Illegal opposition

9. Orientation: Cabralist socialism

13. History: Following the overthrow of President Cabral and his replacement by a purely Guinea PAIGC led by Major Joao Vieira, the former prime minister, some Guinean PAIGC leaders who were displaced became dissatisfied. At the end of 1981 they denounced Vieira and called for the re-establishment of a government based on the ideas of PAIGC's deceased founder, Amilcar Cabral.

FRONT CONGOLAISE POUR LA RESTAURATION DE LA DEMOCRATIE (FCD-Congolese Front for the Restoration of Democracy-CFRD: Zaire)

2. Republic of Zaire (33,927,000)

3. Date Established: 1 October 1982

4. Organisational Type: Coalition

6. Membership: Several thousand indirect individual members as members of the constituent organisations

7. Status: Illegal (now defunct)

9. Orientation: Elements of left-nationalism, Marxism, socialism, liberalism and conservatism

10. Strategy: Revolution

11. Internal Affiliations: PRP, Union pour la democratie et le progres social (UDPS)

13. History: Formed on 1 October 1982 in Brussels when Nguza Karl-I-Bond (ex-premier for Mobutu) announced his leadership of the coalition, the FCD was, in effect,

dissolved when Karl-I-Bond returned to Mobutu's bosom in June 1985.

14. Leadership: Nguza Karl-I-Bond, Spokesman and Executive Secretary (1982-85)

FRONT DE LA LIBERATION NATIONALE CONGOLAISE (FLNC-Congolese National Liberation Front-CNLF: Zaire)

2. Republic of Zaire (33,927,000)

3. Date Established: c.1975

4. Organisational Type: Mass party

6. Membership: Several thousand (during the late 1970s), many from the Lunda people

7. Status: Illegal

9. Orientation: Left nationalist; elements of Marxism

10. Strategy: Armed overthrow of Mobutu

11. Internal Affiliations: FCD, MNC, PRP

12. External Affiliations: MPLA-Angola, Guinea-Bissau

13. History: The FLNC was formed in the wake of the 1975-76 Angolan civil war. Zairean President Mobutu had supplied troops, etc. to one of the parties trying to overthrow the MPLA government of Angola. When the attempt of Mobutu and allies failed, the Angolan MPLA allowed the FLNC to create an army around a core of exile Katangese gendarmes (who had supported Tshombe's attempt to have Katanga/Shaba province secede) and to invade Shaba province in March 1977 and May 1978. The FLNC established nominal military liason with the PRP who have been militarily active in the north-east.

14. Leadership: General Nathaniel Mbumba, leader; Major Mufu

FRONT DE LIBERATION NATIONAL TCHADIEN (Frolinat-National Liberation Front of Chad)

2. Republic of Chad (5,308,000)

3. Date Established: 1966

4. Organisational Type: Extremely variable grouping of civil war factions but based on the national liberation model

7. Status: Because of Chadian history, Frolinat has been a government as well as one or more of the opposition factions.

9. Orientation: The various factions have contained a wide variety of orientations including left nationalism, eclectic socialism and personalist anti-imperialism.

10. Strategy: Negotiations and civil war

11. International Affiliations: Since the fragmentation of Frolinat, the various factions have been involved in a complicated and shifting set of alliances.

12. External Affiliations: The factions have varied from being allied with Libya to being allied with France. The FAP faction (see below) has been pro-Libyan.

13. History: Since Frolinat's founding in 1966, its history has been one of fragmentation and being in and out of power over varying parts of the country. The two main factions have been those led by Habre (e.g. FAN: Forces Armees du Nord - Armed Forces of the North) and Woddei (FAP: Forces Armees Popularies - People's Armed Forces created in 1976). Frolinat-FAP went on to join GUNT in 1979 and the CSR in 1985. In 1984 Habre's Frolinat-FAN joined UNIR.

14. Leadership: Abrahim Abatcha (1966-d.1969), then Dr. Abba Siddick, then Hissein Habre in FAN/UNIR against Goukouni Woddei (a.k.a. Oueddei, Weddeye) in FAP/GUNT/CSR.

FRONT DE LIBERATION NATIONALE (FLN-National Liberation Front-NLF:Algeria)

2. Democratic and Popular Republic of Algeria (24,847,000)

3. Date Established: 1 November 1954

4. Organisational Type: Mass party

5. Organisational Nature: The FLN Congress (some four thousand members) which meets every five years, elects a Central Committee (one hundred and sixty full members and thirty to forty alternate members) and a Secretary-General (who becomes the FLN's only presidential candidate) who chooses the Politburo (seven to eleven members) but who are confirmed by the Central Committee. Mass organisations include the Union Nationale de la Jeunesse Algerienne (UNJA-National Union of Algerian Youth), the Union Nationale des Femmes Algeriennes (UNFA-National Union of Algerian Women), and the Union Generale des Travailleurs Algeriens (UGTA-General Union of Algerian Workers).

6. Membership: Thousands

7. Status: Ruling, sole legal party

8. Publications: _El-Moudjahid_ (FLN-250,000 daily in French), _al-Jumhuriyah_ (FLN-70,000 daily in Arabic) as well as the three government newspapers and radio and television (all government owned)

9. Orientation: Social democracy (Islamic socialism)

10. Strategy: Electoral, regime maintenance

12. External Affiliations: Despite the ties that the Soviet Union maintains with the outlawed PAGS, the FLN and the Communist Party of the Soviet Union have party-to-party relations.

13. History: Formed in 1954, the FLN fought an ultimately successful war of liberation against French colonialism until independence was won on 3 July 1962. President Ahmed Ben Bella began to institute a number of socialist, even Marxist measures, but was overthrown on 19 June 1965 by a military officers' social democratic faction of the FLN which has remained in power despite the death of its original leader (Col. Houari Boumedienne, died 27 December 1978; succeeded by Col. Bendjedid Chadli on 7 February 1979).

14. Leadership: Secretary-General - Col. Bendjedid Chadli (President of the Republic); Other Politburo members - Col. Mohamed Ben Ahmed Abdel-Ghani, Boualem Baki, Col. Abdallah Belhouchet, Boulalem Benhamouda, Rabah Bitat, Dr. Ahmed Taleb Ibrahimi, Mohamed Cherif Messaadia, Mohamed Hadj Yala

FRONT DEMOCRATIQUE (FD-Democratic Front: Comoros)

2. Federal Islamic Republic of the Comoros (410,000)

3. Date Established: Existed in 1985

7. Status: Exile group based in Paris

13. History: The FD was accused of organising the March 8, 1985 attempted coup. Numbers of its members, including the Secretary-General, in the Comoros were arrested and sentenced to life imprisonment. Some were amnestied later in the year.

14. Leadership: Mohamed Monjoin (in Paris); Secretary General: Moustapha Said Cheikh (jailed in 1985 in the Comoros)

FRONT DEMOCRATIQUE POUR LA LIBERATION DE DJIBOUTI (FDLD-Djibouti Democratic Liberation Front: Djibouti)

2. Republic of Djibouti (588,000)

3. Date Established: 1 June 1979

4. Organisational Type: Mass party

7. Status: Illegal opposition party

9. Orientation: Nationalist/Marxist

10. Strategy: Electoral, negotiations

12. External Affiliations: Reflecting the Afar ethnic composition of the FPLD, the party was in exile in Ethiopia

13. History: The FPLD was created by the Marxist-oriented Mouvement Populaire pour la Liberation (MPL) and the

Union Nationale pour l'Independance (UNI) on 1 June 1979 in opposition to Gouled's RPP government which they accused of being for annexation to Somalia and of being a tool of French imperialism. In 1982 some of the former MPL accepted Gouled's amnesty.

14. Leadership: Mohamed Kamil Ali

FRONT DES FORCES SOCIALISTES (FFS-Socialist Forces Front: Algeria)

2. Democratic and Popular Republic of Algeria (24,847,000)

3. Date Established: Existed in 1963

4. Organisational Type: Mass party

6. Membership: Several hundred, mainly Berber

7. Status: Illegal

9. Orientation: Socialist

10. Strategy: Revolution

11. Internal Affiliations: The FFS and the pro-Ben Bella group, the Organisation Clandestine de la Revolution Algerienne - OCRA, formed in 1967 a coalition entitled the Mouvement Algerien pour l'Unite Nationale et la Democratie (MAUND-Algerian Movement for National Unity and Democracy) which existed in the late 1960s.

13. History: While the FFS revolted against Ben Bella's FLN regime in 1963 and 1964, following his 1965 overthrow the FFS joined with the pro-Ben Bella group, OCRA, to create the MAUND. The FFS has continued to maintain its own organisation.

14. Leadership: Hocine Ait Ahmed

FRONT NATIONAL POUR LA DEFENSE DE LA REVOLUTION SOCIALISTE MALGACHE (FNDR-National Front for the Defense of the Malagasy Socialist Revolution: Madagascar)

See also: AREMA; AKRM; VITM/VONJY; MPP/MFM; MONIMA; VSM; UDECMA/KMTP

2. Democratic Republic of Madagascar (9,490,000)

4. Date Established: 21 December 1975

5. Organisational Nature: The FNDR was responsible to the CSR (Conseil Supreme de la Revolution) which in turn was controlled by its Chairman who was also President of the Republic. The FNDR selected from the constituent parties' lists of candidates for the FNDR's final list of candidates who were then directly elected by the citizenry.

7. Status: Ruling coalition

8. Publications: The FNDR influences the government-owned newspaper (Atrika, circulation 13,000), radio and television.

9. Orientation: Socialist

10. Strategy: Building and administering a socialist state, regime maintenance, electoral, mixed economy

11. Internal Affiliations: The FNDR was composed of the following 'revolutionary associations' or parties: AREMA, AKRM, VITM/VONJY, MPP/MFM, MONINA, VSM, UDECMA/KMTP.

12. External Relations: Nonaligned with pro-Soviet, pro-Palestinian and anti-apartheid components

13. History: The FNDR was established as the official governing party mechanism by the 21 December 1975 constitution. The FNDR organised the candidates lists for the 1982 presidential election and the 1977 and 1983 National Assembly elections.

14. Leadership: Admiral Didier Ratsiraka (President of the Republic and Secretary General of AREMA)

FRONT NATIONAL PROGRESSISTE POUR LA LIBERATION DE LA TUNISIE (FNPLT–National Progressive Front For the Liberation of Tunisia: Tunisia)

2. Republic of Tunisia (7,224,000)

3. Date Established: Existed in 1980

4. Organisational Type: Mass party - clandestine

7. Status: Illegal

9. Orientation: Libyan eclectic socialism

10. Strategy: Revolution

12. External Affiliations: Libya

13. History: The FNPLT was a clandestine organisation that supposedly organised the raid on the city of Gafsa.

FRONT NATIONAL UNI DES KOMORES (FNUK-Comoran National United Front: Comoros)

See Also: CNSP, UNIKOM and FNUK-UNIKOM

2. Federal Islamic Republic of the Comoros (410,000)

3. Date Established: Existed in 1982

7. Status: Exile group

11. Internal Affiliations: In 1981, FNUK joined with Unikom and CNSP to form a coalition, FNUK-Unikom.

13. History: Emerging out of the aftermath of the 1978 overthrow of Ali Soilih's National United Front, the FNUK joined with Unikom during the middle of 1981 and with the CNSP on October 3, 1981. This coalition operates from Paris.

14. Leadership: Abukar Ahmed Nurdin.

FRONT PATRIOTIQUE OUBANGUIEN - PARTI TRAVALLAISTE (FRP-PT: Ubangi Patriotic Front-Labour Party: Central African Republic)

See also: PRC, MLPC, MCLN.

2. Central African Republic (2,734,000)

3. Date Established: Pre-1983

7. Status: Illegal

9. Orientation: Socialist

10. Strategy: Negotiations, coalition

11. Internal Affiliations: The FPO-UT in coalition with the MLPC and the MCLN created the PRC.

12. External Affiliations: Congo-Brazzaville; European socialist parties

13. History: The FPO-PT has been based for some time in the Congo. In 1981 the FPO-PT rejected the Dacko regime, calling for the creation of democracy and French military withdrawal. In 1983 it joined in coalition with the MLPC and the MCLN to create the PRC. The leadership has been detained several times. In 1985, the President and Secretary General were released from their northern internal exile.

14. Leadership: Abel Goumba, President and founder; Patrice Endjimoungou, Secretary General.

FRONT PROGRESSISTE VOLTAIQUE (FPV-Voltaic Progressive Front: Burkina Faso)

2. Republic of Burkina Faso (8,130,000)

3. Date Established: Existed in 1978

4. Organisational Type: Mass party

7. Status: Illegal party

9. Orientation: Socialist

10. Strategy: Regrouping in exile after a failed coup plot, formerly electoral

13. History: The FPV was created by dissatisfied members of the then (1978-1980) ruling party, the Union Democratique Voltaique - Rassemblement Democratique Africain (UDV-RDA). The FPV won nine National Assembly seats in the 1978 elections. After the 1980 coup the FPV was marginalised. Its main leaders went in exile, at least one of them (Joseph Ki-Zerbo) being accused of plotting to overthrow Sankara's CNR in May 1984.

14. Leadership: Joseph Ki-Zerbo, Leader; Joseph Ouedraogo

GAMBIA SOCIALIST REVOLUTIONARY PARTY (GSRP: Gambia)

2. Republic of the Gambia (770,000)

7. Status: Banned on November 1, 1980

9. Orientation: Socialist

10. Strategy: The GSRP was critical of the Jawara'a People's Progressive Party government and may have advocated its overthrow.

14. Leadership: Pingon Georges

GOUVERNEMENT D'UNION NATIONAL DE TRANSITION (GUNT-Transitional Government of National Unity: Chad)

2. Republic of Chad (5,308,000)

3. Date Established: August 20-21, 1979

4. Organisational Type: National liberation/civil war movement

7. Status: Government from 1979 to 1982, 1982-85 in opposition

10. Strategy: Negotiation and civil war.

11. Internal Affiliations: Woddei's Frolinat-FAP and Kamougue's southern FAT (Forces Armees Tchadiennes: Chadian Armed Forces, latter known as the MRP (Mouvement Populaire et Revolutionnaire du Tchad-People's Revolutionary Movement) were the most important forces to join GUNT.

12. External Affiliations: Pro-Libyan

13. History: Formed on August 20-21, 1979, GUNT ruled much of Chad until it was militarily pushed out of the capital by Habre's Frolinat-FAN in June 1982. Following a period of extreme fragmentation, elements of GUNT reformed around Woddei's Frolinat-FAP on August 7, 1984 to create the CNL (Conseil National de la

Liberation - National Council of Liberation). In August 1985 the CNL was transformed into the CSR.

14. Leadership: Goukouni Woddei, President; Lt. Col. Wadal Abdekader Kamougue, Vice President.

GROUPE COMMUNISTE (GC-Communist Group: Burkina Faso)

2. Republic of Burkina Faso (8,130,000)

3. Date Established: Existed in 1983

7. Status: Part of the ruling CNR

9. Orientation: Marxism-Leninism

10. Strategy: Building revolutionary socialist regime

11. Internal Affiliations: The GC, ULC, UCB, ROC and LIPAD were part of Sankara's CNR government.

13. History: The minister of culture and information was Ouattamou Lamien, a GL leader.

14. Leadership: Ouattamou Lamien

GROUPE COMMUNISTE REVOLUTIONNAIRE (GCR-Revolutionary Communist Group-RCG:Algeria)

2. Democratic and Popular Republic of Algeria (24,847,000)

3. Date Established: Existed in 1980

6. Membership: Few

7. Status: Illegal

9. Orientation: Trotskyist interpretation of Marxism-Leninism

10. Strategy: Revolution, party-building

12. External Affiliations: Section of the Fourth International (Trotskyist)

13. History: In the early 1980s the GCR expressed their support for the national rights of Berbers and Arabs as opposed to the French language which, the GCR argued, was used by the FLN leadership to exclude proletarians from power.

GROUPE DE LA REVOLUTION SOCIALISTE ARABE (GRSA-Arab Socialist Revolution Group: Tunisia)

2. Republic of Tunisia (7,224,000)

3. Date Established: Existed in 1981

4. Organisational Type: Pre-party formation

6. Membership: Students and youth

7. Status: Illegal

9. Orientation: Trotskyist interpretation of Marxism-Leninism

10. Strategy: Leninism Revolution, party-building

12. External Affiliations: Trotskyist Fouth International parties

14. Leadership: K. Said (pseudonym)

GROUPE D'ETUDES ET D'ACTION SOCIALISTE TUNISIEN (GEAST-Tunisian Socialist Study and Action Group: Tunisia) a.k.a. PERSPECTIVISTES

2. Republic of Tunisia (7,224,000)

3. Date Established: 1963

4. Organisational Type: Vanguard party

6. Membership: Included students

7. Status: Illegal

8. Publications: <u>Perspectives Tunisiennes</u> (Tunisian Perspective), <u>Tunisian Worker</u>

9. Orientation: Maoist interpretation of Marxism-Leninism

10. Strategy: Revolution

13. History: After GEAST was founded in France in 1963, members began to return in 1964. Numbers of GEAST members were arrested in 1968 and 1974.

14. Leadership: Ahmad ben 'Uthman Raddam, publisher of (8) above

HIZB AL-'AMAL AL-ISHTIRAKI (HAI-Egypt) a.k.a. SLP

HIZB AL-TAJAMMU 'AL-WATANI AL-TAQADDUMI AL-WAHDAWI (HTWTW-Egypt) a.k.a. NPUP

ISLAMIC SOCIALIST PARTY (ISP: Sudan)

2. Republic of Sudan (23,089,000)

3. Date Established: Existed in 1985

4. Organisational Type: Mass party

6. Membership: Muslims, mainly Northern

7. Status: Legal

9. Orientation: Eclectic socialism (Islamic socialism)

JAMAHIRIYA (Libya)

2. Socialist People's Libyan Arab Jamahiriya (4,108,000)

3. Date Established: March 1977 developing from the September 1, 1969 revolution.

4. Organisational Type: Mass party

5. Organisational Nature: A series of committees from the grassroots upwards and spread throughout Libyan society and government were created in 1977 in an attempt to permeate revolutionary values throughout Libya and prevent bureaucrats from dominating the people. The

People's Committees are organised through a number of levels and congresses until they culminate in the General People's Congress whose de facto executive is the General Secretariat which is chaired by the Secretary General, who is also de jure head of state. The de facto cabinet is the General People's Committee which is chaired by its Secretary.

6. Membership: Nominally all adult Libyans are members.

7. Status: Sole legal ruling organisation.

8. Publications: <u>al-Fajr al-Jadid</u> (40,000 weekly, Arabic) is published by the Jamahiriya News Agency. The Socialist People's Libyan Arab Jamahiriya Broadcasting Corporation broadcasts in Arabic and English using television and radio.

9. Orientation: Distinctive combination of left nationalism, Islamic socialism and anti-imperialism as defined by Qadhafi.

10. Strategy: Domestic economic policy has arrived at socialisation in order to improve the standard of living of the ordinary Libyan. Politically the creation of people's committees was aimed at preventing or overcoming the bureaucratization and corruption of the Libyan revolution. Internationally, Jamahiriyan Libya has sought to fight imperialism around the world, hence it has supported national liberation movements and promoted Arab and African unity. Consequently Libya has been extensively involved in a number of countries.

11. Internal Affiliations: Trade unions, professional bodies, etc. have been incorporated into the revolutionary committee structure.

12. External Affiliations: Jamahiriya is allied with Syria, Iran, pro-Syrian PLO elements, Woddei's CSR in Chad, and a number of national liberation movements and revolutionary forces around the world. The Soviet Union has not always been responsive to Libyan overtures.

13. History: On September 1, 1969 the Libyan revolution was initiated by military officers. Colonel Mu'ammar al-Qadhafi emerged as the leader of the Revolutionary Command Council (R.C.C.). In order to overcome a

number of problems within the revolution during March 1977 Libya was politically refocussed and reorganised as the Socialist People's Libyan Arab Jamahiriya.

14. Leadership: Col. Mu'ammar Abu Minyar al-Qadhafi, Leader of the Revolution; Miftah al-Usta '<u>Umar</u>, Secretary of the General People's Congress; Jadallah 'Azzuz al-<u>Talhi</u>, Secretary of the General People's Committee (de facto prime minister).

JUNE FOURTH MOVEMENT (JFM: Ghana)

See also, UNITED FRONT (Ghana)

2. Republic of Ghana (12,205,000)

3. Date Established: c.1979

4. Organisational Type: Mass party

6. Membership: Several hundred to one thousand

7. Status: Illegal

8. Publications: <u>Workers' Banner</u> (September 1981-1982), <u>Kpano</u> (special edition for the Northern and Upper Regions)

9. Orientation: Marxist-Leninist (Pro-Soviet)

10. Strategy: Revolution; party-building

11. Internal Affiliations: After December 31, 1981 (the start of the PNDC), the JFM and the PRLG came to form the United Front.

13. History: The JFM was formed in the aftermath of the first Rawlings' government (the AFRC) by some elements that had rejected the PRP's merger into the PNP Indeed the JFM's name commemorates the 4 June 1979 uprising that started with the freeing of Rawlings from jail. The JFM took part in the revolution that started on 31 December 1981 with Rawlings' second coming. Sharp differences with Rawlings and the NDM over the JFM's desire (1) to have an immediate transition to socialism and (2) to reject an economic strategy based on the IMF and World Bank, and (3) to create a united vanguard

party (this also called into question Rawlings' leadership) led the JFM to cooperate with the PRLG in a (possibly pre-emptive?) coup attempt in October 1982 against Rawlings. After its failure, numbers of JFM members went into exile and began to revive the United Front in London. Another wing of the JFM continued to cooperate with the PNDC.

14. Leadership: Chris Atim, Secretary General (former PNDC member); Kwasi Adu (former Chairman of the PNDC's Democratic Youth League of Ghana); Zeeya Yeebo (former secretary for Youth and Sports)

KWAME NKRUMAH REVOLUTIONARY GUARDS (KNRG: Ghana)

2. Republic of Ghana (12,205,000)

3. Date Established: 21 September 1980

4. Organisational Type: Mass party

6. Membership: Several thousand in seven southern regions

7. Status: Legal

9. Orientation: Socialist (Nkrumahist), left nationalism

10. Strategy: Peaceful; working within (formerly) the PNP and later the PNDC; popular mobilisation

11. Internal Affiliations: The KNRG was affiliated first with the PNP and then the PNDC.

13. History: Founded on Nkrumah's birthday in 1980, the KNRG was initially intended to act as a "ginger group" pushing for Nkrumahist socialism within the governing PNP of President Limann. Following Limann's fall, the KNRG attempted to play a similar role within the PNDC.

14. Leadership: H.S.T. (Sonny) Provencal, General Secretary; Johnny Hansen, former Acting National Chairman (former PNDC Secretary of the Interior); F.A. Jantuah (former PNDC Regional Secretary for Ashanti) and C.S. Takyi (former PNDC Regional Secretary for Brong-Ahafo)

LABOUR LEAGUE (LL-Wez Ader: Ethiopia)

2. Socialist Ethiopia (35,210,000)

3. Date Established: Existed in 1975

4. Organisational Type: Vanguard party

6. Membership: Some recruitment success in the trade unions

7. Status: Legal, aid to PMAC from c.1975 to 1977, illegal afterwards

9. Orientation: Marxism-Leninism

10. Strategy: Party-building with PMAC until mid-1977, overthrow PMAC after that

11. Internal Affiliations: LL joined with RF, MEISON, EORS and MLRO to form the short-lived UEMLO in February 1977 in an attempt to unify the pro-PMAC left into a vanguard party

13. History: For some time PMAC used LL to counter MEISON, however, LL later unsuccessfully tried to use the trade unions to supplant the PMAC.

LEAGUE, THE (Ghana) a.k.a. PRLG

LIGUE COMMUNISTE DES TRAVAILLEURS (LCT-Communist Workers League: Senegal)

2. Republic of Senegal (6,710,000)

3. Date Established: 1982

4. Organisational Type: Trotskyist pre-party formation

6. Membership: few

7. Status: Legal

9. Orientation: Trotskyist Marxism-Leninism

10. Strategy: Party-building for socialist revolution

12. External Affiliation: Fourth International

13. History: The LCT has differed with the OST over the question of the Soviet Union.

14. Leadership: Mahmoud Saleh

LIGUE DEMOCRATIQUE-MOUVEMENT POUR LE PARTI DU TRAVAIL (LD-MPT: Democratic League - Movement for the Party of Labour: Senegal)

See also, ADS

2. Republic of Senegal (6,710,000)

3. Date Established: Existed in 1979; 1981 registered

4. Organisational Type: Trotskyist pre-party formation

6. Membership: Numbers amongst students and teachers

7. Status: Legal opposition party

9. Orientation: Trotskyist Marxism-Leninism

10. Strategy: Party-building by broadening its trade union and intelligentsia base; promotion of the anti-imperialist national democratic phase of the revolution by joining tactical alliances such as the ADS.

11. Internal Affiliations: One of the LD-MPT leaders, Mamadou N'Doye was also the Secretary General of the Syndicat Unifie et Democratique des Enseignants du Senegal (SUDES-United Democratic Union of Senegalese Teachers). The LD-MPT was allied with the MRDN, the OST, the PDS and the UDP in the ADS alliance.

12. External Affiliations: Fourth International/Trotskyist

13. History: Following the 1976 creation of the PAI as the only officially-recognised Marxist party, the LD-MPT joined with the PAI in 1979. However, following the PS government's decision to allow any other parties to be registered officially, the LD-MPT left the PAI and registered on 9 July 1981. In 1985 it joined the ADS alliance and one of the LD-MPT leaders, Dr. Abdoulaye Bathily, became chairman of the ADS.

14. Leadership: Mamadou N'Doye, Secretary General; Dr. Abdoulaye Bathily; Amadou Top; Babacar Sane

LIGUE PATRIOTIQUE POUR LA DEVELOPPEMENT (LIPAD–Patriotic League for Development: Burkina Faso)

2. Republic of Burkina Faso (8,130,000)

3. Date Established: 1973

7. Status: August 4, 1983-August 1984 - party of the CNR government; August 1984 - Opposition

9. Orientation: Pro-Soviet Marxism Leninism

10. Strategy: 1983-84 building LIPAD's version of a revolutionary socialist state; 1984-87 onwards trying to pressure Sankara's CNR government to respond to its wishes and to release its leaders; party-building.

11. Internal Affiliations: LIPAD, ULC, GC, UCB and the ROC participated in the establishment of Sankara's CNR government. LIPAD was closely associated with the Confederation Syndicale Voltaique (CSV), the most influential trade union congress in Burkina Faso.

12. External Affiliations: Soviet-allied parties

13. History: LIPAD was formed in 1973 by a dissident group in the PAI (BF). By 1983 LIPAD had eclipsed its progenitor. LIPAD has gained considerable support amongst the military and in the trade unions. It had influence amongst Sankara and his fellow junior ranks in the left wing of the government that preceded Sankara's CNR (i.e. the CSP-Conseil de Salut du Peuple: 7 November 1982 - 5 August 1983) as well as in trade unions such as the CSV. However, LIPAD's influence in Sankara's CNR government was short-lived. LIPAD lost its ministerial posts in August 1984, only one year after the inauguration of Sankara's revolution. Some leaders such as Arba Diallo, formerly external affairs minister, and Soumane Toure, a CSV trade union leader, were jailed, charged with corruption. The CNR government released some of these jailed leaders in February 1985 in response to CNV pressure. More, but not Toure, were released in 1986.

14. Leadership: Hamidou Coulibaly, President; Arba Diallo; Soumane Toure (Secretary General of the CSV)

LIGUEURS, LES (The League: Benin)

2. People's Republic of Benin (4,102,000)

3. Existed in 1981

7. Status: Faction within the ruling party, the PRPB.

9. Orientation: Maoist

10. Leaguers worked within the ruling party on the basis of critical support for Kerekou's PRPB. They have sought to maintain Benin's distance from the Soviet Union, which is regarded as perpetuating 'Soviet imperialism'. Leaguers try to increase their influence by placing their members in key positions. In 1981 the League attempted to establish their own trade union as a base from which they could challenge first the official unions and then the regime. This was stopped by the regime. Several arrests occurred, but some sort of a reconciliation was conducted.

12. External Affiliations: Pro-China

13. Leadership: Gratien Capochichi (PRPB Politbureau member) and Simon Goumba, the former Benin foreign minister.

MALAWI FREEDOM MOVEMENT (MAFREMO: Malawi)

2. Republic of Malawi (6,782,000)

3. Date Established: Existed in 1981

7. Status: Illegal opposition party in exile

9. Orientation: Left nationalist

10. Strategy: Ending the rule of Banda's Malawi Congress Party; negotiations with other opposition groups; underground party-building in Malawi

12. External Affiliations: Exile headquarters in Dar es Salaam, Tanzania

13. History: In December 1981 the leader, Orton Chirwa (a former Banda cabinet minister) and his wife, Vera Chirwa, were abducted from Zambia by the Banda government. Chirwa was sentenced to death for treason but in 1984 sentence was commuted to life imprisonment after an international pressure was applied on Banda. During June 1983, MAFREMO took part with LESOMA and the Congress for the Second Republic in the unsuccessful Lusaka-based attempt to unite the opposition in the Save Malawi Committee.

14. Leadership: Orton Chirwa (abducted 1981)

MARXIST-LENINIST REVOLUTIONARY ORGANISATION (MLRO-Ma.Le.Ri.De.: Ethiopia)

2. Socialist Ethiopia (35,210,000)

3. Date Established: Existed in 1975

6. Membership: Few, mainly youth and students

7. Status: Legal during the mid-1970s

9. Orientation: Marxism-Leninism

10. Strategy: Party-building with PMAC (during 1977-78 through the UEMLO mechanism

11. Internal Affiliations: MLRO joined with EORS, LL, RF and MEISON to form the short-lived UEMLO in February 1977 in an attempt to unify the pro-PMAC left into a vanguard party.

13. History: MLRO supported PMAC

MAURITIAN WORKERS' MOVEMENT (MWM-Mauritius)

2. Mauritius (1,023,000)

3. Date Established: February 1984

4. Organisational Type: Mass Party

7. Status: Member of MSM-led coalition government

9. Orientation: Left nationalist/Social democratic

10. Strategy: Electoral, coalition

11. Internal Affiliations: Member of the MSM-led coalition government.

13. History: When the MLP decided to leave the MSM government in early 1984 because their leader had lost his cabinet position, eleven MLP elected members decided to form their own party, the MWM, and remain in the coalition government. The new MWM leader was made a cabinet member.

14. Leadership: Beergoonath Ghurburran, Leader.

MAURITIUS LABOUR PARTY (MLP-Mauritius)

2. Mauritius (1,023,000)

3. Date Established: c.1967

4. Organisational Nature: Mass party

6. Membership: Most of its strength is drawn from the Hindu community.

7. Status: Legal opposition party

9. Orientation: Social democratic, left nationalist

10. Strategy: Electoral, coalitions

11. Internal Affiliations: The MLP is supported by a number of trade unions. During the 1970s the MLP formed a coalition with the Muslim Action Committee (CAM) to create the Independence Party. In 1983 the MLP joined the MSM government but left in 1984.

13. History: The MLP formed the core of the government from 1967 (independence 1968) to 1982. Following a short period in opposition, the MLP joined the MSM government but left in 1984 after the MLP leader lost his cabinet portfolio.

14. Leadership: Sir Satcam Boolell, Leader; Vijay Venkatasamy, Secretary General.

MAURITIUS PEOPLE'S PROGRESSIVE PARTY (MPPP-Mauritius)

2. Mauritius (1,023,000)

3. Date Established: Existed in 1985

4. Organisational Type: Mass Party

7. Status: Legal opposition party

9. Orientation: Soviet interpretation of Marxism-Leninism

10. Strategy: Electoral, emphasizing the demilitarization of the Indian Ocean

12. External Affiliations: member of the international Afro-Asian People's Solidarity Organisation, pro-Soviet parties

13. History: The MPPP lost numbers of its members to the MMM during the 1980s.

14. Leadership: Teekaram Sibsurun, Secretary General

MEISON (All Ethiopian Socialist Movement-AESM: Ethiopia)

2. Socialist Ethiopia (35,210,000)

3. Date Established: Exited in 1975

6. Membership: Recruitment successes amongst the Oromo people included one of the MEISON leaders, Haile Fida.

7. Status: Legal from 1975 to 1977, illegal since then

8. Publications: <u>The Voice of the Masses</u> (c. mid 1970s)

9. Orientation: Marxism-Leninism

10. Strategy: 1975-1977 - attempted to direct the creation of socialist and an official vanguard party through participation in the PMAC-created Political Bureau; 1977 onwards - armed overthrow of the PMAC.

11. Internal Affiliations: In February 1977, MEISON joined the short-lived (and at first five member) UEMLO. During 1977-1978 MEISON tried to gain control of the "Kebeles" (urban community committees) before MEISON members were literally hunted down by the PMAC loyalists in the Kebeles.

14. Leadership: Haile Fida, Negedde Gobeze

MNCL (Zaire) a.k.a. MNC

MNCR (Zaire) a.k.a. MNC

MOUVEMENT CENTRAFRICAINE POUR LA LIBERTE NATIONALE (MCLN-Central African Movement For National Liberation: Central African Republic) See also, PRC, MLPC, FPO-PT

2. Central African Republic (2,734,000)

3. Date Established: Existed in 1983

4. Organisational Type: National liberation movement

7. Status: Illegal

9. Orientation: Left nationalist, socialist

10. Strategy: Coalition, armed struggle

11. Internal Affiliations: The MCLN joined in coalition with the MLPC and the FPO-PT to create the PRC.

12. External Affiliations: Libya, Chad's CSR.

13. History: The MCLN was founded in Paris by dissident FPO-PT elements. The MCLN has conducted guerrilla warfare in the northern part of the country that borders with Chad. Chad's CSR has aided the MCLN.

14. Leadership: General Alphonse M'Baikoua and General Francois Bozize.

MOUVEMENT D'ACTION POUR LA RESURRECTION AU CONGO (MARC-Action Movement for Congolese Revival - AMCR: Zaire)

2. Republic of Zaire (33,927,000)

3. Date Established: 1974

6. Membership: Mainly students in Belgium

7. Status: Illegal

8. Publication: Miso Gaa (published in the 1970s)

9. Orientation: Left nationalist, socialist

10. Strategy: Revolution

11. Internal Affiliations: MARC was involved with the CLC

13. History: MARC grew out of the student movement. MARC elements were part of a 1979 coup attempt that was to be launched from Rwanda. MARC was based in Belgium.

14. Leadership: Monguya Mbenge, Secretary-General

MOUVEMENT DEMOCRATE SOCIALE CONGOLAISE (MDSC–Congolese Social Democratic Movement - CSDM: Zaire)

2. Republic of Zaire (33,927,000)

3. Date Established: Existed in 1985

4. Organisational Type: Mass party

6. Membership: Few

7. Status: Illegal

9. Orientation: Social democracy

10. Strategy: Revolution

11. Internal Affiliations: MNCR, MNCL

13. History: The MDSC was based in Switzerland. The MDSC, the MNCR and MNCL proposed in September 1985 that opposition groups join a new coordinating body in order to overthrow the Mobutu regime.

14. Leadership: Allah Fior Muyinda

MOUVEMENT DEMOCRATIQUE POPULAIRE (MDP-People's Democratic Movement: Senegal)

2. Republic of Senegal (6,710,000)

3. Date Established: 1981 (registered)

4. Organisational Type: Mass party

7. Status: Legal opposition party

8. Media: <u>Ande Sopi</u> (monthly, founded in 1977 by Mamadou Dia)

9. Orientation: Socialist

10. Strategy: Electoral, worker self-management (autogestion)

13. History: The MDP was founded legally in 1981 by breakaway elements of the underground pro-Soviet faction of the PAI, most notably Mamadou Dia (a former PS/UPS prime minister) as well as left nationalists such as another former PS/UPS interior minister, Valdiodio N'diaye. The MDP ran Dia as its presidential candidate in 1983 but boycotted the 1984 municipal elections. Its success in recruiting intellectuals has not been matched amongst the proletariat or the peasantry.

14. Leadership: Mamadou Dia, Valdiodio N'Diaye

MOUVEMENT DE RESISTANCE NATIONALE (MORENA-Movement for National Resistance: Gabon)

2. Gabonese Republic (1,551,000)

3. Date Established: 1981

4. Organisational Type: Exile party with underground wing in Gabon.

7. Status: Illegal, in exile and in underground

9. Orientation: Social Democratic

10. Strategy: Peaceful agitation and external lobbying for the ending of Bongo's one-party state and the reinstatement of multi-party democracy.

12. External Affiliations: The French Socialist Party has provided assistance to MORENA.

13. History: MORENA was formed in 1981 and has been active within Gabon and in exile in France. MORENA developed links with the French Socialist Party, including French President Mitterand. In 1982, Mitterand intervened on behalf of twenty MORENA members and had their sentences shortened. Numbers of those imprisoned, for distributing leaflets, were pardoned in 1985. In August 1985 MORENA declared itself to be a government-in-exile, based in France.

14. Leadership: Max Anicet Koumba-Mbabinga, Simon Adolphe Evouna (based in Paris) and Paul Mba-Abessole.

MOUVEMENT DES DEMOCRATES SOCIALISTES (MDS-Social Democratic Movement: Tunisia)

2. Republic of Tunisia (7,224,000)

3. Date Established: October 1977

4. Organisational Type: Mass party

7. Status: Legal

9. Orientation: Social democratic

10. Strategy: Electoral

13. History: The MDS was formed in October 1977, initially titled as the Democratic Socialist Group, by dissident PSD cabinet ministers. Denied recognition by the Bourguiba PSD government in 1978, the MDS won 3.28 per cent of the stated vote in the 1981 legislative elections. Bourguiba granted legal status to the MDS in November 1983.

14. Leadership: Ahmed Mestiri (Secretary General); Mohammed Moadda; Hammouda Ben Salama; Dali Jazi

MOUVEMENT DU 17 (dix-septieme) JANVIER (MDJ-Movement of 17 January: MSJ: Zaire)

2. Republic of Zaire (33,927,000)

3. Date Established: Exited in 1982

6. Membership: Few

7. Status: Illegal

9. Orientation: Left nationalist (Lumumbist)

10. Strategy: Revolution

11. Internal Affiliations: The MDJ had some relations with the PRP.

13. History: The MDJ appears to have been based in Belgium. The name stems from the day when Premier Patrice Lumumba was assassinated (17 January 1961).

MOUVEMENT D'UNITE POPULAIRE (MUP-Popular Unity Movement: Tunisia)

2. Republic of Tunisia (7,224,000)

3. Date Established: c.1973

4. Organisational Type: Mass party

7. Status: Illegal external faction, legal internal faction

9. Orientation: Left nationalist, some Marxist and socialist elements.

10. Strategy: External faction - revolution; internal faction - electoral

11. Internal Affiliations: The internal faction has had links to one faction of the PDS.

12. External Affiliations: External factions has had contact with Iraq.

13. History: MUP was formed by dissidents from the PDS (including Ahmed Ben Salah who had been responsible for the PDS' further turn to the left as economics minister in the 1960s and who escaped from prison in 1973) and other groups including the PCT. MUP's June 1978 attempt to register as a political party was rejected by Bourguiba's PDS government. However, the government successfully used registration as a tactic to split MUP. The internal faction led by Mohamed Bel Hadj Amor had their members amnestied by the government and were allowed to contest the 1981 elections where they won 0.81 per cent of the stated vote. Bourguiba granted them legal status in 1983. The external faction, led by Salah (who was not pardoned nor allowed to return from exile) has opposed collaboration with the PDS regime. This led to the continuation of support for Salah's MUP, especially by the youth and students.

14. Leadership: External faction - Ahmed Ben Salah, Secretary General; Brahim Hayder; Hamidi Cherif; Internal faction - Mohamed Bel Hadj Amor, leader; Mohammed Daouad

MOUVEMENT MILITANT MAURICIEN (MMM-Mauritian Militant Movement: Mauritius)

2. Mauritius (1,023,000)

3. Date Established: c.1967

4. Organisational Type: Mass party

7. Status: Legal opposition party.

9. Orientation: Marxist

10. Strategy: Electoral, coalitions, non-racial.

11. Internal Affiliations: The MMM has received significant trade union support.

13. History: The MLP government seized the MMM leaders during the 1971 communal disturbances; however, the MMM remained a legal opposition party. The 1976 elections gave it official opposition status. The MMM alliance won the June 15, 1982 elections. Policy differences, mainly over economics and language, caused the party to

split in March 1983. The MMM leader and prime minister, Aneerood Jugnauth was expelled from the party. He formed the MSM which defeated the MMM in the August 21, 1983 election. However, the MMM rebounded somewhat in 1985 when it won a plurality of votes in the December 8 municipal elections.

14. Leadership: Paul Berenger, Leader; Dharam Fokeer, President; Allan Ganoo, Secretary General.

MOUVEMENT MILITANT MAURICIEN SOCIAL PROGRESSISTE (MMMSP-Mauritian Social Progressive Militant Movement: Mauritius)

2. Mauritius (1,023,000)

3. Date Established: Existed in 1985.

4. Organisational Type: Mass party

6. Membership: Originally drawn from former MMM members.

7. Status: Legal opposition party

9. Orientation: Maoist-Marxist

10. Strategy: Electoral

13. History: The MMMSP was created by proponents of a Maoist outlook in the MMM.

14. Leadership: Dev Veraswamy

MOUVEMENT NATIONAL DEMOCRATIQUE (MND-National Democratic Movement: Mauritania)

2. Islamic Republic of Mauritania (1,888,000)

3. Date Established: Early 1970s, existed in 1984

4. Organisational Type: Mass party

6. Membership: Both black and Moorish ethno-linguistic groups

7. Status: Tolerated

9. Orientation: Left nationalist, socialist

10. Strategy: Revolution; united front; organising labour, military officers, workers and peasants

11. Internal Affiliations: The MRD has some influence in the leadership of the Union des Travailleurs Maurtianiens (UTM-Mauritanian Workers' Union) and especially amongst the rank and file workers of Harratine descent (children, etc. of black slave ancestors).

13. History: The MND had been very active in the early 1970s but lost some influence after the 1978 coup

MOUVEMENT NATIONAL DU CONGO (MNC - Congo National Movement - CMM: Zaire) a.k.a. MNCL, a.k.a. MNCR

2. Republic of Zaire (33,927,000)

3. Date Established: 1958

4. Organisational Type: Mass party

5. Organisational Nature: The MNC fractured after Lumumba's death. In 1982 there was a seven-member Secretariat headed by Secretary General Mosamete Sekola. By September 1985, the MNC had split into the Mouvement National du Congo Reforme (MNCR) and the Mouvement National du Congo - Lumumba (MNCL)

6. Membership: Few but growing

7. Status: Illegal

9. Orientation: Left nationalism

10. Strategy: Revolution

11. Internal Affiliates: MDSC, FLNC, member of the FCD

13. History: Formed in 1958 as a non-ethnic party the MNC's first National President was Patrice Lumumba. In July 1959 the MNC split into the MNC-L led by Lumumba and the MNC-K led by Albert Kalonji. Lumumba became Prime Minister of the Congo, 30 June to 5 September 1960 when he was overthrown first by President Kasavubu and then by Colonel Mobutu on 14 September 1960.

Mobutu and his allies then proceeded to destroy nearly all of the MNC and murdered Patrice Lumumba on 17 January 1961. The MNC reappeared from its ashes during the 1970s. In 1984 the MNC stated that it had set off a number of bombs in Kinshasa, Zaire's capital. By 1985 the MNC had split into the MNCL and MNCR. The MNC was a member of the FCD. Upon its demise, the MNCR, MNCL, the FLNC and the MDSC called for the creation of a new opposition coalition.

14. Leadership: Leader and Secretary General - Francois-Emery Lumumba-Tolenga (son of P. Lumumba); President - Paul Roger Mokede; Albert Onawelho (MNCL)

MOUVEMENT NATIONAL POUR L'INDEPENDENCE DE MADAGASCAR (MONIMA - National Movement for Madagascar's Independence: Madagascar)

2. Democratic Republic of Madagascar (9,490,000)

3. Date Established: 1958

4. Organisational Type: Mass party

7. Status: Constituent 'revolutionary association' of the ruling FNDR coalition

9. Orientation: left nationalist, socialist

10. Strategy: Electoral

11. Internal Affiliations: MONIMA was associated with the AKRM, AREMA, MFM/MPP, VSM, VONJY and UDECMA/KMTP as constituent parts of the FNDR.

13. History: The oldest existing party in Madagascar has been led by the venerable sole surviving party leader of the anti-colonial fight. Monja Jaona originally built the party's base amongst the southern peasantry, however, the 1982 Presidential and the 1983 National Assembly elections demonstrated that this base had been eroded and replaced by sections of the urban poor in the capital. Jaona was the sole presidential candidate opposing Ratsiraka and obtained twenty per cent of the vote. MONIMA's two seats (2/137) were both located in the capital. Tension had consistently existed between MONIMA and Ratsiraka's FNDR. In 1977 MONIMA accused

the FNDR of defrauding MONIMA of its votes and subsequently left the FNDR. Jaona was under house arrest from November 1980 to March 1982. He was released after he agreed to bring MONIMA back into the FNDR. After having run for President and having called for a general strike, he was put under house arrest in December 1982 and released again on 15 August 1983 to run successfully for the National Assembly.

14. Leadership: Monja Jaona

MOUVEMENT POUR LA DEMOCRATIE D'ALGERIE (MDA-Movement for Democracy in Algeria: Algeria)

2. Democratic and Popular Republic of Algeria (24,847,000)

3. Date Established: May 1984

4. Organisational Type: Mass party

6. Membership: Few

7. Status: Illegal

9. Orientation: Left nationalism

13. History: Founded in France, the MDA's goal was to create pluralistic democracy in Algeria.

14. Leadership: Ahmed Ben Bella (Algerian President from 1962 until 1965 when he was overthrown, and also former FLN leader).

MOUVEMENT POUR LA LIBERATION DE DJIBOUTI (MLD-Djibouti Liberation Movement: Djibouti)

2. Republic of Djibouti (588,000)

3. Date Established: 1964

7. Status: Illegal opposition party in exile

9. Orientation: Marxist

10. Strategy: Negotiations

12. External Affiliations: Based in Ethiopia

13. History: Founded in 1964, the MLD has built its support among the Afar people in Djibouti. The MLD rejected the negotiations of the LPAI/RPP with the French as well as the pre-independence elections.

14. Leadership: Shehem Daoud

MOUVEMENT POUR LA LIBERATION DU PEUPLE CENTRAFRICAINE (MLPC-Movement for the Liberation of the Central African People: Central African Republic)

See also, PRC, FRO-PT, MCLN

2. Central African Republic (2,734,000)

3. Date Established: 1979

4. Organisational Type: Mass party

7. Status: Illegal

9. Orientation: social democratic, socialist

10. Strategy: Negotiations, alliance

11. Internal Affiliations: coalition with FPO-PT and MCLN to form the PCR.

13. History: The MLPC was formed in Paris during the middle of 1979 at the instigation of Ange Patasse, a former Chadian prime minister (September 1976 to July 1978). He was replaced as leader by a nine-member directorate at the 14-18 September 1983 extraordinary congress which marked the MLPC's shift from nationalism to social democracy-socialism. In 1983 the MLPC joined in coalition with the FPO-PT and MCLN to create the PRC.

14. Leadership: Francis Albert Oukanga, Secretary-General; Raphael Nambele, Secretary for External Relations.

MOUVEMENT POUR LE POUVOIR PROLETARIAN (MPP-Movement for Proletarian Power: Madagascar) a.k.a. MFM

MOUVEMENT POUR L'INDEPENDENCE DE REUNION (MIR: Movement for the Independence of Reunion: Reunion)

2. Reunion (French occupation) (543,000)

3. Date Established: Existed in 1985

4. Organisational Type: Nationalist movement

7. Status: Legal

9. Orientation: Left nationalist for full independence.

10. Strategy: The MIR campaigns for the full independence of Reunion.

11. Internal Affiliations: The Maoist OCMLR helped to establish the MIR.

13. History: The MIR was established by the OCMLR.

MOUVEMENT PROGRESSIVE DE LA GAUCHE (MPG-Progressive Left Movement: Reunion)

2. Reunion (French Occupation) (543,000)

3. Date Established: Existed in 1985.

9. Orientation: Marxism-Leninism

10. Strategy: Electoral

11. Internal Affiliations: The MPG had relations with the PCR, but these were broken in August 1985

13. History: The PCR accused the MPG of obstructing the Sainte-Marie Deputy Mayor, who was PCR, and his party from participating in the administration of the municipality.

MOUVEMENT REVOLUTIONNAIRE NATIONAL POUR LE DEVELOPPEMENT (MRND-National Revolutionary Movement for Development: Rwanda)

2. Republic of Rwanda (6,023,000)

3. Established: July 5, 1975

4. Organisational Type: Mass party

5. Organisational Nature: National party of unification incorporating both military and civilian membership to overcome ethnic cleavage between the Hutu and Tutsi

7. Status: Sole legal, governing party

8. Publications: There are three government newspapers (Imahvo, Kinyamateka, La Releve), as well as a government news agency and radio station.

9. Orientation: Left Nationalist

10. Strategy: Following a coup designed to prevent inter-ethnic warfare, the creation of the MRND was designed to prevent the reoccurrence of such ethnic hostilities. Consequently the MRND has focussed on national unification and development through an electoral strategy that is guaranteed by the participation of the armed forces.

12. External Affiliations: During the pre-MRND phase (1973-75) following Habyarimana's coup, Rwanda shifted from a pro-Western orientation to one that incorporated non-aligned and anti-imperialist elements. Rwanda supported the liberation movements in both southern Africa and Palestine, breaking relations with Israel in 1973.

13. History: the present leadership took power on July 5, 1973 in an effort to stop inter-ethnic violence. Previously existing political parties were banned. On July 5, 1975 General Habyarimana announced the creation of the MRND. Under the new December 1978 constitution, the MRND became the only legal party.

14. Leadership: President of the Republic and MRND-Major-General Juvenal Habyarimana; MRND Secretary-General Bonaventure Habymana.

MOUVEMENT REVOLUTIONAIRE POUR LA DEMOCRATIE NOUVELLE/AND JEF (MRDN/And Jef-Revolutionary Movement for New Democracy/Work Together: Senegal)

See also, ADS; AND JEF; ODP; UDP; PRA-SENEGAL

2. Republic of Senegal (6,710,000)

3. Date Established: 1981 (registered)

4. Organisational Type: Mass party

5. Organisational Nature: The MRDN biennial Congress elects the General Council which in turn elects the twenty-five member National Executive Committee, the two Deputy Secretary General and the Secretary General. Congresses are called by the General Council. Besides the Congress, the main units of the MRDN in descending order are: region, federation, section and committee (five to fifty members).

7. Status: Legal

8. Publications: Jaay Doole Bi (The Proletarian: monthly)

9. Orientation: Maoist Marxism-Leninism

10. Strategy: Party-building amongst workers and peasants to fight imperialism and liberate the masses, especially those in rural areas; joined the ADS alliance; has boycotted elections

11. Internal Affiliations: Allied with the LD-MPT, the OST, the PDS and the UDP in the ADS alliance

12. External Affiliations: Pro-China

13. History: Before 1981 the pro-Albanian UDP broke away from And-Jef. In 1981, the Proletarian Democratic Organisation (ODP) led by Abdoulaye Ly (a former PS minister) joined Karebi-And-Jef (Work Together) to form the MRDN. The organisation attempted to draw Ly's former comrades in the defunct PRA to join. The MRDN was registered as a party in 1981. In July 1985 the MRDN helped create the ADS alliance.

14. Leadership: Landing Savane, Secretary General and editor of Jaay Doole Bi and the 1980-banned Le Communist; Alioune Sene, Deputy Secretary General; Mamadou Diop, Deputy Secretary General; Abdoulaye Ly; Abdoulaye Gueye

MOUVEMENT SOCIALISTE MAURICIEN (**MSM-Mauritian Socialist Movement: Mauritius**)

See also, MOUVEMENT SOCIALISTE MILITANT-MSM: Mauritius

2. Mauritius (1,023,000)

3. Date Established: April 8, 1983

4. Organisational Type: Mass party

7. Status: Ruling party

8. Publication: Le Socialist

9. Orientation: Non-aligned socialist/social democratic

10. Strategy: Politically, the MSM follows an electoral strategy, while in the economic sphere policy is dominated by social welfare and a mixed economy.

11. Internal Affiliations: The original MSM merged with the PSM to form the presently-named MSM. In 1983, the MSM allied itself with the MWM (Mauritian Worker's Movement, a MLP off-shoot), the right-wing PMSD (Parti Mauricien Social-Democrate), the OPR (Organisation du Peuple Rodriquais), and the MLP.

13. History: In March 1983, the MMM expelled Aneerood Jugnauth who was both leader and prime minister. Jugnauth responded by forming the Mouvement Socialiste Militant on April 8, 1983. When the MSM merged with the PSM on May 1, 1983, the name of the MSM became the Mouvement Socialiste Mauricien. Jugnauth's governing coalition retained power in the August 1983 election.

14. Leadership: Aneerood Jugnauth, Leader and Prime Minister; Harish Boodhoo.

MOUVEMENT SOCIALISTE MILITANT (**MSM-Mauritius**)

See also, MOUVEMENT SOCIALISTE MAURICIEN (MSM-Mauritius)

MOVEMENT FOR JUSTICE IN AFRICA (**MOJA-Gambia**)

2. Republic of the Gambia (770,000)

3. Date Established: Late 1979

7. Status: Banned on November 1, 1980.

9. Orientation: Left Nationalist-Pan Africanist

10. Strategy: MOJA opposed both the Jawara regime, accusing it of corruption, and Senegalese attempts to absorb Gambia. MOJA may have advocated the overthrow of the Jawara government.

11. Internal Affiliations: In December 1980 the National Liberation Party defended MOJA from Jawara's banning of it.

12. External Affiliations: MOJA-Gambia adopted its name from a Liberian party of similar orientation.

13. History: MOJA was founded in 1979, banned on November 1, 1980 and accused by Jawara of taking part in the July 1981 military coup attempt. During the suppression of the coup, it was reported that the MOJO leader, Koro Sallah, was killed. Since then MOJO has maintained a public presence with a series of communiques.

14. Leadership: Koro <u>Sallah</u> (possibly killed in 1981)

MOVEMENT FOR JUSTICE IN AFRICA-LIBERIA (MOJA-Liberia: Liberia)

2. Republic of Liberia (1,800,000)

3. Date Established: 21 March 1973

4. Organisational Type: Mass party

7. Status: Illegal

9. Orientation: Left-nationalism, Pan-Africanism, anti-imperialism

10. Strategy: Negotiations, electoral

11. Internal Affiliations: Union of Liberian Associations in the Americas

13. History: Formed in 1973, MOJA-Liberia grew during the rest of the 1970s. After Master Sergeant (later General) Samuel Doe overthrew the government of President W. Tolbert in April 1980, the leader of MOJA-Liberia, Dr. Togba-Nah Tipoteh was invited to become Minister of Planning and Economic Affairs. However, MOJA and all political groups were banned and Tipoteh resigned in July 1981 and went into exile after Doe decisively turned to the right. MOJA-Liberia has since called for the removal of the Doe regime.

14. Leadership: Dr. Togba-Nah Tiopteh, President

MOVEMENT ON NATIONAL AFFAIRS (MONAS: Ghana)

2. Republic of Ghana (12,205,000)

3. Date Established: c.1979

4. Organisational Type: Mass party

6. Membership: Few, mainly military, youth and students

7. Illegal, defunct

9. Orientation: Elements of left nationalism, liberalism and Marxism

10. Strategy: Revolution

13. History: MONAS was formed in the aftermath of the first Rawling government, the Armed Forces Revolutionary Council (AFRC) that ruled from 4 June to 24 September 1979. One of the founders of MONAS was Capt. Boakye-Djan who had been number two to Rawlings in the AFRC. MONAS contained both right- and left-wing elements, but in any case both wings later came into conflict with Rawlings. When the PNDC came to power, it made it quite clear to MONAS elements within Ghana that they were not welcome. Another wing of MONAS led by then Major Boakye-Djan established itself in London and later went on to found the anti-PNDC group, the Campaign for Democracy. By the end of 1982, MONAS was effectively defunct.

MOVIMENTO DE LIBERATACAO DE SAO TOME E PRINCIPE (MLSTP - Movement for the Liberation of Sao Tome and Principe - MLSTP: Sao Tome and Principe)

2. Democratic Republic of Sao Tome and Principe

3. Date Established: September 1960

4. Organisational Type: Vanguard party emerging from a national liberation movement.

5. Organisational Nature: The MLSTP Congress elected the Central Committee (fifty-one members including ten alternates) which elected the Political Bureau (nine members) which elected the President of the MLSTP. Party mass organisations include those for women, youth and children as well as the trade unions and the militia.

6. Membership: Several hundred to one thousand

7. Status: Ruling, sole legal party

8. Publications: Diario da Republica (weekly); Revolucao (weekly); Povo (weekly), radio

9. Orientation: Marxism-Leninism, socialism, social democracy

10. Strategy: Electoral; building socialism and the party; regime maintenance

12. External Affiliations: MPLA (Angola), Cuba, Soviet Union and other pro-Soviet parties

13. History: The MLSTP was formed during September 1960 in Ghana as the CLSTP. At first the MLSTP was primarily an exile organisation but it was able to tap into and consolidate its support amongst the growing number of Sao Tomeans critical of Portuguese colonialism. In 1972 the CLSTP changed its name to the MLSTP and elected Dr. Manuel Pinto da Costa as its General Secretary. The MLSTP were able to negotiate independence following the 25 April 1974 overthrow of the Portuguese dictatorship. The MLSTP's overwhelming victory at the pre-independence elections ensured that the MLSTP led Sao Tome to independence on 12 July 1975, with da Costa as the islands' President. Following

independence, the MLSTP emphasized improving the conditions of its people, developing security ties with the MPLA of Angola, and after 1985 attempting a Lenin-style NEP, i.e. trying to use selectively capitalism in order to revive the economy devastated by the hostile nature of the Portuguese withdrawal.

14. Leadership: MLSTP President - Dr. Manual Pinto da Costa; Political Bureau - Dr. Manuel Pinto da Costa, Alda Neves Graca do Espirito Santo, Tome Dias da Costa, Antonio Amado Vaz, Oscar Aguiar Sacramento e Soua, Romao Pereira do Couto. Maj. Raul Braganca Neto, Francisco Fortunato Pires, Manuel Quaresma Costa

MOVIMENTO POPULAR DE LIBERTICAO DE ANGOLA - PARTIDO DO TRABALHO (MPLA-PT: Popular Movement for the Liberation of Angola - Party of Labour: Angola)

2. People's Republic of Angola (8,340,000)

3. Date Established: 1956

4. Organisational Type: Vanguard party (national liberation movement until 1977)

5. Organisational Nature: The party is led by a Chairman, a thirteen member Politburo (including three alternates), an eight-member Central Committee Secretariat, and a seventy-five member Central Committee. Congresses are the supreme legislative party body. The party operates on the basis of democratic centralism.

6. Membership: 31,000

7. Status: Ruling, sole legal party

8. Publications: (_A Celula_ (MPLA-PT), _A Voz do Trabalhador_ (UNTA) State-run newspapers (_Jornal de Angola_, 50,000; _Provincia de Angola_, 35-40,000 daily; _Diario de Republica_, 8,500), radio and television have been controlled by the party

9. Orientation: Soviet interpretation of Marxism-Leninism

10. Strategy: Party building; building socialism; regime maintenance; repulsing and defeating the apartheid South African troops that occupy parts of Angola and

all of Namibia; extending proletarian internationalist support to SWAPO (Namibia) and the ANC (South Africa); elements of a NEP-style economic programme.

11. Internal Affiliations: JMPLA (MPLA Youth), OMA (Organisation of Angolan Women) and UNTA (National Union of Angolan Workers)

12. External Affiliations: The communist parties of the Soviet Union, Cuba and the rest of the Soviet Bloc; the MLSTP; the ANC, SWAPO; the ruling parties of the Frontline States

13. History: Formed in 1956, the MPLA in 1961 launched the armed struggle which lasted until 1974 when the Portuguese dictatorship was overthrown. During this period Augustinho Neto as President led the MPLA in its development as a national liberation movement. The transitional government (December 1974-1975) which was a coalition of the MPLA and two western-backed groups, UNITA and the FNLA, broke down in late 1975 when the FNLA (funded by the American CIA) and troops from Zaire attacked the MPLA government from the northern border with Zaire, and UNITA rode on the backs of apartheid South African armoured columns that attacked from the southern border with Namibia. The MPLA declared Angola independent on 11 November 1975 and called for Soviet material and Cuban personnel assistance. This combination broke the FNLA and UNITA, forcing the apartheid armour back, temporarily, into Namibia by early 1976. The MPLA then embarked on its present strategy (see '10' above). In May 1977 the Minister of Internal Administration, N. Alves, made a coup attempt based on the non-party mass organisation, neighbourhood committees, that he had established in 1974-1975 in Luanda, the capital. Following his defeat, during 4-11 December 1977, Neto called the First Congress of the MPLA. Party control was strengthened by completely restructuring the neighbourhood committees, subordinating them and other mass organisations to the MPLA. The MPLA formalised the transition of itself from a national liberation movement to a Marxist-Leninist vanguard party by calling itself a workers party, MPLA PT, and adopting the necessary structures. Upon Neto's death in Moscow from health problems in September 1979, the MPLA-PT Central Committee elected Jose Eduardo dos Santos to the Chairmanship of the MPLA-PT and Presidency of the People's Republic. The

Central Committee (CC) was expanded to seventy-five members at the First Extraordinary Congress of the MPLA-PT during 17-23 December 1980. During March 1985 the MPLA-PT held its First (ordinary) Congress.

14. Leadership: Chairman - Jose Eduardo dos Santos; Central Committee Secretariat - Jose Eduardo Dos Santos, Lucio Lara, Roberto Antonio de Almeida, Col. Juliao Mateus Paulo, Henrique de Carvalho Santos Onambwe, Maria Mambo Cafe, Santana Andre Pitra, Afonso van Dunem

MPITOLONA HO AMIN'NY FANJAKAN'NY MADINIKA. (MFM-Proletarian Power Party: Madagascar) a.k.a. MPP a.k.a. Pouvoir Aux Petits

2. Democratic Republic of Madagascar (9,490,000)

3. Date Established: post May 1972

5. Organisational Nature: MFM has a Central Committee

7. Status: Constituent 'revolutionary association' in the FNDR ruling coalition

9. Orientation: Marxist-Leninist

10. Strategy: Electoral, building a socialist society, party building

11. Internal Affiliations: MFM was associated with the AKFM, AREMA, MONIMA, VSM, VONJY and UDECMA/KMTP as constituent parts of the FNDR.

13. History: Intellectuals established the MFM after the transfer of power in May 1972 from President Tsirana to Major General Ramantsoa. Much of the MFM's organisational has been built amongst students and northern peasants. Joining the FNDR after the 1977 National Assembly elections, the MFM translated this support during the 1983 elections into 11% of the popular vote and four seats (4/137). By the end of 1983, two of the MFM Central Committee members, Manandafy Rakotonira (a professor in sociology) and Michel Mahatsanga (a professor) were appointed by President Ratsiraka to the republic's Supreme Revolutionary Council (Conseil Supreme de la Revolution - CSR).

14. Leadership: Manandafy Rakotonira, leader and Central Committee member; Michel Mahatsanga, Central Committee member

MWAKENYA (UNION OF NATIONALISTS TO LIBERATE KENYA: Kenya) possibly a.k.a. UKENYA

2. Republic of Kenya (19,583,000)

3. Date Established: 1982

6. Membership: Members present in many rural and urban parts of the country

7. Status: Illegal

9. Orientation: Socialist

10. Strategy: Revolution

13. History: MWAKENYA has operated as a very clandestine organisation. Its publications have been distributed, apparently by hand. MWAKENYA is the acronym in Swahi for the Union of Nationalists to Liberate Kenya.

NATIONAL ALLIANCE PARTY (NAP: Sierra Leone

2. Republic of Sierra Leone (4,105,000)

3. Date Established: Existed in 1982, 1986

6. Membership: Small number of exiles

7. Status: Illegal exile party

9. Orientation: Left nationalist

13. History: The NAP has been based in the USA.

NATIONAL COALITION (NC-Libya)

2. Socialist People's Libyan Arab Jamahiriya (4,108,000)

3. Date Established: Existed in 1981

7. Status: Illegal opposition group in exile.

8. Publications: <u>El Jihad</u>

9. Orientation: Left nationalists, liberals, social democrats

NATIONAL DEMOCRATIC MOVEMENT (NDM-L: Libya)

2. Socialist People's Libyan Arab Jamahiriya (4,108,000)

3. Date Established: 1977

7. Status: Illegal opposition group in exile

8. Publications: <u>Sawt Libya</u> (Voice of Libya)

9. Orientation: Left nationalists, liberals, social democrats

14. Leadership: Fadel Masoudi

NATIONAL LIBERATION PARTY (NLP-Gambia)

2. Republic of The Gambia (770,000)

3. Date Established: October 1975

4. Organisational Type: Rural-based mass party

7. Status: Legal opposition party, subject to government harassment.

9. Orientation: Left Nationalist

10. Strategy: The NLP contests elections, so far without winning a seat, in order to fight unemployment, inflation and corruption.

11. Internal Affiliations: The NLP has opposed the government's banning of MOJA.

13. History: Formed in 1975, the NLP followed an electoral strategy. Following the 1981 coup attempt, its leader was arrested and ordered executed in June 1982.

14. Leadership: Cheyassin Papa Secka.

NATIONAL PROGRESSIVE UNION PARTY (NPUP - Hizb al-Tajammu 'al-Watani al-Taqaddumi al-Wahdawi: Egypt)

2. Arab Republic of Egypt (48,832,000)

3. Date Established: 1976

4. Organisational Type: Mass party

5. Organisational Nature: NPUP has a Central Committee.

6. Membership: 160,000

7. Status: Legal opposition party

8. Publications: al Ahali (weekly: 100,000)

9. Orientation: Left nationalist, socialist and Marxist-Leninist elements; anti-imperialist, pro-Palestinian

10. Strategy: Electoral

11. Internal Affiliations: Unofficial relationships by NPUP elements to the EWCP, ECP, RC, RECP and the OCEP - January 8.

12. External Affiliations: Pro-Soviet, Syria, Libya and South Yemen

13. History: Originally formed in 1976 as a subordinate association of the Arab Socialist Union during one of Sadat's minor relaxations of control, the NPUP evolved into the major left-legal opposition of the Sadat-Mubarak regimes. President Mubarak has harassed the NPUP. Its parliamentary representation dropped from three in 1979 to one Presidential appointee in 1984 (4.2% of the official vote). The NPUP's First Congress was held in Cairo in April, 1980.

14. Leadership: Khalid Muhi al-Din (a.k.a. Mohieddin), Secretary General; Dr. Rif'at el-Said, Deputy Secretary; Qabbari 'Abdallah; Abu al-'Izz al-Hariri

NATIONAL RESISTANCE ARMY (NRA; Uganda)

See NRM

NATIONAL RESISTANCE MOVEMENT (NRM: Uganda)

2. Republic of Uganda (13,198,000)

3. Date Established: 1981

4. Organisational Type: National liberation movement

6. Membership: Tens of thousands

7. Status: Ruling, sole legal party

9. Orientation: Left nationalist, socialist/Marxist elements

10. Strategy: Revolution, regime maintenance reconstruction

13. History: Yoweri Museveni's forces took an active military part as auxiliaries to the Tanzanian army's 1979 overthrow of the brutal Idi Amin regime. In 1980 Museveni formed the UPM to contest the December 1980 elections in which they won one seat. Museveni declared that the results were rigged. Consequently he and his forces formed in 1981 the National Resistance Army and the NRM. Following a period of guerrilla warfare, the NRM/NRA overthrew General Okello (who had overthrown Obote's UPC on 27 July 1985) on 27 January 1986. The NRM has followed a policy of reconstruction and finishing off the remnants of rebel forces.

14. Leadership: Yoweri Museveni, President (President of the Republic)

NEW DEMOCRATIC MOVEMENT (NDM: Ghana)

2. Republic of Ghana (12,205,000)

3. Date Established: 1 May 1980

4. Organisational Type: Vanguard party

6. Membership: Several hundred

7. Status: Legal, but one wing now in opposition

8. Publications: <u>Direction</u>

9. Orientation: Marxism-Leninism

10. Strategy: Revolution; building towards socialism by building the national democratic revolution

11. Internal Affiliations: PNDC

13. History: From 1982 to 1985 all of the NDM was closely allied with the PNDC, however, one wing began to move into opposition to the policies of the PNDC.

14. Leadership: Dr. Kwesi Botchwey (PNDC Secretary for Finance and Economic Planning); Abraham Dodoo; F. Tsikata; T. Tsikata

NON-EUROPEAN UNITY MOVEMENT (NEUM: South Africa), later known as UMSA

NUBA MOUNTAINS UNION (NMU: Sudan)

See also, PNF

2. Republic of Sudan (23,089,000)

3. Date Established: Existed in 1985

4. Organisational Type: Mass party

6. Membership: The Nuba of the south

7. Status: Legal

9. Orientation: Left nationalism, southern regionalism

10. Strategy: Electoral

11. Internal Affiliations: The NMU was a member of the PNF.

13. History: The NMU had been led by Father Philip Abbas Ghabboush who later broke away to form the Sudan

National Party. The NMU joined the PNF to contest the 1986 elections.

OPPOSITION REVOLUTIONNAIRE (OR-Revolutionary Opposition: Morocco)

2. Kingdom of Morocco (23,207,000)

3. Date Established: Existed in 1983

7. Status: Illegal

9. Orientation: revolutionary socialist

10. Strategy: Revolution

11. Internal Affiliations: Close to the anti-election wing of the USFP.

12. History: The OR believed that the government-manipulated elections serve only to legitimise the monarchy and to block real change. Consequently they have been opposed to being co-opted and strive instead for revolution.

ORGANISATION COMMUNISTE MARXISTE-LENINIST DE REUNION (OCMLR - Marxist-Leninist Communist Organisation of Reunion: Reunion)

2. Reunion (543,000)

3. Date Established: 1975

4. Organisational Type: Marxist-Leninist vanguard party.

5. Organisational Nature: Democratic centralism

7. Status: Legal party

9. Orientation: Maoist Marxist-leninist; nationalist

10. Strategy: Party-building, broadening support for the aims of the party by creating organisations such as the MIR which, along with the OCMLR, advocates full independence for Reunion.

11. Internal Affiliations: The OCMLR helped to create the MIR.

13. History: The OCMLR was created in 1975 by PCR members who preferred Maoist analysis and strategy.

ORGANISATION DE CAMEROUN LATTER POUR DEMOCRATIE (OCLD - Cameroon Organisation to Fight for Democracy: Cameroon)

2. Republic of Cameroon (9,852,000)

3. Date Established: Existed in 1985

7. Status: Illegal exile group

9. Orientation: Elements of left nationalism, socialism

10. Strategy: Exile organising, negotiations

13. History: An attempt by the OCLD to organise a gathering of all Cameroonians living in France opposed to the Biya RNPC/UNC regime was stopped in February 1985 by the French government.

ORGANISATION DE L'ACTION DEMOCRATIQUE ET POPULAIRE (OADP-Democratic and Popular Action Organisation: Morocco)

2. Kingdom of Morocco (23,207,000)

3. Date Established: May 1983

4. Organisational Type: Mass party

7. Status: Legal

9. Orientation: Socialism, elements of Marxism-Leninism

10. Strategy: Electoral, winning the left of the USFP

13. History: The OADP was organised by dissident members of the PPS and USFP in May 1983. Just over a year later the OADP had one of its members directly elected (1/206 + 100 'indirectly elected').

14. Leadership: Mohamed Bensaid, Secretary General

ORGANISATION DEMOCRATIQUE PROLETARIENNE (ODP-Proletarian Democratic Organisation: Senegal)

See also, AND-JEF: MRND/And-JEF

2. Republic of Senegal (6,710,000)

3. Date Established: Dissolved 1981

7. Status: Illegal party

9. Orientation: Maoist

13. History: The ODP joined the And-Jef, which later in 1981 became the MRND/And Jef.

14. Leadership: Abdoulaye Ly

ORGANISATION OF THE EGYPTIAN COMMUNIST PARTY - JANUARY 8 (OCEP - January 8)

2. Arab Republic of Egypt (48,832,000)

3. Date Established: 1975

7. Status: Illegal

9. Orientation: Marxism-Leninism

10. Strategy: Revolution

11. Internal Affiliations: Unofficial but close relations with elements of the NPUP

13. History: The OECP-January 8 was created on 8 January 1975 by the militant Workers and Peasants' Organisation and the Egyptian Communist Party Organisation. It was an offshoot of the ECP. Eighty-five members were arrested on 7 October 1978.

ORGANISATION SOCIALIST DU TRAVAILLEURS (OST-Socialist Workers' Organisation: Senegal)

See also, ADS

2. Republic of Senegal (6,710,000)

3. Date Established: 1982

4. Organisation Type: Trotskyist pre-party formation

6. Membership: Few

7. Status: Legal

9. Orientation: Trotskyist Marxism-Leninism

10. Strategy: Party-building, participation in the ADS alliance of five parties, promotion of the 'permanent revolution to socialism' strategy

11. Internal Affiliations: Allied with the PDS, MRDN, LD-MPT and UDP in the ADS alliance.

12. External Affiliations: Fourth International

13. History: Formed in 1982, the OST helped create the ADS alliance in July 1985. Despite attempts by the PS Senegalese government to suppress this potential electoral coalition, the member parties have continued to cooperate.

14. Leadership: Mbaye Bathily

PAN AFRICANIST CONGRESS OF AZANIA (PAC-South Africa)

2. Republic of South Africa (34,577,000)

3. Date Established: April 1959

4. Organisational Type: Mass party in exile, some underground elements

5. Organisational Nature: The PAC had a Chairman and a Central Committee.

6. Membership: few

7. Status: Illegal

8. Publications: previously the <u>Africanist</u>

9. Orientation: Pan-Africanist left nationalism, anti-Soviet, pro-Maoist, African exclusionist, black consciousness, social democracy

10. Strategy: Revolution

11. Internal Affiliations: The PAC has had contact with elements of the black consciousness movement.

12. External Affilitions: Pro-China, past ties to ZANU (Zimbabwe) and TANU (Tanzania)

13. History: The PAC was formed by a group of ANC members led by Robert Sobukwe, A.P. Mda and Potlako Leballo who rejected the Freedom Charter as being too leftist and not Africanist enough. Following their failure in November 1958 to become the ANC leaders in the Transvaal, they organised the founding congress of the PAC (April 1959) where Robert Sobukwe was elected President. Refusing to join the ANC's anti-pass campaign set to start on 30 March 1960, the PAC set its own campaign to start nine days earlier. In April 1960 the PAC and the ANC were banned. Sobukwe was arrested and imprisoned where he died in 1978. In 1962 Potlako Leballo became Acting President and went into exile in Lesotho. The 1962 consultative conference decided to take up armed struggle by forming POQO units that were to attack South African police and whites in 1963. Leballo's premature press conference announcement resulted not in armed struggle but a security forces crack-down that wiped out the PAC's organisation in South African. In exile the PAC under Leballo allied itself with China and seemed to adopt elements of a Maoist approach. The PAC had some influence in the black consciousness movement from the late 1960s onwards. The PAC in exile has been plagued by a series of hostile leadership battles. In 1977 the Leballo faction was able to oust from the leadership the Templeton Ntantala faction which then created the APRP. However, Leballo after having been elected Chairman in 1978 upon Sobukwe's death, was himself ousted in May 1979 by two of his former supporters, David Sibeko and Vusi Make (who became Chairman) and replaced by a three-person Presidential Council which included Sibeko who was assassinated one month later by Leballo forces. In 1981 Make lost the chairmanship to John Nyati Pokela who readmitted the APRP but died in June 1985. Johnson Mlambo became the Chairman.

14. Leadership: Johnson Mlambo (Chairman); D. Mantshontsho (Administrative Secretary)

PARTI AFRICAIN DE L'INDEPENDENCE (B) (PAI-B: African Independence Party: Benin)

2. People's Republic of Benin (4,102,000)

3. Existed in 1986

7. Status: Now a faction within the ruling party, PRPB

9. Orientation: Pro-Soviet Marxist-Leninist Nationalist

10. Strategy: Promotion within the ruling (PRPB) of its members and policies, including closer links with the Soviet Union. The PAI supports President Kerekou.

11. Internal Affiliations: informal links with numerous junior army officers and intelligentsia.

12. External Affiliations: Pro-Soviet but some non-alignment as a measure of respect for France

PARTI AFRICAIN DE L'INDEPENDENCE (SENEGAL) (PAI(S)-African Independence Party: Senegal)

2. Republic of Senegal (6,710,000)

3. Date Established: 1957

4. Organisational Type: Vanguard party

5. Organisational Nature: Democratic centralism; the Central Committee has a Politburo, five of whose eight members were workers in 1980.

6. Membership: 1000

7. Status: Legal opposition party

8. Media: La Lutte (Struggle: monthly); Monsarev (Independence: weekly)

9. Orientation: Pro-Soviet Marxism-Leninism

10. Strategy: Electoral, unification of the left

11. Internal Affiliations: The PAI(S) attempted to form the Bok Sa Pew Unity Front in 1979 but was rebuffed by the rest of the left.

12. External Affiliations: Until 1976/77 the PAI(S) was closely oriented to the Soviet Union. Following the cooption of the PAI(S) by the PS government in 1976, the PAI(S) was virtually expelled from the Soviet bloc and the PIT substituted for the PAI(S) by Moscow.

13. History: Created in 1957 as an organisation for all of French West Africa, the PAI was forced underground in Senegal by the UPS/PS government in 1960. In 1962, at its first congress, the PAI established itself as a separate Senegalese party. During its underground existence it toyed with the possibility of armed revolution, some members being sent for military training in Cuba, and also conducted exile actions from Mali. The party was split by the Sino-Soviet break-up. One part of the party interpreted the 1976 legislation of the PAI(S) as being cooption by the PS government. They split in 1976 to form what became the PIT. Others split to form the PPS, the PAI-Masses, and the LD-MPT, all of which were formally registered in 1981. This fragmentation has hurt the PAI(S). The PAI(S) abstained from the 1976 regional elections, contested the 1979 and 1983 presidential and legislative elections (failing to get a seat) and then boycotted the 1984 municipal elections.

14. Leadership: Majhemout Diop, President and 1983 presidential candidate; Balla N'Diaye, Vice-President; Bara Goudiaby, Secretary General.

PARTI AFRICAIN DE L'INDEPENDENCE-MASSES (PAI-M: African Independence Party - Masses: Senegal)

2. Republic of Senegal (6,710,000)

3. Date Established: Existed in 1983

4. Organisation Type: Mass party

7. Status: Legal

9. Orientation: Social democracy

10. Strategy: Electoral

13. History: While its programme is similar to that of the PS, the PAI-Masses was critical of the PS for not implementing it.

PARTI AFRICAIN POUR L'INDEPENDENCE (BF) (PAI-BF: African Independence Party-BF: Burkina Faso)

2. Republic of Burkina Faso (8,130,000)

3. Date Established: 1957

4. Organisational Type: Mass party

7. Status: Illegal party

9. Orientation: Pro-Soviet Marxism-Leninism

10. Strategy: Party-building

12. External Affiliations: Pro-Soviet

13. History: In 1973, some PAI members broke away to form the LIPAD. The PAI has not participated in the CNR government.

PARTI AFRICAIN POUR L'INDEPENDENCE DU PEUPLE (PAIP-African Party for the Independence of the People: Senegal)

2. Republic of Senegal (6,710,000)

3. Date Established: August, 1982 (registered)

4. Organisational Type: Vanguard party

7. Status: Legal opposition party

9. Orientation: Marxist-Leninist

10. Strategy: Electoral; party-building

13. History: Legalised in August 1982, the PAIP did not take part in the 1983 general election or the 1984

municipal elections, objecting as it did to PS control of the electoral process.

14. Leadership: Aly Niane, Secretary General; Abdou Bane, Issa Diop, Abdoulaye Slaye

PARTI COMMUNISTE DAHOMEEN (PCD-Communist Party of Dahomey: Benin)

2. People's Republic of Benin (4,102,060)

3. Existed in 1981

4. Organisational Type: Vanguard party

7. Status: Ambiguous - both clandestine and a faction within the PRPB

8. Publication: <u>En Avant</u> which is published by the Bainsite Communist Party of Canada-Marxist Leninist and then illegally imported to Benin.

9. Orientation: formerly Maoist, then pro-Albanian. Linked to the Bainsite Communist Party of Canada-Marxist Leninist. Anti-Soviet

10. Strategy: Quasi-clandestine, expansion of their influence in the ruling PRPB. PCD is against President Kerekou's 'revisionist' policies.

11. Internal Affiliations: Some trade union members and intellectuals.

12. External Affiliations: Was pro-Albania. The PCD is allied with the PCT (Togo), the PCRV (Burkina Faso) and the Bainsite Communist Party of Canada-Marxist Leninist.

PARTI COMMUNISTE GUINEEN (PCG-Guinea Communist Party: Guinea)

2. Republic of Guinea (5,873,000)

3. Date Established: Existed in 1986

4. Organisational Type: Underground vanguard party

6. Membership: Mainly students and intelligentsia abroad

7. Status: Illegal, mainly in exile

9. Orientation: Albanian/Maoist/Bainsite version of Marxism-Leninism

12. External Affiliations: Albania; Bainsite Communist Party of Canada (Marxist-Leninist)

PARTI COMMUNISTE MAROCAINE (PCM-Moroccan Communist Party: Morocco) a.k.a. PPS

PARTI COMMUNISTE REUNIONNAIS (PCR-Communist Party of Reunion: Reunion)

2. Reunion (French occupation) (543,000)

3. Date Established: 1959

4. Organisational Type: Vanguard party

5. Organisational Nature: Democratic centralism. The cells were organised into nineteen sections. At the executive level there was the Central Committee (thirty-two members), the Poliburo (twelve members), the Secretariat (five members) and the Secretary General.

6. Membership: 10,000 claimed (2,000 est.)

7. Status: Legal party, mainly opposition but some government

8. Publications: _Temoignages_ (24 page daily, est. circulation: 10,000); _Travailleur reunionnais_ (CGTR union bimonthly); _Combat Reunionnais_ (UGTRF irregular)

9. Orientation: Pro-Soviet revision of Marxism-Leninism

10. Strategy: Electoral, party-building, auxiliary-building, alliances, autonomy but not independence for Reunion.

11. Internal Affiliations: The PCR helped build the Reunion Peace Committee, the Reunion General Confedera-

tion of Workers (CGTR-Confederation Generale du Travailleurs Reunionnais), the Reunion Youth Front for Autonomy, the Committee for the Rally of Reunionese Youth (CORJ), the Reunion Union of Women (UFR), the Christian Witness Union, the Anti-colonialist Front for Reunion Autonomy (Front Anti-colonialiste Pour L'Autonomie Reunionnaise-FAAR), Reunion General Union of Workers in France (UGTRF), Reunion General Confederation of Farmers and Cattlemen (CGPER - Confederation Generale des Planteurs et Eleveurs Rennionnais) and the Reunion Intercommunal Syndicate for Multiple Vocations. The PCR was in alliances with the SPR and the MPG.

12. External Affiliations: The PCR has close relations with PCF (Parti Communiste Francais-PCF French Communist Party) and other parties allied to the Communist Party of the Soviet Union. The PCR supports and has relations with a number of national liberation movements, e.g. the African National Congress of South Africa, SWAPO-Namibia and the Palestine Liberation Organization.

13. History: The PCF established a section in Reunion that was known as the Reunion Federation of the PCF. In May 1959 this section achieved autonomy and became the PCR. The Fifth Congress was held July 12-14, 1980. The PCR built auxiliary organizations and a substantial electoral base. Indeed for a time the only indigenous party organization was the PCR. The PCR has elected members to the European Parliament, the French Parliament, the Regional Council, the Reunion General Council and municipalities. In this sense, the PCR has had a share in government.

14. Leadership: Secretary General - Paul Verges; Politburo - twelve members including Julien Ramin; Secretariat - six members including Paul Verges, Elie Hoarau, Jean-Baptiste Ponona; Central Committee - thirty-two members including Bruny Payet, Roger Hoarau, Daniel Lallemand, Hippolite Piot, Ary Yee Chong Tchi-Kan, Laurent Verges.

PARTI COMMUNISTE REVOLUTIONNAIRE VOLTAIQUE (PCRV-Voltaic Revolutionary Communist Party: Burkina Faso)

2. Republic of Burkina Faso (8,130,000)

3. Date Established: Existed in 1981

4. Organisational Type: Vanguard party

7. Status: Quasi-legal party independent of the CNR regime

9. Orientation: Formerly Maoist Marxism-Leninism then pro-Albanian Marxism-Leninism with links to the Bainsite Communist Party of Canada - Marxist Leninist

10. Strategy: Quasi-clandestine, party-building

12. External Affiliations: Albania, PCT (Togo), PCD (Benin); Bainsite Communist Party of Canada - Marxist-Leninist

PARTI COMMUNISTE TOGOLAISE (PCT-Communist Party of Togo (Marxist-Leninist): Togo)

2. Republic of Togo (2,928,000)

3. Date Established: Existed in the 1970s

4. Organisational Type: Bainsite version of Marxist-Leninist vanguard party

6. Status: illegal, underground opposition party

9. Orientation: Bainsite version of Albanian interpretation of Maoist Marxism-Leninism

10. Strategy: Revolution

12. External Affiliation: "Bainsite" Communist Party of Canada (Marxist-Leninist); Albania; the PCD (Benin); the PCRV (Burkina Faso)

PARTI COMMUNISTE TUNISIEN (PCT-Tunisian Communist Party)

2. Republic of Tunisia (7,224,000)

3. Date Established: 1934 (1920)

4. Organisational Type: Vanguard party

5. Organisational Nature: The PCT national executive consisted of a Secretary General, a Politburo (six members), a Secretariat (three members and a Central Committee (twelve members). The PCT has a Congress and operated on the basis of democratic centralism.

6. Membership: 2,000-4,000

7. Status: Legal

8. Publications: Al-Tarik al-Jadid (The New Path, newspaper); the PCT formerly published L'Espoir (Hope, monthly 1963) and al-Tariq (The Way, January 1968)

9. Orientation: Soviet interpretation of Marxism-Leninism

10. Strategy: Electoral; progressive coalitions, critical support for the PDS since 1981

12. External Affiliations: Pro-Soviet parties

13. History: The roots of the PCT date to 1920 when a branch of the French communist party was established by Europeans, mainly French. The PCT became independent in 1934 and was active in the resistance against fascist forces in the Second World War. The PCT was a legal party following Tunisian independence in 1956 but was outlawed in 1963 by the PDS government. Bourguiba re-legalised the PCT on 18 July 1981 and allowed it to contest the 1981 legislature elections where it won an officially stated 0.78 per cent, but may have won some five per cent. The Eighth Congress was held in Tunis during February 1981.

14. Leadership: Secretary General - Muhammad Harmel; Politburo - Muhammad Harmel, Muhammad al-Nafa'a, 'Abd al-Hamid ben Mustafa, Hisham Sakik, 'Abd al-Majid Tariki, Salah al-Hajji

PARTI DE L'ACTION (PA-Action Party: Morocco)

2. Kingdom of Morocco (23,207,000)

3. Date Established: December 1974

4. Organisational Type: Mass party

6. Membership: Small, mainly Berber intellectuals and professionals

7. Status: Legal

9. Orientation: Elements of left nationalist but elitist

10. Strategy: Electoral, creating a new elite that would build a new society

13. History: The PA won two seats in the 1977 national chamber elections but lost both of them in the 1984 elections.

14. Leadership: Abdallah Senhaji, Secretary General

PARTI DE LA LIBERATION ET DU SOCIALISME (PLS-Socialist Liberation Party: Morocco) a.k.a. PPS

PARTI DE LA REVOLUTION CENTRAFRICAINE (PRC-Central African Revolutionary Party: Central African Republic)

See also: MLPC, FPO-PT, MCLN)

2. Central African Republic (2,734,000)

3. Date Established: late 1983

4. Organisational Type: Coalition or front of three parties: the MLPC, the FPO-PT, the MCLN.

7. Status: Illegal

9. Orientation: social democratic

10. Strategy: Negotiations, coalition armed struggle

13. History: Following the refusal by General Andre-Dieudonne Kolingba (who came to power following the 1981 coup) to implement the multi-party provisions of the 1980 constitution, the PRC was formed as a coalition by the MLPC, the FPO-PT and the MCLN at Moyenne-Sido near the border with Chad at a clandestine meeting.

14. Leadership: General Francois Bozize (MCLN leader), General Alphonse M'baikoua (MCLN leader).

PARTI DE LA REVOLUTION POPULAIRE (PRP-Popular Revolutionary Party - PRP: Zaire)

2. Republic of Zaire (33,927,000)

3. Date Established: 1967

4. Organisational Type: Vanguard party

5. Organisational Nature: The PRP has political and armed wings.

6. Membership: Thousands

7. Status: Illegal

9. Orientation: Marxism-Leninism (Maoist but not Deng-revisionism)

10. Strategy: Revolution, protracted people's war, political mobilisation, party-building

11. Internal Affiliations: FCD (1982-1985), FLNC, MNC, ECP, UFPCK, FOCK, MDJ

12. External Affiliations: In the past, Maoist China

13. History: The PRP had its roots in the Comite National de Liberation (CNL-National Liberation Committee) that was formed in 1963 by the Lumumbist (or "Nationalist") alliance. The CNL formed, in the eastern Congo, a People's Republic of the Congo government, led by Christopher Gbenye (MNC-L) that lasted from mid-1964 to November 1964, when it fell to Belgian paratroops and mercenaries. One of the CNL leaders, Laurent Kabila, and others retreated to the mountains of southern Kivu and northern Shaba provinces, and linked up to local people opposed to the Mobutu regime. Out of this combined force, the PRP was born in 1967. The PRP became, as Mao advocated, fish swimming in the water. The PRP developed a thorough political analysis based on Congolese experience and the Maoist interpretation of Marxism-Leninism. The PRP has endured through the 1960s, 1970s and the 1980s.

14. Leadership: Laurent Kabila, leader; Richard Ismael

PARTI DE LA REVOLUTION POPULAIRE DU BENIN (PRPB-Benin People's Revolutionary Party: Benin)

2. People's Republic of Benin (4,102,000)

3. Date Established: December 1975

4. Organisational Type: The PRPB has categorized itself as a Marxist-Leninist vanguard party.

5. Organisational Nature: The PRPB operates on Leninist principles, as interpreted by advisers from the German Democratic Republic. Democratic centralism is practiced, but is strongly influenced by the Central Committee's Chairman, Brig. Gen. Kerekou. The PRPB has a forty-five member Central Committee which elects a Political Bureau ('Politburo') of thirteen, which in turn elects the Chairman. The degree to which ordinary party members participate has been questioned. The Politburo selects the candidates for the Central Committee, who are then put up for approval by the party members. The Politburo also selects delegates to PRPB Congresses: First Ordinary Congress, November 13-15, 1979; Second Ordinary Congress, November 18-24, 1985.

6. Membership: 2,000 (est.), mainly drawn from the military and radical civilian intelligentsia, some trade unionists.

7. Status: Governing party

8. Publications: PRPB controls the government-owned press, radio and television.

9. Orientation: Marxist-Leninist vanguard party with strong personalist component.

10. Strategy: Having seized power by the military coup of November 26, 1972, paratroop Captain Mathieu Kerekou sought out a political strategy. He began the establishment of the formal framework of Marxism-Leninism by creating on November 30, 1975 the PRPB as a Soviet-style vanguard party to maintain control and guide the country. Despite the setting-up of mass auxiliaries such as the Cuban-style Revolutionary

Defense Organizations, as well as youth and women's organizations, the degree of popular participation in the revolution remains problematic. Economic strategy, while based on substantial state involvement in the non-agricultural sectors of the economy, relies on significant participation by European-based companies and French aid.

11. Internal Affiliations: Mass organizations of the PRPB include the Committees for the Defence of the Revolution (CDR's), the Revolutionary Youth Organization of Benin (ORJB) and the Women's Revolutionary Committee (CRFB). Additionally a number of political groups take part in the PRPB party. The pro-Soviet "Parti Africain de l'Independance" (PAI) has many sympathisers amongst the officer corps. The League ("Les Ligueurs"), which is pro-Chinese, included Capochichi (a PRPB Poliburo member and Mass Education Minister) and Simon Goumba (former Foreign Minister).

12. External Affiliations: While the PRPB government is non-aligned, the party has close ties with both the Soviet Bloc and China. The SED of East Germany assisted in the drafting of the original PRPB statutes. The North Korean and Cuban parties have also provided political resources. The PRPB government has had friendly relations with Libya and Nicaragua.

13. History: Following his November 26, 1972 coup, Kerekou announced on December 3, 1974 that a Marxist-Leninist party would be established and that the country would be modelled on the 'people's republic' form. The PRPB was created on November 30, 1975, while Dahomey was renamed Benin. The PRPB held its first congress on May 15-17, 1976, and its second on November 13-15, 1979. Using its control of the laws state, the PRPB issued a new revolutionary strategy in August 1977 which stated that Benin would move through three revolutionary stages: (1) revolutionary national liberation movement, (2) democratic people's revolution and (3) socialist revolution.

14. Leadership: PRPB Chairman of the Central Committee - Brig. Gen. Ahmed (Mathieu) Kerekou (President of the Republic); other members of the Politburo included Lt. Col. Michel Alladaye (one of the original coup-makers and until 1986 Education Minister), Baba Moussa (Information Minister), Armand Monteiro (Higher Education

Minister), Gratien Capochichi (Mass Education Minister), and Tiamiou Adjibade (Foreign Minister).

PARTI DE L'AVANT-GARDE SOCIALISTE (PAGS-Socialist Vanguard Party - SVP: Algeria)

2. Democratic and Popular Republic of Algeria (24,847,000)

3. Date Established: 1920 (1965)

4. Organisational Type: Vanguard party

5. Organisational Nature: PAGS had a First Secretary, Poliburo, Secretariat and Central Committee. Its last (the sixth) congress was held in February 1952.

6. Membership: Several hundred to a thousand

7. Status: Illegal

8. Publications: Sawt al-Sha'b (Voice of the People, in Arabic and French: irregular), formerly Alger Republicain (PCA) and Muqawamah (ORP monthly)

9. Orientation: Soviet interpretation of Marxism-Leninism

10. Strategy: Negotiating a coalition with the FLN, and party-building amongst the members of the FLN's mass organisations.

12. External Affiliations: Pro-Soviet parties, especially the Soviet and French communist parties

13. History: In 1920, the French Communist Party established a branch in Algeria that became independent in October 1936. The Parti Communiste Algerien (PCA) was banned in November 1962, shortly after independence by Ben Bella's FLN. However, following Ben Bella's 1965 overthrow by what were essentially social democratic forces in the military critical of Marxist policies, some elements of the FLN's left wing joined with PCS to form the Organisation de la Resistance Populaire (ORP a.k.a. FLN-ORP) ORP adopted the name of PAGS on 26 January 1966. The last and Sixth Congress was held in 1952.

14. Leadership: Sadiq Hadjeres, First Secretary; Larbi Bukhali, former Secretary-General; 'Ali Malki

PARTI DE L'INDEPENDENCE ET DU TRAVAIL (PIT-Independence and Labour Party: Senegal)

2. Republic of Senegal (6,710,000)

3. Date Established: 1976

4. Organisational Type: Vanguard party

5. Organisational Nature: Democratic centralism; the Congress elects the fifty-five member Central Committee which elects the seven-member Secretariat and the fourteen-member Politburo. The Secretary-General is elected at the Congress by the Central Committee.

6. Membership: c.1000

7. Status: Legal

8. Publications: _Monarev_ (PIT version: Independence; occasional), _Ande Sopi_ (Unite for Change: monthly, 7000 circulation); _Daan Deole_, _Gestu_

9. Orientation: Pro-Soviet Marxism-Leninism

10. Strategy: Electoral; promotion of left unity against the PS government; party building

11. Internal Affiliations: In 1985, the Women's Democratic Union was established to assist the PIT.

12. External Affiliations: Soviet-allied parties

13. History: In 1976 a group of PAI(S) members reformed themselves as the underground 'real' PAI, charging that the then just legalised version of the PAI(S) had been corrupted. The 'real' PAI operated underground from 1976 to 1981 when it became the PIT upon registration with the government. The PIT unsuccessfully fought the 1983 legislative elections and the 1984 municipal elections. PIT was left out of the ADS. PIT's Constituent Congress was held in August 1981. Eight hundred and thirty-five delegates attended PIT's Second Congress

(28 September - 2 October 1985). In 1981, Mamadou Dia's faction broke away to form the MDP.

14. Leadership: Secretary General: Amath Dansoko; Politburo - Seydou Cissoko (previous Secretary General), Amath Dansoko, Samba Dioulde Thiam, Maguette Thiam, Mady Danfaka, Sadio Camera, Seydou Ndongo, Semon Pathe Gueye, Makhtar Mbaye, Bouma Gaye, Mohamed Laye and three others.

PARTI DEMOCRATIQUE DE GUINEE (PDG-Democratic Party of Guinea)

2. Republic of Guinea (5,873,000)

3. Date Established: June 1947

4. Organisational Type: Mass Party

6. Membership: Every adult Guinean while the PDG was in power (1,800,000 in 1961)

7. Status: Ruling party 1958-1984, Dissolved 1984.

8. Publications: <u>Horoya</u>

9. Orientation: African socialism, elements of Marxism

10. Strategy: Political -- Create a unity of all the people, the party and the state, non-recognition of class antagonism, series of attempts to mobilise politically the people, the supremacy of politics over economics. Economic -- Creation of state corporations, attempt at economic planning, restriction of private investment except for foreign investment.

11. Internal Affiliations: Party auxiliaries included the Revolutionary Democratic African Youth Movement (JRDA), the Pioneers (children), a women's organisation, production brigades, service civique, the militia and trade unions.

12. External Affiliation: Non-aligned except for a period of time with Nkrumah's Ghana.

13. History: The PDG was founded in June 1947 as the Guinea section of the inter-territorial (French West Africa) Rassemblement Democratique African (RDA). The

PDG became independent of the RDA after the 28 September 1958 independence referendum. Guinea became independent on 2 October 1958 under the leadership of Sekou Toure's PDG. The Bloc Africain de Guinee (BAG - founded 1954) and the Democratie Socialiste e Guinee (DSG - founded 1954) joined the PDG after independence. As in the pre-independence 1957 elections, the PDG had won fifty-eight out of sixty seats in the assembly, and as the PDG had absorbed the BAG, Guinea became a one-party state: the PDG. President Toure maintained control of the PDG and Guinea until his death during heart surgery in the USA on March 26, 1984. His prime minister, Lansana Beavogui became Acting President of Guinea and the PDG, but he was overthrown and the PDG dissolved by the military coup on 3 April 194.

14. Leadership: Sekou Toure, Leader 1947-1984; Lansana Beavogui, leader March 26-April 3, 1984.

PARTI DEMOCRATIQUE SENEGALAIS (PDS-Senegalese Democratic Party: Senegal)

See also, ADS

2. Republic of Senegal (6,710,000)

3. Date Established: October 1974

4. Organisational Type: Mass party

7. Status: Legal opposition party

8. Publications: <u>Takusaan</u> (Evening: three times a week), <u>Le Democrat</u> (The Democrat: monthly)

9. Orientation: Elements of left nationalism

10. Strategy: Electoral, member of the five party ADS alliance

11. Internal Affiliations: Allied with the LD-MPT, the MRDN, the OST and the UDP in the ADS alliance

13. History: The PDS was first formed in October 1974. Under the March 1976 amendment to the Senegalese constitution it was compelled to re-establish itself to the right of the ruling PS. In July 1985 the PDS

joined four socialist organisations to create the ADS alliance. This has created a split in the PDS. The PDS has had modest but insufficient electoral results in PS-controlled state elections.

14. Leadership: Abdoulaye Wade, Secretary General and Presidential candidate; Alassane Cissoko (anti-ADS); Serigne Diop (anti-ADS); Ardo Sow (anti-ADS)

PARTIDO AFRICANO DA INDEPENDENCIA DA GUINEE CABO VERDE (PAIGC-African Party for the Independence of Guinea and Cape Verde: Guinea-Bissau)

2. Republic of Guinea-Bissau (873,000)

3. Date Established: 19 September 1956

4. Organisational Type: National liberation movement in transition to vanguard party

5. Organisational Nature: PAIGC has declared that it is committed to "the principles of democratic centralism and collective leadership, unity and struggle, revolutionary democracy, criticism and self-criticism." Applicants to join the party must meet "strict criteria" of revolutionary and moral standards. The party congress was the supreme decision-making body. In between congresses, the Secretary-General, the Political Bureau (eleven full and four supplementary members) of the Central Committee, and the Central Committee (fifty-one full and ten assistant members) and its Secretariat chaired by the Permanent Secretary act as PAIGC's executive. Mass organisations include the village committees (five members, two of whom must be women) with their regional counterparts, the Women's Democratic Union of Guinea-Bissau, the Amilcar Cabral Youth Organization and the National Union of Workers of Guinea-Bissau.

7. Status: Ruling party

8. Media: Through its control of the government, PAIGC controls the government radio and newspapers (_Vozda Guine_, circulation 6,000 daily; _No Pintcha_, three times a week)

9. Orientation: Cabralist socialism, elements of Marxism

10. Strategy: Consolidation of the national liberation struggle, party building, building of socialism, state elections, regime maintenance, women's participation.

11. Internal Affiliations: Mass organisations include village committees with their regional counter-parts, the Women's Democratic Union of Guinea-Bissau, the Amilcar Cabral Youth Organization and the National Union of Workers of Guinea-Bissau.

12. External Affiliations: PAIGC has maintained its alliance with the other parties of the former Portuguese territories: FRELIMO (Mozambique), MPLA-PT (Angola), MLSTP (Sao Tome) and since the 1980 break, PAICV (Cape Verde). PAIGC has kept its relationship with Soviet-oriented parties as well as with China. PAIGC's policy of non-alignment has led it to maintain its relations with a variety of neutralist countries (Scandinavian countries), western bloc countries (Holland) and international non-governmental organisations (World Council of Churches) that date back to the days of the liberation struggle.

13. History: PAIGC was founded on 19 September 1956. In 1963 PAIGC launched the armed phase of the national liberation struggle against Portuguese occupation. The first leader of the PAIGC, Amilcar Cabral, was murdered by Portuguese forces on 20 January 1973. PAIGC, having liberated two-thirds of Guinea Bissau's territory, declared the country to be independent of Portugal on 24 September 1973. Following the overthrow of the quasi-fascist Portuguese government, on 10 September 1974 the new government recognised Guinea-Bissau's independence under the leadership of President Luiz Cabral and PAIGC. Following strained relations between the Cape Verde and Guinea wings of the party over the proposed merger of the two geographic administrations and whether the development strategy should be primarily urban-industrial (this had been adopted at PAIGC Third Congress in 1977) or primarily rural-agrarian, prime minister Brig. Gen. Vieira (of Guinea) ousted President Cabral (of Cape Verde) on 14 November 1980. Relations were broken between the two wings. The party in Guinea held its First Extraordinary Congress to reaffirm its name and a Cabralist political mobilisation and rural development strategy. Following the Congress, new elections for the National Assembly, the Regional Councils and the Presidency were ordered

for early 1982. The 1984 state constitution established the supremacy of PAIGC over the state institutions.

14. Leadership: Brig. Gen Joao Bernardo Vieira, Secretary-General (President of the Republic); Dr. Vasco Cabral, Permanent Secretary of the Central Committee; other Political Bureau full members: Vitor Saude Maria, Commander Iafai Camara, Col. Paulo Correia, Col. Manuel Saturnino da Costa, Commander Buota N'Batcha, Commander Joao da Silva, Samba Lamine Mane, Carlos Correia, Tiago Aleluia Lopes, Carmen Pereira; Supplementary members: Captain Benghate Na Beate, Dr. Fidelis Cabral d'Almada, Joseph Turpin, Manuel Des Santos

PARTIDO AFRICANO DA INDEPENDENCIA DE CABO VERDE (PAICV-African Party for the Independence of Cape Verde: Cape Verde)

2. Republic of Cape Verde, (308,000)

3. Date Established: 19 January 1981 (predecessor party was PAIGC, which was formed in 1956)

4. Organisational Type: Founded as a national liberation movement, PAIGC became increasingly an anti-imperialist, bi-national vanguard party after independence. After the split between Guinea-Bissau and Cape Verde in 1981, PAICV retained much of the organizational nature of PAIGC.

5. Organisational Nature: PAICV combines elements of democratic centralism with that of a national liberation movement. The party is composed of a number of layers of committees starting at the local level, then the region, then to the thirty-two member National Council with its executive, the Permanent Committee. PAICV has vanguard party-type membership criteria.

6. Membership Number: limited

7. Status: Governing party of one-party state.

8. Publications: (a) party: Unidade e Luta, (b) official: Boletim Informativo, Boletim oficial da Republica de Cabo Verde, Voz di Povo, Emissora Oficial

da Republica de Cabo Verde (radio); Voz de Sao Vicente (radio).

9. Orientation: left national liberation movement with anti-imperialist outlook.

10. Strategy: PAICV's political strategy since independence from Portugal on July 5, 1975 has been to continue and expand all dimensions of the populist, broadly-based, anti-imperialist national liberation movement which leads the revolution. Attention is paid to the development of the party. Party policy is government policy.

PAICV, as the governing party, has shown considerable sensitivity to local conditions. Much effort has been devoted to rehabilitating the economy, which has especially suffered from the recurrent droughts. PAICV has encouraged all patriotic classes to contribute to the economy. Consequently public solutions have been utilised where gains could be made. For example, in contrast to the Portuguese empire's response to previous droughts where 15% to 44% of the population were allowed to die, the PAICV has mobilised international food aid and the extremely limited local resources to create work-for-food programmes that have fed nearly 40% of the rural people. Public resources have been extended to small-scale fishermen and to the peasantry, most of whom were landless before PAICV nationalised the plantations (but the former owners were compensated) and abolished share-cropping. Politically and economically, the PAICV has followed a non-aligned strategy.

11. Internal Affiliations: The party has a number of mass organizations. The youth wing is the JAAC (the Amilcar Cabral African Youth). Workers are organised into the UNTC (the National Union of Cape Verdian Workers. The women's organisation is the National Organising Commission of Cape Verdian Women. There is some debate about the actual significance of women in the party.

12. External Affiliations: The PAICV has long-standing relations with the other ruling parties of Lusophone Africa, i.e. MPLA-PT of Angola, FRELIMO of Mozambique, PAIGC of Guinea-Bissau, MLSTP of Sao Tome and Principe. PAICV was an integral part of the PAIGC until the November 14, 1980 mainland coup against the joint

government of PAIGC under President Luiz Cabral (a Cape Verdian) which had been moving towards greater unification of the two country parts (i.e. Guinea and Cape Verde). Consequently PAICV was formed on 19 January 1981. Fraternal relations were established with the 'new' PAIGC on June 18, 1982 after negotiations encouraged and mediated by President Machel of Mozambique.

13. History: The horrors of Portuguese imperialism helped to produce a vigorous nationalist movement in both Cape Verde and Guinea. In 1956 the PAIGC was established as the national liberation movement for both Portuguese colonies. Numbers of Cape Verdians under Amilcar Cabral's leadership joined PAIGC. They fought and organised mainly on the mainland. PAIGC had freed most of the mainland by 1973. Following the start of the April 1974 Portuguese revolution, PAIGC made significant organizational gains on the islands. Portugal recognized the independence of Guinea-Bissau on September 10, 1974 and that of Cape Verde on July 5, 1975. The joint party, PAIGC remained intact until the mainlanders' 1980 coup against the joint government. PAICV was then established on January 19, 1981. Besides the above-mentioned tensions with the mainlanders, some other intra-Cape Verde party opposition elements did emerge. In April 1979, a small number of party members, supposedly Trotskists, were purged for opposing the party leadership's decisions to accept more relations with the western powers and to pay compensation to the landowners for the expropriation of the plantations.

13. Leadership: Secretary-General Aristides Maria Pereira (President of the Republic); Deputy Secretary-General, General Pedro Pires (Prime Minister of the Republic).

PARTIDO SOCIALISTA DE GUINEA ECUATORIAL (PSAGE - Socialist Party of Equatorial Guinea)

See also, Social Democratic Convergence: Equatorial Guinea

2. Republic of Equatorial Guinea (336,000)

3. Date: Existed in 1984

4. Organisational Type: Exile Party

7. Status: Exiled

9. Orientation: Social Democratic

10. Strategy operating from exile, PSAGE advocated the end of Obiang's military regime and the creation of democracy. Accordingly in 1984 PSAGE allied with RDLGE to form the Social Democratic Convergence.

13. Based in Spain, in 1984 the PSAGE with the RDLGE created the Social Democratic Convergence.

PARTI DU CENTRE SOCIAL (PCS-Social Centre Party: Morocco)

2. Kingdom of Morocco (23,207,000)

3. Date Established: Existed in 1984

7. Status: Legal

9. Orientation: Right-wing socialism

10. Strategy: Electoral

13. History: The PCS won one seat in the 1984 elections for the Majlis Al-Muwab (Chamber of Representatives - 1/206 directly elected and another 100 by 'indirect election')

PARTI DU CONGRES DE L'INDEPENDANCE DE MADAGASCAR (KDRSM: Madagascar) a.k.a. AKFM

PARTI DU PROGRES ET DU SOCIALISME (PPS-Party of Progress and Socialism: Morocco) a.k.a. PCM and PLS

2. Kingdom of Morocco (23,207,000)

3. Date Established: 1943

4. Organisational Type: Vanguard party

5. Organisational Nature: Democratic centralism; the congress was the ultimate decision making body. The executive was led by the Secretary General, a

four-person Secretariat, a twelve-member Politburo, and a sixty-five member Central Committee.

6. Membership: 2000

7. Status: Legal party

8. Publications: al-Kifah al Watani, the Patriotic Struggle: Arabic weekly, French excerpted version monthly; both suppressed in 1969); al Bayane (The Bulletin, daily, Arabic and French editions, 1972 onwards) and al-Mukafih (The Fighter, Arabic daily, French monthly, 1970s)

9. Orientation: Pro-Soviet interpretation of Marxism-Leninism, elements of progressive revolutionary Islam

10. Strategy: Electoral for the national-democratic revolution, party building, creation of a united front of 'national, progressive and revolutionary forces' to build political democracy (i.e. directly elected national assembly) and economically the 'non-capitalist' way to socialism in order to defeat feudalism, the large bourgeoisie and imperialism. The party supported annexation of the Western Sahara.

12. External Affiliations: Pro-Soviet parties, especially the French CP

13. History: Intriguingly, when the PPS was first formed in 1943 as a section of the French C.P., it had no Moroccan members, mainly French and Spanish residents. However, the localisation of the PCM proceeded quickly and in 1945 'Ali Yata became the Secretary General of the PCM (and its successors: the PLS in 1968 and PPS in 1974). The PCM was suspended in 1959 and banned in 1960. In 1964 the PCM became a clandestine organisation. In 1968 it reconstituted itself as the PLS but was banned in 1969, along with its al-Kifah al-Watani and the jailing of its leader/editor, 'Ali Yata, for ten months. During the early 1970s Yata proceeded to lead the revival of the PLS until it was legalised in August 1974 as the PPS, following Yata's tour of East-bloc capitals to argue the king's case for annexing Western Sahara (a position opposed by Cuba and the Soviet Union). The PPS has participated in the November 1976 national elections (no seats won), the 1977 national chamber elections (one seat) and the 1984

elections (two directly elected, no indirectly elected seats; 2/306 seats; 2.3% of votes cast). PPS has been an opposition party, but Yata has frequently acted as an unofficial envoy of the king on the issue of annexing Western Sahara.

14. Leadership: Secretary: 'Ali Yata; Politburo: 'Ali Yata, Ismail Alaoui, Mohamed Ben Bella, Abdeslem Bourquia, Mohamed Rifi Chouaib, Abdelmajid Douieb, Omar El Fassi, Thami Khyari, Abdallah Layachi, Simon Levy, Mohamed Moucharik, Abdelwahed Souhail; Secretariat: Yata, Chouaib, Fassi, Moucharik

PARTI DU REGROUPEMENT AFRICAIN-SENEGAL) (PRA-African Realignment Party: Senegal)

See also, MRDN/AND-JEF; ODP

2. Republic of Senegal (6,710,000)

3. Date Established: September 1958

4. Organisation Type: Mass party

7. Status: Legal party 1958-1963, illegal 1963-1966

10. Strategy: Electoral

13. History: Founded in 1958 by Abdoulaye Ly as a left split from the UPS (later PS), the PRA was enveloped back into the UPS in 1966. Abdoulaye Ly joined the ODP and later the MRND/And-Jef. MRND/And-Jef courted other PRS members.

14. Leadership: Abdoulaye Ly

PARTI LIBERAL PROGRESSISTE (PLP-Progressive Liberal Party: Morocco)

2. Kingdom of Morocco (23,207,000)

3. Date Established: 1974

4. Organisation Type: Mass party

7. Status: Legal

9. Orientation: Left nationalist

10. Strategy: Electoral

13. History: Founded in 1974 after King Hassan II decided to allow limited elections, the PLP was unsuccessful in the 1984 national Chamber elections.

14. Leadership: Akmouch Ahmed Oulhaj

PARTI OUVRIER ET PAYSAN DU CONGO (PDP-Congolese Workers' and Peasants' Party: CWPP: Zaire)

2. Republic of Zaire (33,927,000)

3. Date Established: 1986

7. Status: Illegal

9. Orientation: Marxism-Leninism

PARTI POPULAIRE SENEGALAIS (PPS-Senegalese People's Party: Senegal)

2. Republic of Senegal (6,710,000)

3. Date Established: December 1981 (registered)

4. Organisational Type: Mass party

7. Status: Legal

9. Orientation: Left nationalist, socialist

10. Strategy: Electoral

11. Internal Affiliations: Some contact with Casamance separatists

13. History: Dissatisfied members of the PAI, the only official Marxist party in Senegal from 1976 to 1981, broke from it in 1981. In 1983, Dr. Oumar Wone was the PPS presidential candidate.

14. Leadership: Dr. Oumar Wone; Magatte Loum

PARTI POUR LA LIBERATION DU PEUPLE (PLP-Party for the Liberation of the People: Senegal)

2. Republic of Senegal (6,710,000)

3. Date Established: July 1983

4. Organisational Type: Mass party

7. Status: Legal opposition

9. Orientation: Anti-imperialist, neutralist, left pan-Africanist and Marxist elements

10. Strategy: Electoral

13. History: The PLP was founded by RND members who accused Diop's RND of serving the interests of the PS government. The PLP ran candidates in the 1984 municipal elections.

14. Leadership: Babacar Niang, Secretary General; Abdoulaye Kane, Assistant Secretary General

PARTI REVOLUTIONNAIRE DU PEUPLE TUNISIEN (PRPT-Revolutionary Party of the Tunisian People: Tunisia)

2. Republic of Tunisia (7,224,000)

3. Date Established: Existed in 1981

6. Membership: Few

7. Status: Illegal

9. Orientation: Left nationalist, Marxist elements

10. Strategy: Revolution

12. External Affiliations: Popular Front for the Liberation of Palestine; 'radical' Arab states

14. Leadership: Abbas Medhkouri (a.k.a. Zine)

PARTI SOCIALISTE (PS-Socialist Party: Senegal)

See also, UPS

2. Republic of Senegal (6,710,000)

3. Date Established: 1949

4. Organisational Type: Mass party (party of notables)

7. Status: Ruling party

8. Publications: Le Soleil (The Sun: PS daily, 35,000 circulation); the PS controls the government-owned radio and television and censors the rest of the media

9. Orientation: Right-wing social democracy

10. Strategy: Electoral, regime maintenance

11. Internal Affiliations: Trade unions - Confederation Nationale des Travailleurs Senegalais (Senegalese National Confederation of Workers); in 1983, President Diouf created a number of committees of intellectuals. The six largest were Professor Iba Der Thiam's Comite des 1500, COSAPAD (le Comite de Soutien a l'Action du President Diouf), ANSAPP (Association Nationale de Soutien a l'Action des Pouvoirs Public), UNSAPAD (Union Nationale a l'Action du President Diouf), MNS (Mouvement Nationale de Soutien a l'Action du President Diouf) and GRESEN (Groupe de Rencontres et d'Echanges pour un Senegal Nouveau).

12. External Affiliations: Socialist International, especially the French Socialist Party

13. History: The PS was founded in 1949 as the UPS by Leopold Senghor from the local branch of the French Socialist Party. The UPS became the governing party at independence in 1960. It swallowed the left opposition contained in the Parti de Regroupement Africain-Senegal (PRA-S) in 1966. From 1963 to 1976, the UPS was the sole legal party. In 1976 the UPS joined the Socialist International, changed its name to the PS, and allowed three other parties to be created as legal entities. Senghor resigned as President of the Republic and PS Secretary in 1981 and was succeeded by Abdou Diouf. Diouf allowed other parties to be registered from 1981 onwards. The PS has governed Senegal since 1960 by

winning a series of elections and controlling electoral rules.

14. Leadership: Abdou Diouf, Secretary General (President of the Republic); M'Baye Jacques Diop, Permanent Secretary; Dr. Daouda Sow (President of the National Assembly)

PARTI SOCIALISTE ARABE (PSA-Arab Socialist Party: Tunisia)

2. Republic of Tunisia (7,224,000)

3. Date Established: Existed in 1981

4. Organisational Type: Mass party

6. Membership: Few

7. Status: Illegal

9. Orientation: Left nationalist (Iraq Baathist)

12. External Affiliations: Iraq

14. Leadership: Brahim Bouderbala

PARTI SOCIALISTE CONGOLAISE (PSC-Congolese Socialist Party - CSP: Zaire)

2. Republic of Zaire (33,927,000)

3. Date Established: Existed in 1985

4. Organisational Type: Mass party

6. Membership: Few

7. Status: Illegal

9. Orientation: Socialist (Lumumbist)

10. Strategy: Revolution

11. Internal Affiliations: The PSC was a member of the CLC coalition.

14. Leadership: Valere Nzamba (associated with Gizenga, Lumumba's Vice-Premier)

PARTI SOCIALISTE DESTOURIEN (PSD-Destourian Socialist Party: Tunisia)

2. Republic of Tunisia (7,224,000)

3. Date Established: 1934

4. Organisational Type: Mass party

5. Organisational Nature: The President, Secretary General, the Political Bureau (twenty members including the Director), and the Central Committee (eighty members) are elected by the PSD congress

6. Membership: Thousands

7. Status: ruling party

8. Publications: al-Amal (52,000), L'Action (50,000)

9. Orientation: Social democratic

10. Strategy: Electoral, regime maintenance

11. Internal Affiliations: Union Generale des Traveilleurs Tunisiens (UGTT-General Union of Tunisian Workers)

12. External Affiliations: The PSD was a member of the Inter-African Socialist Organisation (IAS).

13. History: In 1934 Habib Bourguiba formed the PSD as the Neo-Destour Party, a split from the Destour (Constitution) Party. After lengthy negotiations and a brief bout of armed struggle with France, the Neo-Destour Party (as the PSD was called until 1964) led Tunisia to independence on 20 March 1956. The PSD was the sole legal party from 1963 to 1981 when the PCT was legalised. Bourguiba was deposed by PSD Political Bureau member General Zine el Abidine Ben Ali on 7 November 1987 who in 1988 changed the party name to the RCD, the Constitutional Democratic Rally.

14. Leadership: PSD President-General Zine el Abidine Ben Ali (President of the Republic)

PARTI SOCIALISTE MAURICIEN (PSM-Mauritian Socialist Party: Mauritius)

2. Mauritius (1,023,000)

3. Date Established: 1979

4. Organisational Type: Mass party

6. Membership: Mainly Hindu

7. Status: Legal opposition to 1982 when it joined the MMM coalition. It merged with the ruling MSM on May 1, 1983.

9. Orientation: Socialist-Social democratic

10. Strategy: Electoral, in coalition with MMM for 1982 election.

13. History: In 1979 Harish Boodhoo took his supporters out of the MLP and created the PSM. On May 1, 1983 the PSM merged with the MSM and went on to win the August 1983 election.

14. Leadership: Harish Boodhoo, Leader.

PARTI SOCIALISTE (REUNION) (PSR-Reunion Federation of the Socialist Party: Reunion)

2. Reunion (French Occupation) (543,000)

3. Date Established: Existed since at least the 1960s.

4. Organisational Type: Mass party

7. Status: Legal party, has shared French state power with its French parent, the PS.

9. Orientation: Social democratic

10. Strategy: Electoral, party-building, alliances, autonomy but not independence for Reunion.

11. Internal Affiliations: The PS(R) has cooperated with the PCR in the various elections (despite problems in the late 1970s) and for increased autonomy.

12. External Affiliations: The PS of Reunion is part of the French PS.

13. History: The electoral alliance with the PCR, while not without problems, has contributed to the electoral success of the PS(R) to the European and French parliaments as well as to the local assemblies and municipalities.

PARTI SOCIALISTE ZAIROIS (PSZ-Socialist Party of Zaire - SPZ: Zaire)

2. Republic of Zaire (33,927,000)

3. Date Established: Existed in 1986

4. Organisational Type: Mass party

6. Membership: Few

7. Status: Illegal

9. Orientation: Socialism

10. Strategy: Revolution

13. History: In 1985 the Mobutu regime arrested six PSZ members in Shaba. The PSZ appears to have been based in Paris.

14. Leadership: Secretary-General - Aime Bitou
14. Leadership: Wilfred Berthile, First Secretary.

PATRIOTIC FRONT (PF: Zimbabwe)

See also: ZANU, ZAPU

PATRIOTIC FRONT-ZIMBABWE AFRICAN PEOPLE'S UNION (PF-ZAPU: ZIMBABWE) a.k.a. ZAPU

PEOPLE'S NATIONAL PARTY (PNP: Ghana)

2. Republic of Ghana (12,205,000)

3. Date Established: 1979

4. Organisational Type: Mass party

6. Membership: Several thousand

7. Status: Illegal, defunct

9. Orientation: Social Democracy

10. Strategy: Electoral

11. Internal Affiliations: The KNRG operated as a group within the PNP during 1980 and 1981.

12. External Affiliations: The PNP was a founding member of the Inter-African Socialist Organisation.

13. History: Formed in early 1979, the PNP won the legislative and presidential elections of that year. The PNP governed from 24 September 1979 until its overthrow on 31 December 1981 by Rawlings.

14. Leadership: Dr. Hilla Limann (former President of the Republic); J.W. de Graft Johnson (former Vice-President of the Republic); the late Imoru Egala

PEOPLE'S REDEMPTION PARTY (PRP: Nigeria)

2. Federal Republic of Nigeria (94,181,000)

3. Date Established: 1978

4. Organisational Type: Mass party

6. Membership: The PRP had offices and members in enough states to be registered as a political party for the 1979 and 1983 elections (the minimum was thirteen out of nineteen states).

7. Status: Illegal

9. Orientation: Social democracy

10. Strategy: Electoral

11. Internal Affiliations: In 1982 the PRP joined the Progressive Parties' Alliance. Plans to merge the coalition partners into one party after the 1983 elections were foiled by the military coup.

13. History: The PRP grew out of the wing of the Movement for People's Democracy (MPD, f. 1976). Upon its break-up in 1978, many of those leftists who believed that cooperation with some business interest was essential to achieve reform joined the PRP which contested the 1979 and 1983 elections with some success. All political parties were banned following the 1983 military coup.

14. Leadership: Alhaji Hassan Yussef

PEOPLE'S REVOLUTIONARY LEAGUE OF GHANA (PRLG: Ghana) a.k.a. THE LEAGUE

See also, UNITED FRONT (Ghana)

2. Republic of Ghana (12,205,000)

3. Date Established: c.1979

4. Organisational Type: Vanguard party

6. Membership: Few, possibly one hundred

7. Status: Illegal

9. Orientation: Marxist-Leninist

10. Strategy: Revolution

11. Internal Affiliations: JFM - The PRLG and the JFM formed a United Front after the creation of the PNDC.

13. History: The PRLG was formed by elements of that faction of the PRP who did not want to merge into the PNP and by university activists. After the coming to power of the PNDC, the PRLG initially supported this Rawlings government and began to drawn close to the JFM as opposed to the NDM. The PRLG and the JFM joined together in the United Front which attempted unsuccessfully to overthrow Rawlings (possibly in response to some of Rawlings' actions) in

October-November 1982. Following this, numbers of PRLG members left Ghana, some going to London where the United Front appears to have been revived.

14. Leadership: T. Kodwo Ababio-Nubuor, General Secretary; George Quaynor-Mettle (formerly); (Under-Regional Secretary for Greater Accra), Ali Yemoh

PEOPLE'S REVOLUTIONARY PARTY (PRP:Ghana)

2. Republic of Ghana (12,205,000)

3. Date Established: 1979

4. Organisational Type: Mass party

7. Status: Legal, defunct

9. Orientation: Socialist (Nkrumahist and Marxist elements)

10. Strategy: Electoral

11. Internal Affiliations: The PRP merged into the PNP.

13. History: Unable to meet the rules set for the 1979 elections that returned Ghana to civilian rule, the PRP faction led by Johnny Hansen merged into the PNP, especially what became the KNRG group. Others who rejected this course of action later formed the JFM and the PRLG.

14. Leadership: Johnny Hansen

PERSPECTIVISTES (Tunisia) a.k.a. GEAST

POLISARIO-FRENTE POPULAR PARA LA LIBERACION DE SAGUIA EL HAMRA Y RIO DE ORO (POLISARIO-Popular Front for the Liberation of Saquia el Hamra and Rio de Oro: Saharan Arab Democratic Republic or SADR)

2. Saharan Arab Democratic Republic (a.k.a. Western Sahara: Moroccan occupation since independence was declared 28 February 1976 (400,000 to 1,000,000 of whom 300,000 were in exile).

3. Date Established: 1973

4. Organisational Type: National Liberation Front

5. Organisational nature: POLISARIO had a Secretary General, an Executive Committee (nine members), a Political Bureau (twenty-five members) and a Sahrawi National Council (forty-one members). POLISARIO formed the Saharan Arab Democratic Republic on 28 February 1976 as the government in exile and previously established an army.

6. Membership: Thousands

7. Status: Sole ruling party, territory under Moroccan occupation

9. Orientation: Left nationalist, socialist and Marxist-Leninist elements

10. Strategy: Armed struggle to oust the occupying powers of Spain (successful 1976), Mauritania (successful 1979) and Morocco (on-going liberation war)

12. External Affiliations: Algeria, Libya (at times), some Soviet support (forty-five countries, including a majority of OAU members, have recognised the SADR).

13. History: POLISARIO was formed in 1973 to liberate the Western Sahara from the Spanish empire. On November 14, 1975 Spain agreed to violate the principle of self-determination by handing over its colony for annexation and occupation to Morocco and Mauritania on 28 February 1976. On that date POLISARIO declared independence for the Saharan Arab Democratic Republic and the establishment of a government in exile. Since the POLISARIO's war of national liberation succeeded in knocking Mauritania out of the war (5 August 1979) and the southern third of SADR, Morocco occupied this and the war has continued since then. SADR was first admitted to the OAU on 22 February 1982.

14. Leadership: Mohamed Abdelaziz, Secretary General (SADR President); Mohamed Lamine Ould Ahmed (SADR Prime Minister)

POUVOIR AUX PETITS (Power to the People: Madagascar) a.k.a. MFM

PROGRESSIVE NATIONAL FRONT (PNF: Sudan)

See also: ASBP-OS, NMU, RCPS, SLP, UDF (Sudan)

2. Republic of Sudan (23,089,000)

3. Date Established: 1985

4. Organisational Type: Coalition of organisations

7. Status: Legal

9. Orientation: Left nationalist (Syrian Baathism amongst others), Marxism-Leninism

10. Strategy: Electoral

11. Internal Affiliations: The PNF was composed of the ASBP-OS, the NMU, the UDF (Sudan), the SLP and the RCPS.

13. History: The PNF was formed to contest the 1986 elections.

PROVISIONAL MILITARY ADMINISTRATIVE COUNCIL (PMAC-Ethiopia a.k.a. DERG a.k.a. DERGUE)

2. Socialist Ethiopia (35,210,000)

3. Date Established: September 12, 1974

4. Organisational Type: Military governing council

5. Organisational Nature: From 1974 to 1977, PMAC was directed by the Derg (or Dergue), the Armed Forces Coodinating Committee which was controlled by Major Mengistu Haile-Muriam. In February 1977, PMAC was restructured. The Central Congress of PMAC had limited legislative powers and elected a Central Committee (thirty-two members). The Central Committee (C.C.) elected eight C.C. members to the Standing Committee. All Derg members (some seventy) are members of the Central Congress. Col. Mengistu as PMAC chairman

chaired the Central Congress, the C.C., the Standing Committee, the Council of Ministers and the National Revolutionary Operations Command. PMAC supervised COPWE, and later WPE.

7. Status: Ruling military council

8. Publications: PMAC controls all government and 'party' (formerly COPWE-1979-1984, and from 1984 onwards WPE) media.

9. Orientation: Pro-Soviet Marxism-Leninism from c.1977 onwards; 1974-1977 debate between elements of varieties of left nationalism, African socialism and Marxism-Leninism over the Ethiopian concept of "hebrettesebawinet"

10. Strategy: Administering the building of socialism, especially the creation of an Ethiopian Marxist Leninist vanguard party loyal to Mengistu.

11. Internal Affiliations: the Kebeles (urban community committees); 28,000 peasant associations, UEMLO (1977 February-1979); MEISON until June 1977; LL until early/mid 1978; RF, EORS, MLRO for the duration); EPRP 1975-1976

12. External Affiliations: Pro-Soviet parties, especially those of the Soviet Union and Cuba

13. History: Provisional Military Government formed 12 September 1974 led by Lt. General Amam who was executed 24 November 1974. The PMAC led by Brig. Gen. Teferi was created by the Derg (led by Major Megistu) on 28 November. Following Teferi's execution on 3 February 1977, Col. Mengistu became PMAC Chairman and Lt. Col. Atnafu, Vice-Chairman. Atnafu was executed on 11 November 1977. POMOA (the Provisional Office for Mass Organisational Affairs) in April was created in 1976 to act as a training school for Marxist-Leninist cadres for a future vanguard party. The PMAC encouraged the formation of UEMLO as a mechanism to unify Marxist-Leninist organisations in February 1977. Following UEMLO's failure, in December 1979 the PMAC created COPWE to form the new vanguard party. This was established on 10 September 1984 as WPE under Mengistu's control.

14. Leadership: Lt. Col. Mengistu Haile-Mariam

PROVISIONAL NATIONAL DEFENCE COUNCIL (PNDC: Ghana)

2. Republic of Ghana (12,205,000)

3. Date Established: 31 December 1981

4. Organisational Type: Ruling council plus quasi-mass party structure

5. Organisational Nature: The PNDC acted as the inner-cabinet executive of the government and the party-like structure of the Committees for the Defence of the Revolution (CDR's) that extend from the region to the locality.

6. Membership: Membership in the actual Council has varied in the range of seven to twelve, but membership in the defence committees has numbered varied from the thousands to possibly the hundreds of thousands at the peak of participation in 1982.

7. Status: Ruling movement

8. Publications: The PNDC controlled the *Daily Graphic*, the *Ghanaian Times* as well as all radio and television broadcasting (through the Ghana Broadcasting Service). The defence committees published *Nsamankow* and *The Eagle*.

9. Orientation: Left nationalism with social democratic, liberal and Marxist elements

10. Strategy: Rehabilitation of the economy, regime maintenance in aid of the national democratic phase of the revolution

11. Internal Affiliations: Student Task Force, the National Youth Organising Commission, the Democratic Youth League, December 31st Women's Movement, All Women's Association of Ghana. In the past a number of political organisations had been associated with the PNDC, most notably: JFM, PRLG, NDM, AYC, KNRG, MOPAD.

12. External Affiliations: Sankara's Burkina Faso

13. History: Rawlings and his supporters seized power from Limann's PNP on 31 December 1981 and established the PNDC on 11 January 1982. Rawlings called for the formation of People's Defence Committees (PDC's) and Workers' Defence Committees (WDC) in early 1982. However, after the attempted coup of October 1982 by the JFM and PRLG (who were against acceptance of the IMF plans and who had been very influential in the defence commitees), Rawlings and others in the PNDC decided to revise the PDC's and WDC's into the less politically prominent CDR's in December 1984.

14. Leadership: PNDC Chairman - Flt. Lt. Jerry J. Rawlings; Other PNDC members - Mrs. Aanaa Enin, Ebo Tawiah, Justice D.F. Annan, Alhaji Iddrisu Mahama, Capt. Kojo Tsikata (Rtd), P.V. Obeng, Maj.-Gen. Arnold Quainoo, Brig. W.M. Mensa-Wood

RASSEMBLEMENT DES FORCES PATRIOTIQUE (RFP-Assembly of Patriotic Forces: Chad

See also, GUNT, FROLINAT and CSR

2. Republic of Chad (5,308,000)

3. Date Established: 11 August 1984

4. Organisational Type: Coalition of civil war factions

7. Status: Civil war participant

10. Strategy: Negotiations and civil war

11. Internal Affiliations: The RFP was composed of anti-Libyan GUNT factions, the National Democratic Union, the Abdel Kader Yacine faction of Original Frolinat, and the Fundamental Frolinat.

13. History: Despite its original (August 1984) opposition to the forces of both Goukouni Woddei (a.k.a. Oueddei, Weddeye) and the then Hissein Habre regime, the RFP joined Woddei's opposition CSR in August 1985.

14. Leadership: Facho Balaam, Chairman.

RASSEMBLEMENT NATIONAL ARABE (RNA: Tunisia) a.k.a. RNDA

RASSEMBLEMENT NATIONAL DEMOCRATIQUE (RND-National Democratic Rally)

2. Republic of Senegal (6,710,000)

3. Date Established: February 1976

4. Organisational Type: Mass party

7. Status: Legal opposition

8. Publications: <u>Taxaw</u> (published in French and Wolof)

9. Orientation: Left nationalist and Pan-Africanist, Marxist elements

10. Strategy: Electoral, reformist

13. History: Founded in 1976 by University of Dakar professor Cheikh Anta Diop, the RND was refused registration in 1977, but was granted registration in 1981 when some of its members split to found the PLP. The RND elected one member in the 1983 legislative elections. Its poor showing foundered rumours of a possible coalition government with the PS. Diop died on February 7, 1986.

14. Leadership: Secretary General 1976-1986: Cheikh Anta Diop

RASSEMBLEMENT NATIONAL DEMOCRATIQUE ARABE (RNDA-National Democratic Arab Rally: Tunisia) a.k.a. RNA

2. Republic of Tunisia (7,224,000)

3. Date Established: May, 1981

4. Organisational Type: Mass party

6. Membership: Few

7. Status: Illegal

9. Orientation: Left nationalist (Iraq Baathist), Libyan eclectic socialism

12. External Affiliations: Libya, Iraq

14. Leadership: Bechir Essed

RASSEMBLEMENT NATIONAL MALGACHE (RNM: Madagascar) a.k.a. UDECMA-KMTP

RASSEMBLEMENT POPULAIRE POUR LE PROGRES (RPP-Popular Rally for Progress: Djibouti)

2. Republic of Djibouti (588,000)

3. Date Established: 4 March 1979

4. Organisational Type: Mass party

5. Organisational Nature: The party chairman selects the twelve members of the Political Bureau.

7. Status: Ruling party

9. Orientation: Socialist

10. Strategy: Electoral, regime maintenance

12. External Affiliations: At the request of the RPP government, France maintains a garrison of 4,500 troops in the country.

13. History: The ruling socialist Ligue Populaire Africaine pour l'Independence (LPAI) brought in other political forces to create the RPP on 4 March 1979. This followed LPAI's electoral success at independence in 1977. In 1981 the RPP ensured its continued electoral success by making Djibouti a one-party state.

14. Leadership: Hassan Gouled Aptidon, RPP chairman (President of the Republic)

REGROUPEMENT DES OFFICIERS COMMUNISTES (ROC-Communist Officers Group: Burkina Faso)

2. Republic of Burkina Faso (8,130,000)

3. Date Established: 1983

7. Status: Part of the CNR government

9. Orientation: Marxism-Leninism

10. Strategy: Building a revolutionary socialist state

11. Internal Affiliations: The ROC, UCB, ULC, GC, and LIPAD participated in Sankara's CNR government.

13. History: The RDC supported Sankara's CNR government.

14. Leadership: Capt. Thomas Sankara

REUNION DEMOCRATICA PART LA LIBERACION DE GUINEA ECUATORIAL (RDLGE-Democratic Movement for the Liberation of Equatorial Guinea)

See also, SOCIAL DEMOCRATIC CONVERGENCE: EQUATORIAL GUINEA

2. Republic of Equatorial Guinea (336,000)

3. Date Established: 1981

4. Organisational Type: Exile party

7. Status: Exiled

9. Orientation: Social democratic

10. Strategy: Operating from exile, it advocated the ending of the Obiang regime by creating a provisional government-in-exile in 1982. This followed the collapse of the 1981 talk with Obiang. In 1984 RDLGE (with PSAGE) formed an alliance, the Social Democratic Convergence.

13. History: Formed in 1981 the RDLGE was based in Paris. In 1982 reconciliation talks by the PDLGE with the Obiang regime broke off. Later that year the RDLGE declared it had formed a provisional government-in-exile. In 1984 the RDLGE allied with the PSAGE to create the Social Democratic Convergence.

REVOLUTIONARY COMMAND-COUNCIL OF SOCIALIST GUINEA PATRIOTS (RCCSGP: Equatorial Guinea)

2. Republic of Equatorial Guinea (336,000)

3. Date Established: 1981

7. Status: Exiled

9. Orientation: Socialist

10. Strategy: Operating from exile, it advocates the ending of the military regime of Colonel Obiang and the establishment of democracy.

14. Leadership: Daniel Oyono

REVOLUTIONARY COMMUNIST PARTY OF THE SUDAN (RCPS: Sudan)

See also, PNF

2. Republic of Sudan (23,089,000)

3. Date Established: 1965

4. Organisational Type: Vanguard party

5. Organisational Nature: Democratic centralism

6. Membership: Few

8. Publications: Views published in papers of fraternal parties - e.g. La Voix du Peuple, Brussels.

9. Orientation: Maoist Chinese-Albanian interpretation of Marxism-Leninism

10. Strategy: Electoral, Revolution

11. Internal Affiliations: The RCPS joined the ASBP-OS, the NMU, the UDF (Sudan) and the SLP in the PNF.

12. External Affiliations: Prior to their split, pro-Chinese and pro-Albanian parties

13. History: The RCPS was initiated in 1965 by SCP members who disagreed with the 1956 thesis of the "peaceful transition" to socialism and numbers of whom, most notably Ahmad Muhammad Jair, were expelled in August 1964 from the SCP. The RCPS may have been related to the Revolutionary Leadership faction of the SCP, which included S.M. Ali (a student in 1968), which existed

at least in the late 1960s. The RCPS was part of the PNF for the 1986 elections.

14. Leadership: Ahmad Muhammad Jair

REVOLUTIONARY CURRENT (RC-Egypt)

2. Arab Republic of Egypt (48,832,000)

3. Date Established: Existed in 1979

7. Status: Illegal

9. Orientation: Maoist Marxism-Leninism

10. Strategy: Revolution

11. Internal Affiliations: Unofficial but close relationship with elements of the NPUP.

13. History: The RC was an off-shoot of the ECP.

REVOLUTIONARY EGYPTIAN COMMUNIST PARTY (RECP-Egypt)

2. Arab Republic of Egypt (48,832,000)

3. Date Established: Existed in 1979

6. Membership: Effective beyond its few numbers

7. Status: Illegal

9. Orientation: Marxism-Leninism

10. Strategy: Revolution, underground party-building amongst students and factory workers. Very low public profile.

11. Internal Affiliations: Unofficial but close relationship with elements of the NPUP.

13. History: the RECP was an off-shoot of the ECP.

REVOLUTIONARY FLAME (RF-Seded: Ethiopia)

2. Socialist Ethiopia (35,210,000)

3. Date Established: Existed in 1975

6. Membership: Mainly soldiers

7. Status: Legal in 1977

9. Orientation: Marxism-Leninism

10. Strategy: Party-building; promote the creation of socialism by the PMAC and the Derg.

11. Internal Affiliations: One of the RF leaders was a Derg member. RF joined with LL, MEISON, EDRS, and MLRO to create the party-building UEMLO.

13. History: RF built a base in the army and had one of its leaders made a member of the Derg. In February 1977, RF joined in creating UEMLO as part of the process of unifying the Marxist-Leninist left.

SAWABA (Freedom Party: Niger)

2. Republic of Niger (6,549,000)

7. Status: Banned in 1959, underground remnants.

9. Orientation: Marxist

13. History: After its banning in 1959, Sawaba was forced to adopt an underground strategy against the Niger Progressive Party led by President Hamani Diori. Sawaba attempted armed resistance during the mid 1960s, but in a sense were surpassed by the military coup of April 15, 1974 that brought to power Lt. Colonel (now Brigadier-General) Senyi Kountche.

SEDED (Ethiopia) a.k.a. RF-REVOLUTIONARY FLAME

SEYCHELLES PEOPLE'S PROGRESSIVE FRONT (SPPF/FPPS-Front Populaire Progressiste des Seychelles: Seychelles)

2. Republic of Seychelles (65,480)

3. Date Established: May 1978

4. Organisational Type: Mass party

5. Organisational Nature: The SPPF is led by Secretary-General, Deputy Secretary-General, Secretariat (thirteen members). Congresses are held on an annual basis.

7. Status: Ruling, sole legal party

8. Publications: The People (monthly, circulation 1000)

9. Orientation: Socialist

10. Strategy: Electoral; regime maintenance; building socialism

12. External Affiliations: CCM (Tanzania)

13. History: Premier F.A. Rene's SPUP overthrew President J.R. Mancham's Seychelles Democratic Party on 5 June 1977. SPUP became SPFF in May 1978 and became the only legal party in June 1978. In May 1984, the post of President of the SPPF was merged into that of the Secretary General.

14. Leadership: Secretary General - France Albert Rene (President of the Republic); Deputy Secretary General - Major James Michel

SEYCHELLES PEOPLE'S UNITED PARTY (SPUP: Seychelles) now k.a. SPPF/FPPS

SHUHADA AL LIBYA (SL-Martyrs of Libya)

2. Socialist People's Libyan Arab Jamahiriya (4,108,000)

3. Date Established: Existed in 1981

4. Organisational Type: Student movement

6. Membership: Draws upon the 4,000 Libyan students in the U.S.A.

9. Orientation: Left nationalist to socialist

10. Strategy: Organises Libyan students in the U.S.A.

SOCIAL DEMOCRATIC CONVERGENCE (SDC-Equitorial Guinea)

See also, RDLGE and PSAGE

2. Republic of Equatorial Guinea (336,000)

3. Date Established: 1984

4. Organisational Type: It is an alliance between the RDLGE (Reunion Democratica para la Liberacion de Guinea Ecuatorial) and PSAGE (Partido Socialista de Guinea Ecuatorial)

7. Status: Exiled

9. Orientation: Social democratic

10. Strategy: Operating from exile, it advocates the ending of the military regime of Colonel Obiang which came to power in 1979 and the establishment of democracy.

13. History: Following the failure of reconciliation talks between the RDLGE and the Obiang regime in 1982, the RDLGE declared that it had created a provisional government. Out of this move, the RDLGE and the PSAGE decided to form an alliance, the Social Democratic Convergence.

14. Leadership: Manuel Ruben Ndongo

SOCIALIST LABOUR PARTY (SLP Hizb al 'Amal al-Istiraki: HAI-Egypt)

2. Arab Republic of Egypt (48,832,000)

3. Date Established: November 1978

4. Organisational Type: Mass party

7. Status: Legal opposition party

8. Publications: al-Shaab

9. Orientation: Islamic social democracy, anti-imperialist, pro-Soviet, left Arab nationalist, pro-Palestinian

10. Strategy: Electoral

11. Internal Affiliations: The SLP allied itself with the NPUP and the Liberal Socialist Party in calling for a boycott of the 1983 municipal elections.

12. External Affiliations: Pro-Soviet, pro-PLO

13. History: The SLP was formed in November 1978 by Ibrahim Shukri, a former agriculture minister. The First Congress was held in 1982. Failing to achieve the 8% electoral threshold in the 27 May 1984 elections for the People's Assembly, the SLP did not receive any seats through that mechanism but President Mubarak gave four of the ten Presidentially-appointed seats to the party which had gotten 7.1% of the vote.

14. Leadership: Ibrahim Mahmud Shukri

SOCIALIST LABOUR PARTY (SLP: Sudan)

See also, PNF

2. Republic of Sudan (23,089,000)

3. Date Established: Existed in 1985

6. Membership: Mainly Northern

7. Status: Legal

9. Orientation: Socialism

10. Strategy: Electoral

11. Internal Affiliations: The SLP belonged to the PNF in order to contest the 1986 elections.

SOCIALIST LEAGUE OF MALAWI (LESOMA: Malawi)

2. Republic of Malawi (6,782,000)

3. Date Established: Pre 1980

5. Organisational Nature: In 1980 LESOMA created a military wing, the People's Liberation Army of Malawi (PLAM).

7. Status: Illegal opposition party in exile

9. Orientation: Pro-Soviet Socialist/Marxist, anti-apartheid

10. Strategy: Armed struggle, negotiations with other opposition groups

12. External Affiliations: Soviet Union, Cuba, Zimbabwe

13. History: LESOMA was based in Zimbabwe. In 1980 LESOMA established the PLAM. Dr. Attati Mpakati, the then leader, was murdered in Harare, Zimbabwe on March 28, 1983. An attempt in June 1983 to unite the opposition groups of LESOMA, MAFREMO and the Congress for the Second Republic into the Save Malawi Committee (SMC) failed during meetings in Lusaka, Zambia.

14. Leadership: Dr. Attati Mpakati (assassinated 1983), leader; Grey Kamunyembeni, leader; Kapote Mwakusula, Secretary General

SOCIALIST PARTY OF WORKERS, FARMERS AND YOUTH (SPWFY: Nigeria)

2. Federal Republic of Nigeria (94,181,000)

3. Date Established: 1978

4. Organisational Type: Vanguard party

6. Membership: Workers, academics, students, youth

7. Status: Illegal

8. Publications: <u>Workers' Vanguard</u>

9. Orientation: Marxism-Leninism (independent)

10. Strategy: Electoral, towards the building of a socialist party capable of leading the national democratic revolution

12. External Affiliations: Independent

13. History: One set of roots of the SPWFY goes back to the Movement for People's Democracy (MPD) that was created by academics and others in 1976 order to unify the left in anticipation of the lifting of military rule. The left met in Zaria in 1976 at the All-Nigerian Socialist Conference to address the same aims. However, in 1978 the MPD split into three main groups: the SWPP, the PRP and the SPWFY. Those forming the SPWFY rejected the notion that the left needed to join a bourgeoisie-dominated party like the PRP or that the left needed to have very close political and resource ties with the Soviet Union as the SWPP wanted. The SPWFY made gains but all political parties were banned in 1983 by the new military government.

14. Leadership: Ola Oni (formerly)

SOCIALIST REVOLUTIONARY YOUTH LEAGUE OF GHANA (SRYLOG: Ghana)

2. Republic of Ghana (12,205,000)

3. Date Established: c.1979

6. Membership: Few

7. Status: Defunct

9. Orientation: Socialist

13. History: SRYLOG was defunct by 1984.

SOCIALIST WORKERS' AND FARMERS' PARTY (SWAFP: Nigeria) later a.k.a. SWPP

SOCIALIST WORKING PEOPLE'S PARTY OF NIGERIA (SWPP: Nigeria)

2. Federal Republic of Nigeria (94,181,000)

3. Date Established: 1963

4. Organisational Type: Vanguard party

5. Organisational Nature: The SWPP has a Secretary General, Poliburo, Secretariat and Central Committee. Its last congress was its "first", refounding congress in 1978 which was actually its second congress (See "13. History" section). Under its previous name, the Socialist Workers' and Farmers' Party (SWAFP) was allied to numerous organisations: the Patrice Lumumba Institute of Political Science and Trade Unionism, the Nigerian Trade Union Congress (NTUC which was merged by a 1978 military government decree into the new Nigerian Labour Congress), the Nigerian Youth Congress, the United Youth Front of Nigeria, the Nigerian Peace Council, the Nigerian Committee of the Afro-Asian People's Solidarity Organisation (NC-AAPSO) as well as a host of Nigeria - (Soviet bloc country) Friendship Societies. The SWAFP had a youth wing, the Nigerian Young Communist Youth League. Following a period of intense internal upheaval in Nigeria which accompanied the civil war and the various military governments, the SWAFP decided in 1978 to restyle itself the SWPP in response to its relegislation and in preparation for the 1979 civilian elections. The party and its allies had, however, been severely disrupted by this period. Certainly the SWPP was able to maintain its influence in the trade union movement, the newly created Nigerian Labour Congress.

6. Membership: Estimates of SWAFP membership ranged from 1000 to 22,000. SWPP membership has been estimated at from under one thousand to several thousand.

7. Status: Illegal

8. Publications: SWAFP - The NTUC published the weekly _Advance_. The independent Council of Ten published the sympathetic _African Statesman_; SWPP published _New Horizon_.

9. Orientation: Soviet interpretation of Marxism-Leninism

10. Strategy: SWAFP and SWPP - electoral where possible in order to build the unity of progressive forces (especially trade unions) for the national democratic phase of the revolution; party building

11. Internal Affiliations: Nigerian Labour Congress

12. External Affiliations: Pro-Soviet parties

13. History: The SWPP was founded as the SWAPF in 1963. The first (and only) SWAPF congress was held in 1965. While all parties were banned by the military government in 1966, SWAPF was able to continue to function, although at a much reduced level of activity and in different ways. Following the military's decision to hold civilian elections for 1979, SWAPF changed its name to the SWPP in 1978. The SWPP had delegations from fourteen out of nineteen states at its "founding congress" (but which was really the party's second congress, counting the 1965 congress). The SWPP was not allowed to run as a party in the 1979 and 1983 elections by the civilian regime which itself was overthrown by the military. All parties were then banned.

14. Leadership: Secretary General - Dapo Fatogun; Politburo - Chaika Anozie, Wahab Goodluck, Hassan Sunmonu (President, NLC), Lasisi A. Osunde

SOMALI DEMOCRATIC ACTION FRONT (SODAF: Somalia) a.k.a. SSF

SOMALI DEMOCRATIC LIBERATION FRONT (SDLF: Somalia) a.k.a. DFLS

2. Somali Democratic Republic (4,450,000)

3. Date Established: Existed in 1980

6. Membership: Few

7. Status: Illegal

8. Publications: The SDLF has access to the Ethiopian-based Radio Halgen (Struggle, previously known as Radio Kulmis).

9. Orientation: Soviet Interpretation of Marxism-Leninism

10. Strategy: Revolution (armed struggle) to overthrow the SRSP government; coalitions

11. Internal Affiliations: The SDLF and the SWP were junior coalition partners with the SSF in the SFSS from 1981 to 1983 when the SSF tried to dismember and absorb the other two. The cooperation of the SDLF and the SFLS continued past their withdrawal from the DFSS.

12. External Affiliations: Ethiopian Derg

13. History: The SDLF was formed by the former Chairman of the Ideological Bureau of the SRSP's Central Committee, Abderahman Aydeed Ahmed, following the split between the Soviet Union and Barre's SRSP. Following the unsuccessful DFSS coalition, the SDLF and the SWP continued to cooperate during a period of reorganisation, but Aydeed defected to the DFSS/SSF.

14. Leadership: Abdullahi Abdirahman "Enlay"; Ahmed Baydhabo

SOMALI DEMOCRATIC SALVATION FRONT (SDSF: Somalia) a.k.a. DFSS

SOMALI REVOLUTIONARY SOCIALIST PARTY (SRSP: Somalia)

2. Somali Democratic Republic (4,450,000)

3. Date Established: July 1, 1976

4. Organisational Type: Vanguard party

5. Organisational Nature: The SRSP has been led by a Secretary General, Politburo and Central Committee (fifty-one members, sixteen bureaux).

7. Status: Ruling, sole legal party

8. Publications: Government newspapers - October Star (daily) published as Xiddigta Oktobar (Somali) and Najmat Oktobar (Arabic), Heegan (Vigilance, English weekly; government radio and television

9. Orientation: Eclectic socialism and social democracy (Soviet interpretation of Marxism-Leninism 1976-1977)

10. Strategy: Electoral; regime maintenance

12. External Affiliations: USA; Inter-African Socialist Organisation

13. History: Major-General Mohamed Siad Barre overthrew the elected government of President Abdira-shid Ali Shermarke (which had been moving to the right) on 21 October 1969. Barre created the Supreme Revolutionary Council (SRC) which ruled Somalia until the SRSP was created at its first congress (28 June - 1 July 1976) as a Marxist-Leninist vanguard party of the Soviet model. While Soviet Marxism-Leninism had grown in influence during the SRC (1969-1976) and the early SRSP (1976-1977) periods, the abrupt 1977 switch of the Soviets from supporting Somalia to the new Ethiopian Derg caused Somalia to break from the Soviet model and to search for new allies. As US-Somalia ties deepened, the SRSP began to jettison Marxism-Leninism as inappropriate to the tastes of its new ally/sponsor. In 1981 the SRSP became a founding member of the social democratic Inter-African Socialist Organisation.

14. Leadership: Secretary General, President of the Politburo, Maj.-Gen. Mohamed Siad Barre (President of the Republic); Bureaux Chairman of the Central Committee - Brig.-Gen. Mohamed Sheikh Osman, Brig.-Gen Mohamed Ali Shire, Col. Abdulkadir Haji Mohamed, Col. Abdirazak Mohamoud Abubakr, Mohamed Abdi Dunkal, Adan Mohamed Ali, Ahmed Ashkir Botan, Warsame Abdullahi Ali, Hamsa Mohamed Gadaweyne, Mohamed Ali Warsame, Mohamed Jama Korey, Mohamed Mahmoud Warsame, Musa Nur Amin, Mohamed Ali Abdi, Abderrahman Hussein Abdi Beydani, Adan Hussein Haile

SOMALI SALVATION FRONT (SSF: Somalia) a.k.a. SOSAF, a.k.a. SODAF, a.k.a. DFSS/SSF

2. Somali Democratic Republic (4,450,000)

3. Date Established: 1976

4. Organisational Type: Mass party

5. Organisational Nature: The SSF had an armed wing.

6. Membership: Several thousand, mainly drawn from the north (especially from the Majerteen clan)

7. Status: Illegal

8. Publications: The SSF has had access to the Ethiopian Radio Halgen (Struggle, previously known as Radio Kulmis).

9. Orientation: Left nationalist elements; elements of regionalism, northern separatism and Majerteen clan dominance

10. Strategy: Armed struggle to overthrow Barre's SRSP

11. Internal Affiliations: The SSF dominated the DFSS coalition with the SWP and the SFLS between 1981 and 1983. When the SSF tried to dismember and absorb its junior partners, they left the coalition.

12. External Affiliations: Ethiopian Derg

13. History: From 1976 to 1979 the SSF was based in Rome and known as the Somali Democratic Action Front (SODAF or Sodaf). Following the SSF move to Ethiopia in 1979, they were able to start guerilla warfare against Barre's government in the north. Following the in-fighting which marked the end of the SSF coalition with the SWP and the SFLS in the DFSS, several hundred soldiers crossed over to the Barre regime and the DFSS effectively became the DFSS/SSF.

14. Leadership: Col. Abdullahi Yusef Ahmed

SOMALI WORKERS' PARTY (SWP: Somalia)

See also, DFSS

2. Somali Democratic Republic (4,450,000)

3. Date Established: Existed in 1980

4. Organisational Type: Vanguard party

6. Membership: Few

7. Status: Illegal

8. Publications: The SWP had access to the Ethiopian-based Radio Halgen (Struggle), previously Radio Kulmis.

9. Orientation: Soviet interpretation of Marxism-Leninism

10. Strategy: Revolution (armed struggle) against the SRSP government, coalitions

11. Internal Affiliations: The SWP and the SFLS were junior coalition partners with the SSF in the DFSS from 1981 to 1983 when the SSF tried to dismember and absorb the other two. The cooperation of the SWP and the SFLS continued past their withdrawal from the DFSS.

12. External Affiliations: Soviet-allied parties, especially that of South Yemen

13. History: Based in South Yemen, the SWP and the SFLS (both were Marxist) combined with the SSF in the DFSS coalition from 1981 to 1983 in order to gain a partner with access to territory and people. The northern based and Majerteen clan-dominated SSF attempted to dissolve the SWP and the SFLS in 1983. South Yemen, Syria and the Soviet Union influenced the SSF to release from jail SWP and SFLS members. The SWP and SFLS, having no confidence in the DFSS coalition, went their own way.

14. Leadership: Hussein <u>Said</u> Jama (former Vice-Chairman of the DFSS), Jama Salah, Yassin Mohamed Mire.

SOSAF (Somalia) SSF

SOUFFLES (Whispers-Morocco)

2. Kingdom of Morocco (23,207,000)

3. Date Established: Existed in 1973

7. Status: Illegal; both clandestine and in exile

8. Publications: <u>Souffles</u> (Whispers: irregular)

9. Orientation: Maoist interpretation of Marxism-Leninism

10. Strategy: Revolution, refuses to be co-opted, youth organising

11. Internal Affiliations: Critical of all other Moroccan parties

12. External Affiliations: Pro-China

13. History: SOUFFLES were founded by a former PCM leader, Abraham Serfaty (born c. 1927 of Jewish parents). Serfaty was a mining engineer, former head of the Moroccan Phosphates Office technical department. SOUFFLES focused its organising efforts on youth in the universities colleges and high schools.

14. Leadership: Abraham Serfaty (**SOUFFLES** editor); Abd-al-Latif-Laabi (**SOUFFLES** editor and high school teacher); both were arrested on January 27, 1973.

SOUTH AFRICAN COMMUNIST PARTY (SACP: South Africa) a.k.a. CPSA

2. Republic of South Africa (34,577,000)

3. Date Established: 1921

4. Organisational Type: Vanguard party

5. Organisational Nature: Democratic centralism, Leninist pro-Soviet party model. The on-going executive consisted of the Secretary General, the Politburo, the Secretariat and the Central Committee.

6. Membership: Several hundred to several thousand

7. Status: Illegal

8. Publications: African Communist (quarterly journal, f.1959), Inkululeko ("Freedom" - underground newspaper, f. 1971)

9. Orientation: Soviet interpretation of Marxism-Leninism

10. Strategy: Revolution - alliance with the ANC to complete the victory of the national democratic revolution (thereby ending apartheid) through armed struggle, mass mobilisation and organisation of the working class

(especially party building), and then moving to socialist transformation.)

11. Internal Affiliations: The SACP is a junior partner in the alliance with ANC. SACP members also belong to the ANC.

12. External Affiliations: Pro-Soviet parties

13. History: The SACP was formed in 1921 as the CPSA by Anglophone whites in the aftermath of the Bolshevik Revolution. By the early 1930s membership reflected South Africa's ethnic composition. By the late 1940s the party had achieved some measure of influence amongst the working class, trade unions, the South African Indian Congress, the African National Congress and the very few Africans who were, at that time, allowed to vote. However, the election of the National Party, which had links with fascism, in 1948 meant the systemisation and deepening of racism and repression. This included attacks on the CPSA which was banned in 1950 under the Suppression of Communism Act. The party reorganised itself at a secret meeting in 1953 as the SACP and participated clandestinely in a number of campaigns, always supporting the ANC. Following the banning of the ANC in 1960, the SACP joined the ANC in establishing the armed wing of the ANC, MK. Following the arrest of much of the top leadership of the ANC and SACP in 1963, much of the SACP joined ANC leaders in exile. The SACP and ANC experiences from 1963 onwards have been similar. The SACP focussed on rebuilding in exile the party and the ANC, expanding its foreign contacts. The 1973 strikes and the 1976 Soweto uprising, especially, enabled the SACP to manifest itself again within South Africa and to launch a successful recruiting drive. Subsequent events have reinforced these trends.

14. Leadership: Chairman - John B. Marks (d.1972), Dr. Yusef M. Dadoo (1972-September 1983 d.), General Secretary - Moses Mabhida (1983-March 1986 d.), General Secretary - Joe Slovo (1986 onwards), Deputy General Secretary - Dan Tloome

SOUTH AFRICAN YOUTH REVOLUTIONARY COUNCIL (SAYRC) a.k.a. AYRC

2. Republic of South Africa (34,577,000)

3. Date Established: July 1979

4. Organisational Nature: Mass party

6. Membership: Few - youth and former senior secondary students

7. Status: Illegal, possibly defunct

9. Orientation: Left nationalist, anti-apartheid

10. Strategy: Revolution

12. External Affiliations: Nigerian government funding in 1981

13. History: The SAYRC (a.k.a. AYRC) was formed in July 1979 by non-ANC, non-PAC elements of the Soweto Student Representative Council (SSRC) who were forced into exile in the aftermath of the 1976 Soweto uprising and the 1977 banning of the SSRC by the apartheid regime. After fund-raising efforts for some two years in the USA, Western Europe and West Africa for their exile organisation, in July 1979 the organisation changed its president from Tsietsi Mashinini to Khotso Seatlhoho, and its name from SSRC to SAYRC. Based in Nigeria the SAYRC attempted to infiltrate its members back into South Africa to raise an army. In 1981 the apartheid regime reported that it had caught SAYRC president (Seatlhoho) and another member, Mary Loate, sentencing them to ten and five years respectively. SAYRC now appears to be defunct.

14. Leadership: President - Khotso Seatlhoho

STRONG FLAME (SF: Tunisia) a.k.a. ECH-CHOOLA-EL-WATAD (a.k.a. FDP: Flame Democratic Patriots)

2. Republic of Tunisia (7,224,000)

3. Date Established: Existed in 1981

6. Membership: Students, youth

7. Status: Illegal

9. Orientation: Marxism-Leninism

10. Strategy: Revolution

11. Internal Affiliations: Ech-Chaab-clandestin was supposedly an armed wing infiltrated by police agents.

SUDAN AFRICAN CONGRESS (SAC: Sudan)

2. Republic of Sudan (23,089,000)

3. Date Established: Existed in 1985

4. Organisational Type: Mass party

6. Membership: Mainly Southern

7. Status: Legal

9. Orientation: Left nationalism

10. Strategy: Electoral

11. Internal Affiliations: The SAC maintained contact with the SPLM.

13. History: The SAC won two seats in the 1986 elections.

14. Leadership: Kunijwok Gwado Ayoker,Lam Akol, Peter Nyok (all three are lecturers at Khartoum university).

SUDAN PEOPLE'S LIBERATION MOVEMENT (SPLM: Sudan)

2. Republic of Sudan (23,089,000)

3. Date Established: May-June 1983

4. Organisational Type: National liberation movement

5. Organisational Nature: The executive of the SPLM consisted of the National Committee, the Central Committee, the Political Committee (or Bureau) and the Executive Committee (five members) as well as a cabinet-like structure of seven working committees. The Sudan People's Liberation Army (SPLA) was the armed forces of the SPLM.

6. Membership: Thousands, mainly Southerners; (the SPLA had some 10,000 troops).

7. Status: Illegal

8. Publications: Radio SPLA

9. Orientation: Socialism, Sudanese Marxism

10. Strategy: Revolution to liberate and unify the Sudanese peoples; protracted people's war

12. External Affiliations: Libya, Ethiopia and South Yemen have provided aid to the SPLM.

13. History: Founded in 1983 following yet another series of betrayals of Southern interests by yet another Northern elite regime, the SPLM founded the SPLA. Using the national liberation strategy of combining political mobilisation and armed struggle, the SPLM has gained much popular support and territory in the south.

14. Leadership: Colonel/Doctor John Garang de Mabior, Chairman of the SPLM Provisional Executive Committee (PEC) and Commander-in-Chief of the SPLA; Joseph Oduho, PEC member and Chairman of the Political and Foreign Affairs Committee; Martin Majier, PEC member and Chairman of the People's Justice and Administration Committee; Lt. Col. Kerubino Kwanyin, PEC member; Lt. Col. William Nyon, PEC member

SUDANESE COMMUNIST PARTY (SCP - Al-Hizb al-Shuyu'i al-Sudani: HSS - Sudan)

2. Republic of Sudan (23,089,000)

3. Date Established: 1944

4. Organisation Type: Vanguard party

5. Organisational Nature: The SCP has been led by the Secretary General, the Politburo (six members), the Secretariat (seven members) and the Central Committee (twelve members). As a frequently forced clandestine organisation, the SCP has held only four congresses but has found the principle of democratic centralism to be of especial importance during period of repression.

6. Membership: Several thousand

7. Status: Legal (presently)

8. Publications: Izz el Din Ali Amer (daily) (previously al-Maydan - Forum; Advance

9. Orientation: Soviet interpretation of Marxism-Leninism

10. Strategy: Revolution during periods of illegality; electoral at other times; at all times promoting the national democratic phase of the revolution and unity with other progressive forces; party-building

11. Internal Affiliations: Sudan Workers' Trade Union Federation, Sudanese Youth Union, Democratic Federation of Sudanese Students, Sudanese Defenders of Peace and Democracy, Federation of Farmers' Unions

12. External Affiliations: Pro-Soviet parties

13. History: Marxist study groups established in 1944 amongst Sudanese students in Cairo were the roots of the SCP. These combined with proletarians to found formally the Sudanese Movement for National Liberation (SMNL) in 1946, the name SCP being adopted at its Third (1956) Congress. 'Abd al-Khaliq Mahjub was the first leader until he was executed in 1971 by President Nimeri after the failure of the three-day communist government to overthrow Nimeri. Party congresses were held in 1950, 1951, 1956 and 1967 (Fourth Congress). Party conferences were held in 1949, 1966 and 1970. The SCP has alternated between having to operate underground and being publically recognised as the popular force that it is. The SCP operated clandestinely from 1944-1956, 1958-1964, part of 1965 and 1971-1985. During the times when it was not banned, the SCP was successful in having a number of its members elected to various levels of government as well as exercising considerable influence over government policy, especially during the 1969-71 period of Nimeri's regime. When Nimeri began to swing considerably to the right, elements of the SCP in the Sudanese army led by Major Hashim al-Ata temporarily overthrew Nimeri when he left the country on 19 July 1971. The three-day communist government was in turn overthrown when Nimeri returned and unleashed a violent wave of purges and executions. By the time Nimeri was overthrown on 6 April 1985, the

SCP had rebuilt a substantial portion of its organisation (although membership was not up to its 1971 peak of 10,000). In the April 1986 elections the SCP won three of the two hundred and sixty-four seats in which elections were possible.

14. Leadership: Secretary General - Muhammed Ibrihim Nugud Mansur; Politburo - Muhammed Ibrihim Nugud Mansur, Ali al-Tijani al-Tayyib Babikar, Dr. Izz-al Din Ali Amir, Sulayman Hamid, Al-Gazuli (Jizuli), Said Uthman, Muhammed Ahmad Sulayman (Suleiman)

SUDANESE MOVEMENT OF REVOLUTIONARY COMMITEES (SMRC)

2. Republic of Sudan (23,089,000)

3. Date Established: May 1985

4. Organisational Type: Mass party

5. Organisational Nature: The SMRC consisted of committees.

7. Status: Legal

9. Orientation: Libyan eclectic socialism

10. Strategy: Electoral, revolution prior fo 1985

12. External Affiliations: Libya

13. History: Revolutionary Committees were funded and partly led by Libyans prior to Nimeri's 1985 overthrow. The SMRC created people's committees to win seats in the 1986 elections.

14. Leadership: Abdullah Zakariya

SUDANESE PEOPLE'S SOCIALIST FRONT (SPSF: Sudan)

2. Republic of Sudan (23,089,000)

3. Date Established: 1984 (middle)

7. Status: Legal

9. Orientation: Socialist

10. Strategy: Electoral

12. External Affiliation: Libya

SUDANESE SOCIALIST UNION (SSU - al-Ittihad al-Ishtiraki al-Sudani: IIS: Sudan)

2. Republic of Sudan (23,089,000)

3. Date Established: October 1972 (defunct April 1985)

4. Organisational Type: Mass party

5. Organisational Nature: Similar to that of the Arab Socialist Union of Egypt

7. Status: Illegal (ruling party 1972-1985)

9. Orientation: Right-wing social democracy

10. Strategy: 1972-1985 - regime maintenance

12. External Affiliations: The SSU was a founding member of the Inter-African Socialist Organisation.

13. History: Col. Gaafar Muhammed Nimeri overthrew the elected government on 25 May 1969 and outlawed all political parties except the SCP. When Nimeri introduced more and more right-wing measures, elements of SCP tried to overthrow him in July 1971. In an attempt to establish a political base, Nimeri created the SSU in 1972, moving continually to the right until his overthrow on 6 April 1985 by a Transitional Military Government which banned the SSU.

14. Leadership: Field Marshal Gaafar Muhammed Nimeri, SSU President (President of the Republic); Mohamed Abdel Qader Omer, First Secretary

SUPREME REVOLUTIONARY COUNCIL (SRC: Somalia)

See, SRSP

SWAPO OF NAMIBIA (SWAPO-South West African People's Organisation of Namibia: Namibia)

2. Namibia (1,202,000) (apartheid of South African occupation)

3. Date Established: 1957

4. Organisational Type: National liberation movement

5. Organisational Nature: President, Secretary General, Vice President, Executive Committee (17 members), Central Committee (35 members); there is also a SWAPO army: PLAN-People's Liberation Army of Namibia.

6. Membership: Tens of thousands

7. Status: Persecuted by the apartheid South African regime; an 'internal wing' of SWAPO has been allowed some legal status by the occupation forces.

8. Publications: _Namibia News_ (1968-76), _Namibia_ (1977) Namibia Today (1977-)

9. Orientation: Left nationalist as well as elements of Christian socialism and Marxism

10. Strategy: National liberation struggle - military action against the forces of the occupation; party building; negotiations

11. Internal Affiliations: SWAPO's 1969 Consultative Congress established the Women's Council, the Youth League and the Elders' Council. The National Union of Namibian Workers (NUNW, draft constitution 1977) was affiliated to SWAPO, paralleling in some ways the relationship between the ANC of South Africa and the South African Congress of Trade Unions (SACTU).

12. External Affiliations: SWAPO and the ANC of South Africa have had a cooperative relationship since SWAPO's founding. SWAPO has received considerable assistance from the East bloc countries, especially in military supplies, but the Organisation of African Unity, as well as a number of African countries in their own right, and Western governments and non-government organisations have also provided significant aid.

13. History: SWAPO grew out of several organisations active in the 1950s such as the S.W.A. Student Body (SWASB founded in South Africa during 1952), the S.W.A. Progressive Association (SWAPA founded in 1955) and bodies of ethnically based traditional leaders such as the Council of Chiefs. The Ovamboland People's Congress (OPC), founded in 1957 by (Herman) Toivo ja Toivo and others, emerged as the core organisation. In 1958 the OPC became OPO, the Ovamboland People's Organisation. In April 1959 Sam Nujoma and Toivo ja Toivo initiated the labour organising strategy of what became SWAPO. In May 1959 OPO cooperated with what were ethnically based organisations (such as the Herero-based Council of Chiefs) to create a nationalist party of the mass party type, the South West Africa National Union (SWANU). Following the inability of SWANU to deal with South African occupation and its crackdown on the ANC and PAC in South Africa, SWAPO was created on 19 April 1960 as a national liberation movement by OPO. Following a 1962 debate SWAPO decided to adopt armed struggle as one of its strategies. SWAPO's PLAN had its first military engagement with occupation forces on 26 August 1966. The Tanga (Tanzania) Consultative Congress (26 December 1969 - 2 January 1970) created the youth, women's and elders' wings of the liberation movement. SWAPO's Central Committee approved the revised constitution and Political Programme at its 28 July - 1 August 1976 meeting in Lusaka. SWAPO has since pursued the policies of politically consolidating internal support by organising workers and others as well as encouraging ethnically based organisations to merge themselves in the new Namibian nationalist identity, manifested organisationally as SWAPO, as well as developing its diplomatic and military capabilities against the occupying power. Much of SWAPO's membership has been drawn from the churches.

14. Leadership: Sam Nujoma, President; Andimba Herman Toivo ja Toivo (political prisoner in South Africa 1968-1984) Secretary General; Pastor Hendrik Witbooi, Vice President; David Meroro, National Chairman; Lucas Pohamba, Finance Secretary; Peter Mueshihange, Foreign Affairs Secretary; Richard Kapelwa, Defense Secretary; Moses Ga'roeb, Administrative Secretary; Theo Ben Guriab, SWAPO Representative to the U.N., USA and Canada; Moses Tjiriange, Secretary for Legal Affairs; Moses Tjitendero, Central Committee member; Hidipo

Hamntenya, Secretary for Information and Publicity; Dimo Amambo, Commander of PLAN. Internal SWAPO leaders include: Daniel Rjongarero, Vice President; Frans Kambangula, Secretary for Transport; Frans Tijirimuje, Treasurer.

SWAZI LIBERATION MOVEMENT (SWALIMO: Swaziland)

2. Kingdom of Swaziland (774,000)

3. Date Established: 1978

7. Status: Illegal

9. Orientation: Elements of left nationalism

10. Strategy: Revolution to end the autocracy and achieve democracy

13. History: Founded in 1978, SWALIMO grew out of the Ngwane National Liberatory Congress (NNLC) which was banned in April 1973. Dr. A.P. Zwane, who had been leader of the NNLC, became the SWALIMO leader.

14. Leadership: Dr. Ambrose P. Zwame; Dumisa Dlami, Secretary General

TANGANIYIKA AFRICAN NATIONAL UNION (TANU: Tanzania)

See, CCM

TIGRE PEOPLE'S LIBERATION FRONT (TPLF-Ethiopia)

2. Socialist Ethiopia (35,210,000)

3. Date Established: 1975

4. Organisational Type: National liberation movement

6. Membership: Thousands amongst ethnic Tigrayans

7. Status: Illegal, civil war participant

9. Orientation: Marxism-Leninism

10. Strategy: Revolution towards a communist Ethiopia, with regional autonomy at least in the short term

11. Internal Affiliations: During the late 1970s and early-mid 1980s the TPLF and the EPLF cooperated politically and militarily. The TPLF has offered military aid to the Oromo Liberation Front (OLF) and the EPDM.

UGANDA PATRIOTIC MOVEMENT (UPM: Uganda)

See, NRM

UGANDA PEOPLE'S CONGRESS (UPC-Uganda)

2. Republic of Uganda (13,198,000)

3. Date Established: 1960

4. Organisational Type: Mass party

5. Organisational Nature: The UPC had a leader, Secretary General and a congress.

6. Membership: Defunct, formerly thousands

7. Status: Illegal, defunct

8. Publications: formerly <u>People</u> (weekly)

9. Orientation: Social democratic

10. Strategy: Electoral

12. External Affiliations: formerly CCM (TANU)

13. History: Formed in 1960, the UPC was the ruling party from independence (9 October 1962) until its overthrow by General Idi Amin on January 25, 1971 and following the 10-11 December 1980 elections (which followed Amin's overthrow on 11 April 1979) until the UPC's overthrow by Brig. Gen. B. Okello on 27 July 1985 (who in turn was overthrown by the NRA/NRM on 27 January 1986. During the UPC's first government, Uganda was declared a one-party state in December 1969 based on the Common Man's Charter. Following Obote's first overthrow, he reorganised the UPC in Tanzania.

UPC forces accompanied the Tanzanian army into Uganda in 1979, resulting in Amin's overthrow and the establishment of several transitional governments culminating in the December 1980 elections which returned to power the UPC. Unable to stabilise the situation, Obote's UPC government was again overthrown by the army.

14. Leadership: Dr. Milton Obote (Prime Minister/President) 1962-1971, 1980-1985), leader; Dr. Luwuliza Kirunda, Secretary General.

UMMA-MRANDA (UM-People's Party: Comoros)

2. Federal Islamic Republic of the Comoros (410,000)

3. Date Established: Existed in 1972

4. Organisational Type: Mass party

7. Status: Leading partner in the 1975 ruling coalition until its overthrow in 1978

9. Orientation: Maoist left nationalism

10. Strategy: Both electoral and coup strategies used.

11. Internal Affiliations: It was the leading partner in the National United Front.

13. History: The Umma-Mranda participated in the French-supervised elections of December, 1972 as part of its strategy to achieve national independence by electoral means. Following the unilateral declaration of independence by the Comoros Assembly on July 6, 1975, the Umma-Mranda was a leading force in the overthrow of the interim government of Ahmed Abdallah on August 3, 1975. As the leading partner in the National United Front government of Ali Soilih, himself the Umma-Mranda leader, a Maoist-style anti-feudal programme was put forward. This government was overthrown on May 12-13, 1978 by some fifty French-led mercenaries who re-installed Abdallah. Ali Soilih was killed on May 29.

14. Leadership: Ali Soilih (executed May 29, 1978) and Prince Said Ibrahim.

UMOJA WA KUPIGANIA DEMOKRASIA KENYA (UKENYA-UKENYA MOVEMENT FOR UNITY AND DEMOCRACY IN KENYA: KENYA), possibly a.k.a. MWAKENYA

UNDC (Comoros)

See also, URDC (Comoros)

UNION DEMOCRATIQUE CHRETIEN MALGACHE (UDECMA-KMTP: Malagasy Christian Democratic Union: Madagascar) a.k.a. RNM

2. Democratic Republic of Madagascar (9,490,000)

3. Date Established: 1976

7. Status: Constituent 'revolutionary association' of the ruling FNDR coalition

9. Orientation: left-wing Christian Democracy

10. Strategy: Electoral

11. Internal Affiliations: UDECMA was associated with the AKRM, AREMA, MFM/MPP, MONIMA and VSM as constituent parts of the FNDR.

13. History: Founded in 1976, the following year UDECMA won two seats in the National Assembly, but lost them in the 1983 elections.

14. Leadership: Solo Norbert Andriamorasata

UNION DEMOCRATIQUE DU PEUPLE MALIEN (UDPM-Mali People's Democratic Union: Mali)

2. Republic of Mali (8,116,000)

3. Date Established: March 30, 1979

4. Organisational Type: Loosely-organised mass party reflecting a personalist leadership

5. Organisational Nature: Self-declared democratic centralism. The party structure consists of a top-down hierarchy. The nineteen member Central Executive

Bureau, led by the Secretary-General, establishes policies which are then articulated through the 137 member National Council to the UDPM Congress and to the administration of the country.

7. Status: One-party state; only legal party

8. Publications: The UDPM publishes a daily: L'Essor-La Voix du Peuple (circulation 40,000)

9. Orientation: Ambiguous right-wing left nationalist.

10. Strategy: The UDPM has adopted a strategy of maintaining power by election backed by military support, and an economic strategy of a mixed economy.

11. Internal Affiliations: There are women's and youth auxiliaries. The Union nationale des femmes du Mali (National Union of Malian Women) claimed 350,000 members. Mme. Soro Satouko was the President. The Malian Youth Union (Union des jeunes du Mali) was led by its Secretary-General, Mahamadou Baba Diallo.

12. External Affiliations: Mali, under Traore's UDPM, has moved to increase its ties with France, the United States, Britain and the rest of the West, thus downgrading Mali's relations with the Soviet Bloc and China that existed under the previous socialist regime of Keita.

13. History: Following elections, President Modibo Keita, leader of the Soudanese Union Party, brought Mali to independence from France on June 20, 1960. Domestically he encouraged the growth of socialist policies. Externally he diversified Malian foreign policy by establishing working relationships with the Soviet Bloc and China, as well as promoting pan-Africanism. He and his party were overthrown in a military putsch on November 1968. After having established the Military Committee of National Liberation (CMLM-Comite Militaire de Liberation Nationale) and having eliminated his rivals, Lt. Col. (now general) Moussa Traore moved to civilianise his regime. He created his party, the UDPM, on March 30, 1979. Since his initial election on June 19, 1979, General Traore was reelected for another five-year term as President of Mali on June 9, 1985. Mali remains a one-party state under the UDPM.

14. Leadership: UDPM Secretary-General and Malian President - General Moussa Traore

UNION DEMOCRATIQUE SENEGALAIS-RENOUVELLEMENT (UDS-R: Senegalese Democratic Union-Revival: Senegal)

2. Republic of Senegal (6,710,000)

3. Date Established: February 1985

4. Organisational Type: Mass party

7. Status: Legal

9. Orientation: Left nationalist

10. Strategy: Electoral

13. History: The UDS-R was founded as a result of the expulsion of its founder, Mamadou Fall (a trade union leader), from the PDS party and legislative caucus.

14. Leadership: Mamadou Fall

UNION DES COMMUNISTES BURKINABE (UCB-Burkinabe Communist Union: Burkina Faso)

2. Republic of Burkina Faso (8,130,000)

3. Date Established: Existed in 1983

7. Status: Part of the CNR government

9. Orientation: Marxism-Leninism

10. Strategy: Building a revolutionary socialist state, party building

11. Internal Affiliations: The UCB, ULC, GC, ROC and LIPAD were part of Sankara's CNR government.

13. History: Pierre Ouedraogo led the UCB in the CNR government.

14. Leadership: Pierre Quedraogo

UNION DES FORCES PROGRESSISTES DU CONGO-KINSHASA (UFPCK-Union of Progressive Forces of Congo - Kinshasa: UPFCK: Zaire)

2. Republic of Zaire (33,927,000)

3. Date Established: Existed in 1982

6. Membership: Few

7. Status: Illegal

9. Orientation: Left nationalist (Lumumbist)

10. Strategy: Revolution

11. Internal Affiliations: The UFPCK had some relations with the PRP.

13. History: The UFPCK appears to have been based in Belgium.

UNION DES KOMORIENS (Unikom - Union of Comorans: Comoros)

See also, FNUK, CNSP, FNUK-UNIKOM

2. Federal Islamic Republic of the Comoros (410,000)

3. Date Established: Existed in 1981

7. Status: Exiled group

11. Internal Affiliations: FNUK, CNSP.

13. History: Unikom joined with the FNUK in mid-1981 to form FNUK-Unikom, based in Paris. This coalition was joined on October 3, 1981 by the CNSP.

UNION DES LUTTES COMMUNISTES (ULC-Union for Communist Struggle: Burkina Faso)

2. Republic of Burkina Faso (8,130,000)

3. Date Established: 1978

7. Status: Part of the ruling CNR government

9. Orientation: Pro-China Marxism-Leninism

10. Strategy: Building revolutionary socialist regime, party building

11. Internal Affiliations: The ULC, LIPAD, GC, UCB and the ROC combined to support Sankara's CNR government.

13. History: The ULC was part of the ruling CNR. External affairs minister Basile Guissou was a ULC leader.

14. Leadership: Basile Laetare Guissou

UNION DES PEUPLES DE CAMEROUN (UPC-Cameroon People's Union: Cameroon)

2. Republic of Cameroon (9,852,000)

3. Date Established: 1948

4. Organisational Type: Varied from mass party to national liberation movement

6. Membership: possibly several thousand

7. Status: Illegal opposition in Cameroon and in exile

8. Publications: The Provisional Committee faction published Le Communiste starting in February 1966 as well as other documentation.

9. Orientation: Provisional Committee faction of the UPC-Maoist Marxism Leninism; Revolutionary Committee - Pro-Soviet Marxism-Leninism

10. Strategy: Revolutionary party building, armed struggle

11. Internal Affiliations: The Provisional Committee of the UPC was associated with the Democratic Youth of Cameroon.

12. External Affiliations: UPC Provisional Committee was affiliated with pro-Maoist/China parties and groups, including Belgium's Communist Youth Movement and the then pre-Mao Albanian Working Youth; UPC Revolutionary Committee was affiliated with the Soviet Union and its

allied parties and groups, especially the French Communist Party.

13. History: Formed in 1948, the UPC was banned in 1955 and forced underground and into exile. Both the Soviet Union and China have materially supported the UPC. However, the UPC fragmented during the 1960s following the murder of the effective UPC leader, Felix Moumie, which reflected the increased aid by France to bolster the Ahidjo regime and coincided with the Sino-Soviet split. The pro-Soviet UPC members formed the Revolutionary Committee of the UPC which had a special relationship with the pro-Soviet French Communist Party. The pro-Maoist UPC members created the Provisional Committee of the UPC. In 1964 Osende Afana was elected Secretary General of the Provisionals. In May 1965 at their first Plenary Session, the Provisionals decided to base their strategy and analysis of Cameroon on Maoist Marxism-Leninism. This included a very significant decision to attempt the replication of the Chinese Communist Party's route to power, including the creation of liberated base areas. Osende Afana led the first armed detachment of Provisionals into Cameroon in September 1965 but this tactic, like that of Che's _foco_ in Bolivia, failed: the armed group was broken up and Afana was killed by Ahidjo's forces in March 1966. The Provisionals then established their own paper, _Le Communiste_, thus entering in a more reflective period trying to understand what had gone wrong and what was to be done. Their conclusion was that the mistake of initiating armed struggle before the creation of a vanguard party with broad popular support had been made. Indeed ZAPU was shortly to make a similar mistake in Ian Smith's Rhodesia (Zimbabwe). The Provisionals have attempted to rectify this error.

14. Leadership: Felix Moumie (killed 1960); Osende Afana (Secretary General, Provisionals 1964-1966); Francois Fosso, (Secretary, Provisionals); William Nguembus, Vice President of the Provisional's Democratic Youth of Cameroon; Robert Ekwalla (Secretary, Provisionals): 1986 Secretary General - Woungly Massaga.

UNION FOR A DEMOCRATIC REPUBLIC IN THE COMOROS (URDC - Comoros/also known as the UNDC - the National Union for Democracy in the Comoros)

2. Federal Islamic Republic of the Comoros (410,000)

3. Date Established: Existed in 1985

7. Status; Exile group

14. Leadership: Mouzaoir Abdallah

UNION NATIONALE DES ETUDIANTS MAROCAINS (UNEM-National Union of Moroccan Students)

2. Kingdom of Morocco (23,207,000)

3. Date Established: Existed in 1982

7. Status: Legal but persecuted

9. Orientation: 23 Mars faction - Marxist; Groupe des Martyres faction - Marxist

13. History: In February 1982, three of the five members of the executive committee of UNEM belonged to the above Marxist factions. The students in Rabat organised a strike to win the release of their leaders who were critical of the government.

UNION NATIONALE DES FORCES POPULAIRES (UNFP-National Unity of Popular Forces: Morocco)

2. Kingdom of Morocco (23,207,000)

3. Date Established: 1959

4. Organisational Type: Mass party

5. Organisational Nature: There was a National Administrative Committee supervising five permanent committees.

7. Status: Legal

9. Orientation: Left nationalism

10. Strategy: Boycotted the 1977 and 1984 national chamber elections as well as the June 1983 municipal elections.

13. History: While the UNFP was an important force during the 1960s and early 1970s, since then it has suffered a considerable decline. At its founding in 1959 the UNFP was able to draw together dissident Istiqlal members and left-wing trade unionists, nationalists and former resistance members. In 1965 Mehdi Ben Barka, the leader, was 'disappeared' in France, apparently by Moroccan secret police. Moreover the UNDP split in 1972. The Politburo and Secretariat General were expelled by the National Administrative Committee. The former became the UNFP-Rabat and the latter the USFP which has since become the dominant left legal opposition. The dominant UNFP faction (National Administrative Committee) was known for a time as the UNFP-Casablanca and later just the UNFP. The UNFP boycotted the 1977, 1983 and 1984 elections.

14. Leadership: Moulay Abdullah Ibrahim

UNION NATIONALE POUR L'INDEPENDENCE ET LA REVOLUTION (UNIR-National Union for Independence and Revolution: Chad)

2. Republic of Chad (5,308,000)

3. Date Established: June 22, 1984

4. Organisational Type: National liberation movement

5. Organisational Nature: UNIR was led by a fourteen-member Executive Bureau drawn from the Central Committee.

7. Status: Ruling and only legal party

9. Orientation: Left nationalist

10. Strategy: Negotiations and civil war.

11. Internal Affiliations: Habre's Frolinat-FAN, the Armed Forces of the North, the National Democratic Popular Assembly, the Assembly for Unity and Democracy in Chad, the Democratic Movement of Chad, Abba Siddick's wing of Original Frolinat and sections of the Popular Party of Chad-Democratic Assembly created UNIR.

13. History: The founding congress of UNIR was held on June 22, 1984. This followed the capture of the

capital, N'Djamena, on June 7, 1982 by Habre's Frolinat-FAN. UNIR was the only legal party of Habre's regime.

14. Leadership: President of the Republic and UNIR Chairman, Hissein Habre; UNIR Executive Secretary, Captain Gouara Lassou.

UNION OF DEMOCRATIC FORCES (UDF-Sudan: Sudan)

See also, PNF

2. Republic of Sudan (23,089,000)

3. Date Established: Existed in 1985

4. Organisational Type: Mass party

6. Membership: Mainly northern

7. Status: Legal

9. Orientation: Left nationalist elements

10. Strategy: Existed in 1985

11. Internal Affiliations: The UDF belonged to the PNF in order to contest the 1986 elections.

UNION OF ETHIOPIAN MARXIST-LENINIST ORGANISATIONS (UEMLO: Ethiopia)

See also, RF/SEDED; LL/WA; MEISON; EORS/I.Ch.A.T.; MLRO/Ma.Le.Ri.De.

2. Socialist Ethiopia (35,210,000)

3. Date Established: February 1977

4. Organisational Nature: Coalition

7. Status: Legal but later dissolved

9. Orientation: Marxism-Leninism

10. Strategy: Create a unified vanguard party for PMAC.

11. Internal Affiliations: UEMLO was created by RF/SEDED, LL/WA, MEISON, EORS/I.Ch.A.T., MLRO/MA.Le.Ri.De.

13. History: Formed in February 1977, the five constituent organisations failed to create a vanguard party. MEISON and LL had left UEMLO by June 1978. UEMLO was superceded by PMAC's COPWE in 1979 and the WPE in 1984.

UNION POUR LA DEMOCRATIE POPULAIRE (UDP-Democratic People's Union: Senegal)

See also, ADS

2. Republic of Senegal (6,710,000)

3. Date Established: 1981 (registered)

4. Organisational Type: Mass party

6. Membership: few

7. Status: Legal party

9. Orientation: Pro-Albanian Maoist Marxism-Leninism

10. Strategy: Party building, joined the ADS as part of the creation of a national democratic revolutionary organisation to promote the transition to socialism skipping over the 'dictatorship of the proletariat' phase.

11. Internal Affiliations: Allied with the LD-MPT, the MRDN, the OST and the PDS in the ADS alliance.

12. External Affiliations: Pro-Albanian

13. History: The UPD was created by a number of former And-Jef/MRDN members who took the Hoxha/Albanian side of the 1970s debate in contradiction to the vast majority of the And-Jef/MRDN who sided with Mao/China. While the UDP is a co-member of the ADS alliance, established in 1985, with the MRDN, this has not stopped the UDP from strenuously debating the MRDN. The UDP has also boycotted PS government-controlled elections.

14. Leadership: Hamedine Racine Guisse

UNION POUR LE PROGRES NATIONAL UNION POUR LE PROGRES NATIONAL (UPRONA - Union for National Progress: Burundi)

2. Republic of Burundi (4,822,000)

3. Date Established: 1958

4. Organisational Type: Mass party with personalist leadership.

5. Organisational Nature: According to the 1979 party constitution, UPRONA has a President, a Central Committee, provincial committees, commune committees, zone or quarter committees and finally, at the base, local committees. The Congress is the supreme decision-making body for UPRONA.

6. Membership Number: One million (claimed in 1980)

7. Status: Ruling party in one-party state.

8. Publications: Through its control of the government, UPRONA influences the three newspapers, the news agency and the radio station.

9. Orientation: Left Nationalist elements

10. Strategy: Electoral in a one-party state. Regime maintenance including massacres of the Hutu commoner majority by the nobility-dominated Tutsi military in 1988.

11. Internal Affiliations: UPRONA has three auxiliary organizations: (a) Union de la Jeunesse Revolutionnaire burundaise (UJRB-Burundi Union of Revolutionary Youth), (b) Union des Femmes burundaises (UFB-Burundi Union of Women) and (c) Union des Travailleurs du Burundi (UTB-Burundi Union of Workers).

12. External Affiliations: At the end of the 1985 visit to Burundi by Libya's leader, Colonel Qadhafi, Burundi and Libya declared the need to form a "World Front of progressive states".

13. History: Formed in 1958 under the original name of Union et Progres National, its victory in the pre-independence 1961 elections encouraged many of the other twenty-three parties to join UPRONA. After inde-

pendence in 1962, UPRONA has served as the sole legal political party for the monarchy, the first republic of Captain Micombero (1966-1976) and the second republic of Colonel Bagaza (1976 to the present). Bagaza initially dissolved the party but reconstituted UPRONA in December 1979 at its first congress. The second congress was held in July 1984. The party was unable to prevent the Tutsi-dominated army from conducting a number of massacres against the Hutu in late 1988.

14. Leadership: UPRONA (and Burundi) President: Colonel Jean-Baptiste Bagaza; UPRONA Secretary-General: Emile Mworoho

UNION PROGRESSISTE SENEGALAISE (UPS-Senegalese Progressive Union: Senegal)

See also PS

UNION SOCIALISTE DES FORCES POPULARIES (USFP-Socialist Union Popular Forces: Morocco)

2. Kingdom of Morocco (23,207,000)

3. Date Established: September 1974

4. Organisational Type: Mass party

6. Membership: 100,000 names

7. Status: Legal party

8. Publications: <u>Al-Moharrir</u> (Arabic, banned in 1982), <u>Liberation</u> (French, banned in 1982)

9. Orientation: Socialism, social democracy

10. Strategy: Electoral, especially after 1976, nationalisation of major industry. One faction close to OR has rejected elections as being only a mechanism for the king to co-opt the left.

11. Internal Affiliations: Some USFP elements were in sympathy with the OR's revolutionary strategy. The USFP is allied with the CDT (Confederation Democratique

des Travilleurs-Democratic Confederation of Workers). The PPS has sought to cooperate with the USFP.

12. External Affiliations: The Muhammed Basri faction was based in Libya.

13. History: The USFP was formed in September 1974 by the former UNFP-Rabat faction, following the 1972 split in UNFP. Participating in the 1977 national chamber elections, the USFP won sixteen seats. This was increased in the 1984 elections to thirty-five directly elected (35/206) but only one 'indirectly elected' (1/100). Even under the monarchial-controlled electoral system, the USFP emerged as the third largest popularly-elected party and the most important left-legal party in Morocco. However, prior to those elections in May 1983 one faction broke off to join with a dissident PPS members to create the OADP.

14. Leadership: Abderrahim Bouabid, First Secretary; Mohammed El-Lyazghi and Mohammed Lahbali (both are related to Bouabid), all three were members of the Political Bureau.

UNITED DEMOCRATIC FRONT (UDF: South Africa)

2. Republic of South Africa (34,577,000)

3. Date Organised: May 1983

4. Organisational Type: Coalition of organisations

6. Membership: Seven hundred community, religious and labour organisations with a total of hundreds of thousands of members

7. Status: Restricted (semi-illegal)

9. Orientation: Left nationalism

10. Strategy: Peaceful mass mobilisation

11. Internal Affiliations: as per (6) above

13. History: The UDF was formed in May 1983 by an initial group of thirty-two organisations including the then Council of Unions of South Africa (CUSA, now COSATU:

Congress of South African Trade Unions) and the Transvaal Indian Congress (TIC). By 1985, the UDF had become one of the two major centres of internal resistance to apartheid, a fact recognised by the apartheid regime, which arrested six of the top leaders of the UDF in February 1985 and banned in March all UDF meetings for three months. Most UDF affiliates have adopted the ANC's Freedom Charter. As UDF pressure mounted and became more effective against the apartheid regime at home and abroad, the regime decided to impose legal measures to cripple the UDF. These were applied in 1987.

14. Leadership: Rev. Dr. Allen Boesak (President World Alliance of Reformed Churches); Archbishop Desmond Tutu (Anglican Primate of South Africa); Albertina Sisulu (UDF Co-President); Oscar Mpetha (UDF Co-President); Archie Gumede (UDF Co-President); Dr. Essop Jassat (TIC President); Azhar Cachalia (UDF National Treasurer).

UNITED FRONT (Ghana)

See also, JFM and PRLG

UNITED NATIONAL INDEPENDENCE PARTY

2. Republic of Zambia (6,788,000)

3. Date Established: September 1959

4. Organisational Type: Mass party

5. Organisational Nature: The main decision making bodies of UNIP were the Secretary General (S.G.) chosen by the President of the Republic), the Central Committee (twenty-four members including the S.G. and the President of the Republic - there were ten sub-committees) and the General Conference which meets every five years. There were also women's and youth auxiliaries.

6. Membership: Thousands

7. Status: Ruling, sole legal party

8. Publications: _Times of Zambia_ (daily 68,000-71,000) as well as the government owned _Zambia Daily Mail_ (44,000), radio and television

9. Orientation: Social democracy (Kaunda's Humanism version of African socialism)

10. Strategy: Electoral

13. History: UNIP was formed as a result of an October 1958 split within the Northern Rhodesia African National Congress. In December 1958 Kenneth Kaunda led his followers into the Zambia African National Congress which became in 1959 the UNIP, winning the January 1964 elections that led to independence on 24 October 1964. Following considerable electoral success, Kaunda's UNIP was able to change the Zambian constitution to that of a one-party state in December 1972, UNIP being the sole legal party. Kaunda and UNIP have been strong opponents of the colonial, racist and apartheid regimes of southern Africa.

14. Leadership: President of the Republic and Central Committee members - Dr. Kenneth David Kaunda; Secretary General - A. Grey Zulu; Sub-Committees of the Central Committee - Alex K. Shapi, Reuben Kamanga, Daniel Lisulo, Clement Mwananshiku, Mary Fulano, Elijah H.K. Mudenda, Axon Soko, Betty Chilunga, J.C. Mutale, Joseph Simuyandi

UNITY MOVEMENT OF SOUTH AFRICA (UMSA: South Africa)

2. Republic of South Africa (34,577,000)

3. Date Established: 1943

4. Organisational Type: Coalition

5. Organisational Nature: The constituent organisations were joined together by a federal leadership.

6. Membership: Few, mainly based in the Western Cape and in one trade union

7. Status: Legal

9. Orientation: Left nationalist, some Trotskyist Marxist Leninist elements, anti-apartheid

10. Strategy: Negotiation, unification of 'non-European' peoples to end apartheid

11. Internal Affiliations: All-African Convention (AAC, f.1935); South African Indian Congress (SAIC, f.1920) from 1943 to 1944, Anti-CAD (Anti Coloured Affairs Department) and the African Peoples' Democratic Union of South Africa (APDUSA, f. January 1961).

12. External Affiliations: Some contact with Trotskyist organisations

13. History: The UMSA was formed in 1943 as the Non-European Unity Movement (NEUM) by the AAC, the Anti-CAD, the SAIC and Trotskyist elements who wished to oppose the ANC and the CPSA. Dadoo (of the CPSA and later the ANC) was successful in getting the SAIC to leave NEUM and to ally the SAIC with the ANC. While the NEUM did oppose apartheid, and did mobilise some support in the Cape, especially amongst African and Coloured teachers, it was unable to develop mass mobilisation campaigns in the 1940s and the 1950s. A series of splits rent the NEUM during the 1950s and 1960s, mainly between I.B. Tabata's AAC and Hosea Jaffe's Anti-CAD. In response to these divisions within the federation, Tabata created in January 1961 the APDUSA as a UMSA affiliated vehicle for individual membership. APDUSA utilised such Trotskyist concepts as the Permanent Revolution but was again unable to mobilise the masses in the Soweto uprising aftermath. APDUSA continued to oppose the ANC.

14. Leadership: I.B. Tabata, President of APDUSA and UMSA

VITM (Madagascar): a.k.a. VONJY

VONDRONA SOSIALISTA MONIMA (VSM-Socialist Monina: Madagascar)

2. Democratic Republic of Madagascar (9,490,000)

3. Date Established: 1977

7. Status: Constituent 'revolutionary association' of the ruling FNDR coalition

9. Orientation: Pro-China Marxism Leninism

10. Strategy: Electoral, party-building, building a socialist society

11. Internal Affiliations: VSM was associated with the AKRM, AREMA, MFM/MPP, MONIMA, VONJY and UDECMA/KMTP as constituent parts of the FNDR.

12. External Affiliations: Pro-China

13. History: VSM was founded in 1977 by dissatisfied MONIMA members who wanted a more Maoist China interpretation of analysis and strategy. VSM did not have a seat in the National Assembly.

14. Leadership: Tsihozony Maharanga Razafindrabe, Andre Tovonaiko Arnault

VONJY IRAY TSY MIVAKY (VONJY-Popular Impulse for National Unity: Madagascar) a.k.a. VITM or EPUN

2. Democratic Republic of Madagascar (9,490,000)

3. Date Established: 1973

4. Organisational Type: Mass party

7. Status: Constituent 'revolutionary association' of the ruling FNDR coalition

9. Orientation: Left nationalist, social democratic

10. Strategy: Electoral

11. Internal Affiliations: VONJY was associated with the AKFM, AREMA, MPP/MFM, MONIMA, VSM and UDECMA/KMTP as constituent parts of the FNDR.

13. History: Founded in 1973 after the 1972 removal of President Tsiranana by former members of his PSD (Parti Social Democratique), VONJY was incorporated into the FNDR in 1975 as a constituent 'revolutionary association'. VONJY's greatest base of support was the

western coast. It won seven seats in the 1977 National Assembly elections but lost one in the 1983 elections (6/137).

14. Leadership: Dr. Jerome Razanabahimy Marojama, leader; Andre Resampa

WESTERN SOMALIA LIBERATION FRONT (WSLF-Ethiopia)

2. Socialist Ethiopia (35,210,000)

3. Date Established: 1975

4. Organisational Type: National liberation movement

5. Organisational Nature: The WSLF has a military wing of some three thousand troops as well as a youth wing, Western Somali Youth League. The WSLF has a Secretary General, Committee and a Congress.

6. Membership: Thousands

7. Status: Illegal, war of independence participant

9. Orientation: left nationalist

10. Strategy: Revolution, war of independence, debate over whether to unite with Somalia or establish separate Western Somalia republic

11. Internal Affiliations: The WSLF has a youth wing, the Western Somali Youth League. The WSLF has cooperated with the OLF (Oromo Liberation Front).

12. External Affiliations: Somalia has supplied, trained and cooperated militarily with the WSLF, besides trying to direct it.

13. History: Formed in 1975 to liberate that portion of the Somali nation conquered by the old Ethiopian empire, the WSLF and the Somali army attacked troops of Socialist Ethiopia in late 1977. After early successes, the Ethiopian, Cuban and other Soviet bloc troops defeated the combined WSLF-Somali forces and in March 1978 pushed them back to the Ethiopia-Somalia border. At its February 1981 Congress the WSLF decided to establish an independent Western Somali republic.

14. Leadership: Secretary General - Issa Shaykh _Abdi_ Nasir Adan

WEZ ADER a.k.a. LL-LABOUR LEAGUE

WORKER'S PARTY OF ETHIOPIA (WPE-Ethiopia)

2. Socialist Ethiopia (35,210,000)

3. Date Established: 10 September 1984

4. Organisational Type: Vanguard party

5. Organisational Nature: The WPE has a Secretary General, a Politburo (eleven full, 6 alternate members), a Secretariat (eight members), and a Central Committee (one hundred and thirty-six full and sixty-four alternate members). COPWE handed over thirty-three regional units, seventy subregional units and two hundred and forty district units to WPE as constituent units. Party schools were set up at the national and regional levels. Mass organisations included the Kebeles (urban community committees), the 28-30,000 peasant associations, the Revolutionary Ethiopia's Women's Association, the Revolutionary Ethiopia's Youth Association, the All-Ethiopia Trade Union and the All-Ethiopian Peasant's Association.

6. Membership: 50,000

7. Status: Ruling party

8. Publications: _Serto_ _Ader_ (Working People: 100,000 weekly), _Meskerem_ (theoretical and organisational newspaper). Through the PMAC, the WPE has access to all the Ethiopian government media.

9. Orientation: Pro-Soviet Marxism Leninism

10. Strategy: Revolution; building socialism by building the party and sharing the administration of socialism

11. Internal Affiliations: The mass organisations of the WPE are noted in (5) above.

12. External Affiliations: Pro-Soviet parties, especially those of the Soviet Union and Cuba

13. History: Founded at the end of the Third Congress of COPWE, the WPE at its founding First Congress inherited all of its predecessor's infrastructure. The PMAC has continued to dominate the WPE, however, the considerable overlap of leaders of the top of both organisations appears to have ameliorated this potential source of conflict.

14. Leadership: Secretary General - Lt. Col. Mengistu Haile-Mariam; Politburo (full members) - Mengistu Haile-Mariam, Lt. Col. Firkre-Selassie Wogderess, Fisseha Desta, Lt. Gen. Tesfaye Gebre-Kidan, Berhanu Bayih, Legesse Asfaw, Addis Tedlay, Hailu Yimenu, Amanuel Amde-Michael, Shimelis Mazengia, Alenu Abebe

ZIMBABWE AFRICAN NATIONAL UNION (ZANU: Zimbabwe) a.k.a. ZANU-PF

2. Republic of Zimbabwe (8,496,000)

3. Date Established: 9 August 1963

4. Organisational Type: Mass party (formerly national liberation movement)

5. Organisational Nature: ZANU's decision making bodies included the President, the First Secretary, the Poliburo (fifteen members), the Central Committee (ninety members) and the Congress. A People's Militia was being established.

6. Membership: Thousands

7. Status: Ruling party

8. Publications: Moto; additionally ZANU exerted influence throughout the government and privately-owned media

9. Orientation: Marxism Leninism, left nationalism

10. Strategy: Electoral (since 1980, but armed struggle before that, c.1965), party building, creation of one

party socialist state, pragmatic NEP-style economic policy

11. Internal Affiliations: From 1976 to February 1980, ZANU and ZAPU were partners in the PF coalition. Following independence in 1980, ZANU and ZAPU discussed ZAPU merging into ZANU. The talks were discontinued in 1983 but resumed in 1985.

12. External Affiliations: ZANU has friendly relations with FRELIMO (who have been their ally since the wars of liberation started), China (who contributed arms during and after the liberation struggle), and North Korea (who trained the Zimbabwe Army's Fifth Brigade). As the Soviet Union backed ZAPU, ZANU's relations with the USSR have been lukewarm.

13. History: ZANU was formed in 1963 by a group led by Rev. Ndabaningi Sithole, who were dissatisfied with Joshua Nkomo's non-militant ZAPU. Following a convoluted series of events, ZANU properly launched the armed struggle in 1972, following FRELIMO's national liberation example in Mozambique. Herbert Chitepo, ZANU's Chairman, was assassinated in 1975 by the Smith regime. By 1976 Robert Mugabe was recognised by the leader of ZANU. In October 1976 ZANU and ZAPU were forced into a coalition, the PF; ZANU adopting the name ZANU-PF. The PF lasted through the remaining armed struggle (in which ZANU played the major role), the ceasefire and constitutional talks until the pre-independence February 1980 elections, when ZANU and ZAPU parted company once more. ZANU won fifty-seven of the eighty commonroll seats, establishing its dominance of Zimbabwean politics that continued through the 1985 election (64/80 seats). ZANU's proposed merger talks with ZAPU have had a difficult history but were resumed in 1985. ZAPU agreed to join ZANU in December 1987. ZANU's Fifth Congress was held on 8-12 August 1984.

14. Leadership: President - Robert Mugabe (Prime Minister of the Republic); Vice President - Simon Muzenda; Politburo - Robert Mugabe (First Secretary), Simon Muzenda (Second Secretary and Foreign Affairs Secretary), Mauriece Nyagumbo, Enos Nkala, Emmerson Munangagwa, Nathan Shamuyarira, Didymus Mutasa, Dzingai Mutumbuka, Teurai Ropa Nhongo, Ernest Kadungure, Sydney Sekeremayi, Rex Nhongo, Josiah Tongamirai, Mayor Uribo

ZIMBABWE AFRICAN NATIONAL UNION-PATRIOTIC FRONT (ZANU-PF: Zimbabwe) a.k.a. ZANU

ZIMBABWE AFRICAN PEOPLE'S UNION (ZAPU: Zimbabwe) a.k.a. PF-ZAPU

2. Republic of Zimbabwe (8,496,000)

3. Date Established: 1961

4. Organisational Type: Mass party

5. Organisational Nature: ZAPU had a President, Secretary General and a Central Committee.

6. Membership: Thousands, mainly in the southwest

7. Status: Legal opposition

9. Orientation: Socialism, left nationalism, some Soviet Marxism Leninism

10. Strategy: Electoral (post 1980; from 1965-1979, armed struggle)

11. Internal Affiliations: From October 1976 until the February 1980 pre-independence elections, ZAPU and ZANU were coalition partners in the PF. They contested the elections separately. Merger talks took place from 1980 to 1983 and again from 1985 onwards.

12. External Affiliations: Soviet bloc countries provided military assistance to ZAPU during the armed struggle. British capitalist Tiny Rowland's Lonrho provided some legal and other assistance to ZAPU's leader, Joshua Nkomo.

13. History: ZAPU was formed, with Joshua Nkoma as its President, in December 1961 but could trace its roots back through a series of parties banned by the racist white Southern Rhodesian government: National Democratic Party (NDP) formed in 1 January 1960, banned 9 December 1961; the African National Congress of Southern Rhodesia (founded September 1957 from earlier organisations) banned February 1959. In 1963, a group of ZAPU members broke with ZAPU and formed ZANU, which was eventually to overtake ZAPU in popular support.

Following the 1965 Unilateral Declaration of Independence by Ian Smith's white settler regime, ZAPU decided to use military tactics to gain power. After a number of military failures in the 1960s and early 1970s, ZAPU began to make progress, although at a slower rate than ZANU. ZAPU's coalition with ZANU, the PF, lasted until just before the independence elections of February 1980. ZAPU won twenty (to ZANU's fifty-seven) out of eighty seats on the common roll. The 1985 election saw ZAPU's seats shrink from twenty to fifteen. The proposal to merge ZAPU into ZANU was raised again between the parties in 1985 and was accepted in December 1987.

14. Leadership: Joshua Nkomo, President; Joseph Msika, Secretary General

PART III
INDEX BY ACRONYM

Explanation of Entries for the Ecronym Index

Organisations which have primary or secondary entry status are listed by their acronyms. The acronyms are listed alphabetically by the letters only in the acronym and not by the letters of the organisation's full name.

After the acronym, the reader is refered to the full title, other names and/or acronyms and country of the organisation. To find further details of the organisation, the reader then uses the full name to locate the organisation.

ADPUSA - African People's Democratic Union of South Africa (South Africa); See also UMSA

ADS - Alliance Democratique Senegalais, or Senegalese Democratic Alliance (Senegal); See also, LD-MPT; MRDM; OST; PDS; UDP

AGAT - Avant-Garde Arabe en Tunisie, or Tunisian Arab Vanguard (Tunisia)

AESM - All Ethiopian Socialist Movement, a.k.a. MEISON (Ethiopia)

AKFM - Antoko'ny Kongresi'ny Fahaleovantenan'i Madagasikara, or Congres Party for an Independent Madagascar, a.k.a. KDRSM (Madagascar)

ANC - African National Congress of South Africa (South Africa)

AND-JEF - Work Together (Senegal), a.k.a. MRDN/AND-JEF

APC - All People's Congress (Sierra Leone)

APRP - Azanian People's Revolutionary Party (South Africa)

AREMA - Avant-Garde de la Revolution Malgache, or Vanguard of the Malagasy Revolution (Madagascar)

ASBP-CS - Arab Socialist Baath Party - Country of Sudan (Sudan)

ASBS-OS - Arab Socialist Baath Party - Organisation of Sudan (Sudan); See also, PNF

ASEC - Association des Stagiares et des Etudiants Comoriens, or Association of Comoron Students and Trainees (Comoros)

ASPI - Afro-Shirazi Party (Tanzania); See also, CCM

AT - el Amal el Tounsi, or Tunisian Worker (Tunisia)

AYB - African Youth Brigade (Ghana)

AYC - African Youth Command (Ghana)

AYRC - Azanian Youth Revolutionary Council, a.k.a. SAYRC (South Africa)

AZAPO - Azania People's Organisation (South Africa)

BATH, le Renaissance (Tunisia)

BCP - Basotho Congress Party (Lesotho)

BCP - Black People's Convention (South Africa)

BIP - Botswana Independence Party (Botswana)

BNF - Botswana National Front (Botswana)

BNP - Basotho National Party (Lesotho)

BPP - Botswana People's Party (Botswana)

CCM - Chama Cha Mapinduzi, or Revolutionary Party of Tanzania (Tanzania); See also, ASP and TANU

CLC - Conseil pour la Liberation du Congo, or Council for the Liberation of Congo (Zaire)

CLSTP - Comite de Libertacao de Sao Tome e Principe, or Committee for the Liberation of Sao Tome and Principe, a.k.a. MLSTP (Sao Tome and Principe)

CNR - Conseil National de la Revolution, or National Revolutionary Council (Burkina Faso)

CNSP - Comite National de Salut Public, National Committee for Public Salvation (Comoros); See also, FNUK, UNIKOM, and FNUK-UNIKOM

COPWE - Commission for Organising the Party of the Working People of Ethiopia (Ethiopia); See also, WPE

CPL - Communist Party of Lesotho (Lesotho)

CPSA - Communist Party of South Africa, a.k.a. SACP (South Africa)

CR - Choix Revolutionnaire, Le or Revolutionary Choice (Tunisia); See also, AT

CSR - Conseil Supreme de la Revolution, or Supreme Revolutionary Council (Chad)

DERG - Armed Forces Coordinating Committee, a.k.a. DERGUE a.k.a. PMAC (Ethiopia)

DFLS - Democratic Front for the Liberation of Somalia, a.k.a. SDLF (Somalia)

DFSS - Democratic Front for the Salvation of Somalia, a.k.a. SDSF (Somalia)

DFSS/SSF - Democratic Front for the Salvation of Somalia/SSF, a.k.a. SSF (Somalia)

Ech-Choola-El-Watad(Tunisia) a.k.a. SF-Strong Flame (pref. trans.); a.k.a. FDP-Flame Democratic Patriots

ECLP - Egyptian Communist Labour Party (Egypt)

ECP - Egyptian Communist Party, or al-Hizb al-Shuyu'i al-Misri (Egypt)

ECP - Etudiants Congolaise Progressiste, or Progressive Congolese Students (Zaire)

ELF - Eritrean Liberation Front (Eritrea)

EL HOR - a.k.a. Free Man: FM (Mauritania)

EORS-I.Ch.A.T. - Ethiopian Oppressed Revolutionary Struggle (Ethiopia)

EPDM - Ethiopian People's Democratic Movement (Ethiopia)

EPLF - Eritrean People's Liberation Front (Eritrea)

EPRP - Ethiopian People's Revolutionary Party (Ethiopia)

EPUN - Elan Populaire pour l'Unite Nationale, a.k.a. VONJY (Madagascar)

EWCP - Egyptian Workers Communist Party (Egypt)

FCD - Front Congolaise Pour la Restauration de la Democratie, or Congolese Front for the Restoration of Democracy (Zaire)

FD - Front Democratique, or Democratic Front (Comoros)

FDLD - Front Democratique pour la Liberation de Djibouti, or Djibouti Democratic Liberation Front (Djibouti)

FDP - Flame Democratic Patriots (Tunisia), a.k.a. SF-Strong Flame (pref. translation) a.k.a. Ech-Choola-El-Watad

FFS - Front des Forces Socialistes, or Socialist Forces Front (Algeria)

FLING - Frente para a Libertacao e Independencia da Guinea-Bissau, or Guinea-Bissau Front for Liberation and Independence (Guinea Bissau)

FLN - Front de Liberation Nationale, or National Liberation Front (Algeria)

FLNC - Front de la Liberation Nationale Congolaise, or Congolese National Liberation Front (Zaire)

FM - Free Man, a.k.a. El Hor (Mauritania)

FNDR - Front National pour la Defense de la Revolution Socialiste Malgache, or National Front for the Defense of the Malagasy Socialist Revolution (Madagascar)

FNLK-UNIKOM (Comoros); See also, FNUK, UNIKOM, and CNSP

FNPLT - Front Nationale Progressiste Pour la Liberation de la Tunisie, or National Progressive Front for the Liberation of Tunisia (Tunisia)

FNUK - Front National Uni des Komores, or Comoron National United Front (Comoros); See also, CNSP, UNIKOM, and FNUK-UNIKOM

FOCK Force des Opprimes du Congo-Kinshasa, Force of the Oppressed of Congo (Zaire)

FPV - Front Progressiste Voltaique, or Voltaic Progressive Front (Burkina Faso)

FRELIMO - Frente da Liberatacao de Mocambique, or Mozambique Liberation Front (Mozambique)

FROLINAT - Front de Liberation National Tchadien, National Liberation Front of Chad (Chad)

FRP-PT - Front Patriotique Oubanguien - Parti Travallaiste, or Ubangi Patriotic Front - Labour Party (Central African Republic); See also, PRC, MLPC, MCLN

FUND - Frente para Unidade Nacional e Desenvolvimento, or Front for National Unity and Development (Guinea Bissau)

GC - Groupe Communiste, or Communist Group (Burkina Faso)

GCR - Groupe Communiste Revolutionnaire, or Revolutionary Communist Group (Algeria)

GEAST - Groupe d'Etudes et d'Action Socialiste Tunisien, a.k.a. PERSPECTIVISTES (Tunisia)

GRSA - Groupe de la Revolution Socialiste Arabe, or Arab Socialist Revolution Group (Tunisia)

GSRP - Gambia Socialist Revolutionary Party (Gambia)

GUNT - Gouvernement d'Union National de Transition, Transitional Government of National Unity (Chad)

HAI - Hizb al-'Amal al-Ishtiraki, a.k.a. SLP (Egypt)

HAKIKA, al - The Truth (Tunisia)

HSM - al-Hizb al-Shuyu'i al-Misri, a.k.a. ECP (Egypt)

HSS - al-Hizb al-Shuyu'i al-Sudani, a.k.a. SCP (Sudan)

HTWTW - Hizb al-Tajammu 'al-Watani al-Taqaddumi al-Wahdawi, a.k.a. NPUP (Egypt)

HURRIYA, al-Liberty - (Tunisia)

HWL - El Haraka el Wataniya Libya, or National Libyan Movement (Libya)

ISP - Islamic Socialist Party (Sudan)

JAMAHIRIYA - (Libya)

JFM - June Fourth Movement (Ghana); See also, UF, United Front

JWD - El Jabha el Wataniya Democratiya, or National Democratic Libyan Front (Libya)

KDRSM - Parti du Congres de l'Independance de Madagascar, a.k.a. AKFM (Madagascar)

KNRG - Kwame Nkrumah Revolutionary Guards (Ghana)

LCT - Ligue Communiste des Travailleurs, or Communist Workers League (Senegal)

LD-MPT - Ligue Democratique-Mouvement pour le Parti du Travail, or Democratic League-Movement for the Party of Labour (Senegal); See also, ADS

LEAGUE, THE - a.k.a. PRLG (Ghana)

LESOMA - Socialist League of Malawi (Malawi)

LIGUEURS, Les - The League (Benin)

LIPAD - Ligue Patriotique pour la Developpement, or Patriotic League for Development (Burkina Faso)

LL - Labour League or Wez Ader (Ethiopia)

MAFREMO - Malawi Freedom Movement (Malawi)

MARC - Mouvement d'Action Pour la Resurrection au Congo, or Action Movement for Congolese Revival (Zaire)

MCLN - Mouvement Centreafricaine pour la Liberte Nationale, Central African Movement for National Liberation (Central African Republic); See also, PRC, MLPC, FPO-PT

MDA - Mouvement pour la Democratie d'Algerie, or Movement for Democracy in Algeria (Algeria)

MDJ - Mouvement du 17 January, or Movement of 17 January (Zaire)

MDP - Mouvement Democratique Populaire, or People's Democratic Movement (Senegal)

MDS - Mouvement des Democrates Socialistes, or Social Democratic Movement (Tunisia)

MDSC - Mouvement Democrate Sociale Congolaise, or Congolese Social Democratic Movement (Zaire)

MEISON - All-Ethiopian Socialist Movement, a.k.a. AESM (Ethiopia)

MFM - Mpitolona Ho Amin'ny Fanjakan' Ny Madinika, or Proletarian Power Party, a.k.a. MPP, a.k.a. Pouvoir Aux Petits (Madagascar)

MIR - Mouvement pour l'Independence de Reunion, Movement for the Independence of Reunion (Reunion)

MLD - Mouvement pour la Liberation de Djibouti, or Djibouti Liberation Movement (Djibouti)

MLP - Mauritius Labour Party (Mauritius)

MLPC - Mouvement pour la Liberation du Peuple Centrafricaine, or Movement for the Liberation of the Central African People (Central African Republic); See also, PRC, FPR-PT, MCLN

MLRO - **Ma.Le.Ri.De.** - Marxist-Leninist Revolutionary Organisation (Ethiopia)

MLSTP - Movimento de Libertacao de Sao Tome e Principe, or Movement of the Liberation of Sao Tome and Principe (Sao Tome and Principe)

MMM - Mouvement Militant Mauricien, or Mauritian Militant Movement (Mauritius)

MMMSP - Mouvement Militant Mauricien Social Progressiste, or Mauritian Social Progressive Militant Movement (Mauritius)

MNC - Mouvement National du Congo, or Congo National Movement, a.k.a. MNCL a.k.a. MNCR (Zaire)

MNCL - Mouvement Nationale du Congo-Lumumba, a.k.a. MNC (Zaire)

MNCR - Mouvement Nationale du Congo-Reforme, a.k.a. MNC (Zaire)

MND - Mouvement National Democratique (Mauritania)

MOJA - Movement for Justice in Africa (Gambia)

MOJA-Liberia - Movement for Justice in Africa-Liberia (Liberia)

MONAS - Movement on National Affairs (Ghana)

MONIMA - Mouvement National pour l'Independence de Madagascar, or National Movement for Madagascar's Independence (Madagascar)

MORENA - Mouvement de Resistance Nationale, or Movement for National Resistance (Gabon)

MPG - Mouvement Progressive de la Gauche, Progressive Left Movement (Reunion)

MPLA-PT - Movimento Popular de Liberticao de Angola - Partido do Trabalho, or Popular Movement for the Liberation of Angola - Party of Labour (Angola)

MPP - Mouvement pour le Pouvoir Proletarian, or Movement for Proletarian Power, a.k.a. MFM (Madagascar)

MPPP - Mauritius People's Progressive Party (Mauritius)

MRDN/AND-JEF - Mouvement Revolutionnaire pour la Democratie Nouvelle/AND-JEF, or Revolutionary Movement for New Democracy/Work Together (Senegal); See also, ADS; AND-JEF; ODP; UDP; PRA-Senegal

MRND - Mouvement Revolutionnaire National pour le Developpment, or National Revolutionary Movement for Development (Rwanda)

MSM - Mouvement Socialiste Mauricien, or Mauritian Socialist Movement (Mauritius); See also, Mouvement Socialiste Militant-MSM

MSM - Mouvement Socialiste Militant (Mauritius)

MUP - Mouvement d'Unite Populaire, or Popular Unity Movement (Tunisia)

MWAKENYA - Union of Nationalists to Liberate Kenya (Kenya), possibly a.k.a. UKENYA

MWM - Mauritian Workers' Movement (Mauritius)

NAP - National Alliance Party (Sierra Leone)

NC - National Coalition (Libya)

NDM - New Democratic Movement (Ghana)

NDM-L - National Democratic Movement - Libya (Libya)

NEUM - Non-European Unity Movement, a.k.a. UMSA (South Africa)

NLP - National Liberation Party (Gambia)

NMU - Nuba Mountains Union (Sudan); See also, PNF

NPUP - National Progressive Union Party, or Hizb al-Tajammu 'al-Watani al-Taqaddumi al-Wahdawi (Egypt)

NRA - National Resistance Army (Uganda); See, NRM

NRM - National Resistance Movement (Uganda)

OADP - Organisation de l'Action Democratique et Populaire, or Democratic and Popular Action Organisation (Morocco)

OCLD - Organisation de Cameroun Latter pour Democratie, or Cameroon Organisation to Fight for Democracy (Cameroon)

OCML - Organisation Communiste Marxiste-Leniniste de Reunion, or Marxist-Leninist Communist Organisation of Reunion (Reunion)

ODP - Organisation Democratique Proletarienne, or Proletarian Democratic Organisation (Senegal); See also, AND-JEF; MRDN/AND-JEF

OECP-January 8 - Organisation of the Egyptian Communist Party - January 8 (Egypt)

OR - Opposition Revolutionnaire, or Revolutionary Opposition (Morocco)

OST - Organisation Socialist du Travailleurs, or Socialist Workers' Organisation (Senegal); See also, ADS

PA - Parti de l'Action, or Action Party (Morocco)

PAC - Pan-Africanist Congress of Azania (South Africa)

PAGS - Parti de l'Avant-Garde Socialiste, or Socialist Vanguard Party (Senegal)

PAI (B) - Parti Africain de l'Independence, or African Independence Party (Benin)

PAI (BF) - Parti Africain pour l'Independence, or African Independence Party (Burkina Faso)

PAI (S) - Parti Africain de l'Independence, or African Independence Party (Senegal)

PAICV - Partido Africano da Independencia do Cabo Verde, or African Party for the Independence of Cape Verde (Cape Verde)

PAIGC - Partido Africano da Independencia da Guinee Cabo Verde, African Party for the Independence of Guinea and Cape Verde (Guinea Bissau)

PAI-M - Parti Africain de l'Independence-Masses, or African Independence Party-Masses (Senegal)

PAIP - Parti Africain pour l'Independence du Peuple, or African Party for the Independence of the People (Senegal)

PCD - Parti Communiste Dahomeen, or Communist Party of Dahomey (Benin)

PCM - Parti Communiste Marocaine, or Moroccan Communist Party, a.k.a. PPS (Moroccan)

PCR - Parti Communiste Reunionnais, or Communist Party of Reunion (Reunion)

PCRV - Parti Communiste Revolutionnaire Voltaique, Voltaic Revolutionary Communist Party (Burkina Faso)

PCS - Parti du Centre Social, or Social Centre Party (Morocco)

PCT - Parti Communiste Togolaise, or Communist Party of Togo (Togo)

PCT - Parti Communiste Tunisien, or Tunisian Communist Party (Tunisia)

PDG - Parti Democratique de Guinee, or Democratic Party of Guinea (Guinea)

PDS - Parti Democratique Senegalais, or Senegalese Democratic Party (Senegal); See also, ADS

PERPSECTIVISTES - a.k.a. GEAST (Tunisia)

PF - Patriotic Front (Zimbabwe); See also, ZANU, ZAPU

PF-ZAPU - Patriotic Front-Zimbabwe African People's Union, a.k.a. ZAPU (Zimbabwe)

PIT - Parti de l'Independence et du Travail, or Independence and Labour Party (Senegal)

PLP - Parti pour la Liberation du Peuple, or Party for the Libertion of the People (Senegal)

PLP - Parti Liberal Progressiste, or Progressive Liberal Party (Morocco)

PLS - Parti de la Liberation et du socialisme, or Socialist Liberation Party, a.k.a. PPS (Morocco)

PMAC - Provisional Military Administrative Council, a.k.a. DERG, a.k.a. DERGUE (Ethiopia)

PNDC - Provisional National Defence Council (Ghana)

PNF - Progressive National Front (Sudan); See also, ASBP-OS, NMU, RCPS, SLP, UDF

PNP - People's National Party (Ghana)

POLISARIO - Frente Popular para la Liberacion de Saguia el Hamra y Rio de Oro, or Popular Front for the Liberation of Saquia el Hamra and Rio de Oro (SADR, a.k.a. Saharan Arab Democratic Republic, a.k.a. Western Sahara)

POP - Parti Ouvrier et Paysan du Congo, or Congolese Workers' and Peasants' Party (Zaire)

POUVOIR AUX PETITS - Power to the People, a.k.a. MFM (Madagascar)

PPS - Parti du Progres et du Socialisme, or Party of Progress and Socialism, a.k.a. PCM, a.k.a. PLS (Morocco)

PPS - Parti Populaire Senegalais, or Senegalese People's Party (Senegal)

PRLG - People's Revolutionary League of Ghana (Ghana); See also, UF, United Front

PRA - Parti du Regroupement Africain, or African Realignment Party (Senegal); See also, MRDN/AND-JEF; ODP

PRP - Parti de la Revolution Populaire, or Popular Revolutionary Party (Zaire)

PRP - People's Redemption Party (Nigeria)

PRP - People's Revolutionary Party (Ghana)

PRPB - Parti de la Revolution Populaire du Benin, or Benin People's Revolutionary Party (Benin)

PRPT - Parti Revolutionnaire du Peuple Tunisien, or Revolutionary Party of the Tunisian People (Tunisia)

PS - Parti Socialiste, or Socialist Party (Senegal); See also, UPS

PSA - Parti Socialiste Arabe, or Arab Socialist Party (Tunisia)

PSAGE - Partido Socialista de Guinea Ecuatorial, or Socialist Party of Equatorial Guinea (Equatorial Guinea)

PSC - Parti Socialiste Congolaise, or Congolese Socialist Party (Zaire)

PSD - Parti Socialiste Destourien, or Destourian Socialist Party (Tunisia)

PSM - Parti Socialiste Mauricien, or Mauritian Socialist Party (Mauritius)

PSR - Parti Socialiste (Reunion), or Reunion Federation of the Socialist Party (Reunion)

PSZ - Parti Socialiste Zairois, or Socialist Party of Zaire (Zaire)

RC - Revolutionary Current (Egypt)

RCCSGP - Revolutionary Command Council of Socialist Guinean Patriots (Equatorial Guinea)

RCPS - Revolutionary Communist Party of the Sudan (Sudan); See also, PNF

RDLGE - Reunion Democratica para la Liberacion de Guinea Ecuatorial, or Democratic Movement for the Liberation of Equatorial Guinea (Equatorial Guinea); See also, Social Democratic Convergence: Equatorial Guinea

RECP - Revolutionary Egyptian Communist Party (Egypt)

RF - Revolutionary Flame, a.k.a. Seded (Ethiopia)

RFP - Rassemblement des Forces Patriotique, or Assembly of Patriotic Forces (Chad); See also, GUNT, FROLINAT, and CSR

RNA - Rassemblement Nationale Arabe, a.k.a. RNDA (Tunisia)

RND - Rassemblement National Democratique, or National Democratic Rally (Senegal)

RNDA - Rassemblement Nationale Democratique Arabe, or National Democratic Arab Rally, a.k.a. RNA (Tunisia)

RNM Rassemblement Nationale Malgache, a.k.a. UDECMA-KMTP (Madagascar)

ROC - Regroupement des Officiers Communistes, or Communist Officers Group (Burkina Faso)

RPP - Rassemblement Populaire pour le Progres, Popular Rally for Progress (Djibouti)

SAC - Sudan African Congress (Sudan)

SACP - South African Communist Party, a.k.a. CPSA (South Africa)

SAWABA - Freedom Party (Niger)

SAYRC - South African Youth Revolutionary Council, a.k.a. AYRC (South Africa)

SCP - Sudanese Communist Party, a.k.a. HSS (Sudan)

SDC - Social Democratic Convergence (Equatorial Guinea); See also, RDLGE and PSAGE

SDLF - Somali Democratic Liberation Front, a.k.a. DFLS (Somalia)

SDSF - Somali Democratic Salvation Front, a.k.a. DFSS (Somalia)

SEDED - (Ethiopia); See also, Revolutionary Flame

SF - Strong Flame (Tunisia), a.k.a. Ech-Choola-El-Watad, a.k.a. FDP-Flame Democratic Patriots (non-pref. trans.)

SL - Shuhada al Libya, or Martyrs of Libya (Libya)

SLP - Socialist Labour Party, or Hizb al-'Amal al-Ishtiraki, a.k.a. HAI (Egypt)

SLP - Socialist Labour Party (Sudan); See also, PNF

SMRC - Sudanese Movement of Revolutionary Committees (Sudan)

SODAF - Somali Democratic Action Front, a.k.a. SSF (Somalia)

SOSAF - a.k.a. SSF (Somalia)

SOUFFLES - Whispers (Morocco)

SPLM - Sudan People's Liberation Movement (Sudan)

SPPF/FPPS - Seychelles People's Progressive Front, or Front Populaire Progressiste des Seychelles, a.k.a. SPUP (Seychelles)

SPSF - Sudanese People's Socialist Front (Sudan)

SPUP - Seychelles People's United Party, a.k.a. SPPF/FPPS (Seychelles)

SPWFY - Socialist Party of Workers, Farmers and Youth (Nigeria)

SRC - Supreme Revolutionary Council (Somalia); See SRSP

SRSP - Somali Revolutionary Socialist Party (Somalia)

SRYLOG - Socialist Revolutionary Youth League of Ghana (Ghana)

SSF - Somali Salvation Front, a.k.a. SOSAF, a.k.a. SODAF, a.k.a. DFSS/SSF (Somalia)

SSU - Sudanese Socialist Union, or al-Ittihad al-Ishtiraki al-Sudani (Sudan)

SWAFP - Socialist Workers' and Farmers' Party, a.k.a. SWPP (Nigeria)

SWALIMO - Swazi Liberation Movement (Swaziland)

SWAPO - South West African People's Organization of Namibia (Namibia)

SWP - Somali Workers' Party (Somalia); See also, DFSS

SWPP - Socialist Working People's Party of Nigeria (Nigeria)

TANU - Tanganyika African National Union (Tanzania); See also, CCM

TPLF - Tigre People's Liberation Front (Ethiopia)

UCB - Union des Communistes Burkinabe, or Burkinabe Communist Union (Burkina Faso)

UDECMA-KMTP - Union Democratique Chretien Malgache, or Malagasy Christian Democratic Union, a.k.a. RNM (Madagascar)

UDF - Union of Democratic Forces (Sudan); See also, PNF

UDF - United Democratic Front (South Africa)

UDP - Union pour la Democratie Populaire, or Democratic People's Union (Senegal); See also, ADS

UDPM - Union Democratique du Peuple Malien, or Mali People's Democratic Union (Mali)

UDS-R - Union Democratique Senegalais-Renouvellement, or Senegalese Democratic Union - Revival (Senegal)

UEMLO - Union of Ethiopian Marxist-Leninist Organisations (Ethiopia); See also, RF/SEDED; LL/WA; MEISON; EORS/I.Ch.A.T.; MLRO/Ma.Le.Ri.De.

UFPCK - Union des Forces Progressistes du Congo-Kinshasa, or Union of Progressive Forces of Congo (Zaire)

UKENYA - Umoja wa Kupigania Demokrasia Kenya, or UKENYA Movement for Unity and Democracy in Kenya (Kenya), possibly a.k.a. MWAKENYA.

ULC - Union des Luttes Communistes, or Union for Communist Struggle (Burkina Faso)

UM - Umma-Mranda, or People's Party (Comoros)

UMSA - Unity Movement of South Africa (South Africa)

UNDC - (Comoros); See also, URDC

UNEM - Union Nationale des Etudiants Marocains, or National Union of Moroccan Students (Morocco)

UNFP - Union Nationale des Forces Populaires, or National Union of Popular Forces (Morocco)

UNIKOM - Union des Komoriens, or Union of Comorans (Comoros); See also, FNUK, CNSP, and FNUK-UNIKOM

UNIP - United National Independence Party (Zambia)

UNIR - Union Nationale pour l'Independence et la Revolution, or National Union for Independence and Revolution (Chad)

UPC - Uganda People's Congress (Uganda)

UPC - Union des Peuple de Cameroun, or Cameroon People's Union (Cameroon)

UPM - Uganda Patriotic Movement (Uganda); See, NRM

UPRONA - Union pour le Progres National, or Union for National Progress (Burundi)

UPS - Union Progressiste Senegalaise, or Senegalese Progressive Union (Senegal); See also, PS

URDC - Union for a Democratic Republic in the Comoros, also known as the UNDC - the National Union for Democracy in the Comoros

USFP - Union Socialiste des Forces Populaires, or Socialist Union of the Popular Forces (Morocco)

VITM - a.k.a. VONJY (Madagascar)

VONJY - Vonjy Iray Tsy Mivaky, or Popular Impulse for National Unity, a.k.a. VITM, a.k.a. EPUN (Madagascar)

VSM - Vondrona Sosialista Monima, or Socialist Monima (Madagascar)

Wez Ader - a.k.a. LL-Labour League (Ethiopia)

WPE - Worker's Party of Ethiopia (Ethiopia)

WSLF - Western Somalia Liberation Front (Ethiopia)

ZANU - Zimbabwe African National Union, a.k.a. ZANU-PF (Zimbabwe)

ZANU-PF - Zimbabwe African National Union - Patriotic Front, a.k.a. ZANU (Zimbabwe)

ZAPU - Zimbabwe African People's Union, a.k.a. PF-ZAPU

PART IV
INDEX BY COUNTRY

Explanation of Entries for the Country Index

The name of the country, the date of independence (or otherwise) and the left organisations are listed for each country in Africa. The countries are listed in alphabetical order by the country's short name. For each country, the organisations are listed alphabetically according to their acronym.

Algeria (3 July 1962)

FFS
FLN
GCR
MDA
PAGS

Angola (11 November 1975)

MPLA-PT

Benin (1 August 1960)

Ligueurs
PCD
PAI-Benin
PRBB

Botswana (30 September 1966)

BIP
BNF
BPP

Burkina Faso (5 August 1960)

CNR
FPV
GC
LIPAD
PAI(BF)
PCRV
ROC

UCB
ULC

Burundi (1 July 1962)

UPRONA

Cameroon (1 January 1960)

OCLD
UPC

Cape Verde (5 July 1975)

PAICV

Central African Republic (13 August 1960)

FPO-PT
MCLN
MLPC
PRC

Chad (11 August 1960)

CSR
Frolinat-FAN
Frolinat-FAP
GUNT
RFP
UNIR

Comoros (6 July 1975)

ASEC
CNSP
FD
FNUK
FNUK-Unikom
UM
Unikom
UNDC; see also URDC

URDC; see also UNDC

Djibouti (27 June 1977)

FDLD
MLD
RPP

Egypt (28 February 1922)

ECLP
ECP
EWCP
HAI, a.k.a. SLP
HSM, a.k.a. ECP
HTWTW, a.k.a. NPUP
NPUP
OECP - January 8
RC
RECP
SLP

Equatorial Guinea (12 October 1968)

PSAGE
RCCSGP
RDLGE
SDC

Eritrea (Ethiopian Occupation)

ELF
EPLF

Ethiopia (antiquity: Italian occupation 1935 1941)

(N.B. Eritrean parties and groups are listed under Eritrea)

AESM, a.k.a. MEISON
COPWE, see also WPE
DERG, a.k.a. DERGUE, a.k.a. PMAC
EORS
EPDM

EPRP
I.Ch.A.T., a.k.a. EORS
LL
Ma.Le.Ri.De., a.k.a. MLRO
MEISON
MLRO
PMAC
RF
SEDED, a.k.a. RF
TPLF
UEMLO
Wez Ader, a.k.a. LL
WPE
WSLF

Gabon (17 August 1960)

MORENA

Gambia (18 February 1965)

GSRP
MOJA
NLP

Ghana (6 March 1957)

AYB
AYC
JFM
KNRG
LEAGUE, THE, a.k.a. PRLG
MONAS
NDM
PNDC
PNP
PRLG
PRP
SRYLOG
UF

Guinea (2 October 1958)

PCG

PDG

GUINEA-BISSAU (24 September 1973/10 September 1974)

FLING
FUND
PAIGC

Ivory Coast (7 August 1960)

Kenya (12 December 1963)

Mwakenya

UKENYA, possibly a.k.a. MWAKENYA

Lesotho (4 October 1966)

BCP
BNP
CPL-Lesotho

Liberia (26 July 1847)

MOJA-Liberia

Libya (24 December 1951)

HWL
JWD
Jamahiriya
NC
NDM-L
SL

Madagascar (26 June 1960)

AKRM
AREMA
EPUN, a.k.a. VONJY
FNDR

KDRSM, a.k.a. AKFM
MFM
MONIMA
MPP, a.k.a. MFM
Pouvoir aux Petits, a.k.a. MFM
RNM, a.k.a. UDECMA-KMTP
UDECMA-KMTP
VITM, a.k.a. VONJY
VONJY
VSM

Malawi (6 July 1964)

LESOMA
MAFREMO

Mali (20 June 1960)

UDPM

Mauritania (28 November 1960)

EL HOR, a.k.a. FM
FM
MND

Mauritius (12 March 1968)

MWM
MLP
MPPP
MMM
MMMSP
MSM (Militant)
MSM (Mauricien)
PSM

Morocco (2 March 1956)

OADP
OR
PA
PCM, a.k.a. PPS

PCS
PLP
PLS, a.k.a. PPS
PPS
SOUFFLES
UNEM (23 Mars faction; Groupe des Martyres faction)
UNFP
USFP

Mozambique (25 June 1975)

FRELIMO

Namibia (occupied by apartheid South Africa)

SWAPO

Niger (3 August 1960)

SAWABA

Nigeria (1 October 1960)

PRP (Nigeria)
SPWFY
SWAFP, later a.k.a. SWPP
SWPP

Reunion (French occupation)

MIR
MPG
OCMLR
PCR
PS(R)

Rwanda (1 July 1962)

MRND

Saharan Arab Democratic Republic (or SADR, a.k.a. Western Sahara: Moroccan occupation, but declaration of independence 28 February 1976)

POLISARIO

Sao Tome and Principe (12 July 1975)

CLSTP, later a.k.a. MLSTP
MLSTP

Senegal (20 July 1960)

And Jef
LCT
MDP
MRDN/And Jef
ODP
OST
PAI(S)
PAI-M
PAIP
PDS
PIT
PLP
PPS
PRA-Senegal
PS
RND
UDP
UDS-R
UPS, a.k.a. PS

Seychelles (29 June 1976)

SPPF/FPPS
SPUP, now k.a. SPPF/FPPS

Sierra Leone (27 April 1961)

APC
NAP

Somalia (1 July 1960)

DFLS, a.k.a. SDLF
DFSS, see also SWP, SFLS, SSF

DFSS/SSF, a.k.a. SSF
SDLF
SDSF, a.k.a. DFSS
SODAF, a.k.a. SSF
SOSAF, a.k.a. SSF
SRC, see SRSP
SRSP
SSF
SWP

South Africa (under apartheid occupation)

ANC
APDUSA, see also UMSA
APRP
AYRC, a.k.a. SAYRC
AZAPO
BPC
CPSA, a.k.a. SACP
NEUM, now k.a. UMSA
PAC
SACP
SAYRC
UDF
UMSA

Sudan (1 January 1956)

ASBP-CS
ASBP-OS
HSS, a.k.a. SCP
IIS, a.k.a. SSU
ISP
NMU
PNF
RCPS
SAC
SCP
SLP
SMRC
SPLM

SPSF
SSU
UDF (Sudan)

Swaziland (6 September 1968)

SWALIMO

Tanzania (9 December 1961, including Zanzibar-10 December 1963; United Republic April 1964)

ASP, see also CCM
CCM
TANU, see also CCM

Togo (27 April 1960)

PCT

Tunisia (20 March 1956)

AGAT
AT
BATH, LE
CR, see AT
Ech-Choola-El-Watad, a.k.a. S.F.
FDP, a.k.a. SF
FNPLT
GEAST
GRSA
HAKIKA, AL
HURRIYA, AL
MDS
PERSPECTIVISTES, a.k.a. GEAST
PCT
PRPT
PSA
PSD
RNA, a.k.a. RNDA
RNDA
SF

Uganda (9 October 1962)

NRA, see NRM
NRM
UPC
UPM, see NRM

Zaire (30 June 1960)

CLC
ECP
FCD
FLNC
FOCK
MARC
MDJ
MDSC
MNC
MNCL, a.k.a. MNC
MNCR, a.k.a. MNC
POP
PRP
PSC
PSZ
UFPCK

Zambia (24 October 1964)

UNIP

Zimbabwe (18 April 1980)

PF
PF-ZAPU, a.k.a. ZAPU
ZANU
ZANU-PF, a.k.a. ZANU
ZAPU